Praise for *The Savv*

David Cutler has opened a floodgate of opportunit
many say the arts are dying, he writes to musicians w
you've ever wondered why someone else succeeds ins
importantly, you will discover countless ways to make sure it's you that people are wondering about the next time! I loved *The Savvy Musician*, and know my students will love it too!

Jeff Nelsen
Hornist, Canadian Brass
Indiana University Jacobs School of Music
www.jeffnelsen.com

The Savvy Musician is an adventure: critical concepts are explained in language that anyone can understand, but the side stories make it real. I found myself bouncing back and forth between the text and referenced websites. This book provides a blueprint for the new wave of musicians eager to understand the power of creating opportunities.

Kevin Woelfel
Director, Lionel Hampton School of Music, University of Idaho
Director, Entrepreneurship Center for Music, University of Colorado at Boulder (2003-07)
www.artsstart.org

The beauty of *The Savvy Musician* is its broad approach. Cutler paints a holistic picture of what it takes to prosper as a contemporary artist. His insistence that musicians look both inward and outward is progressive and needed.

Gary Beckman
Founder, Arts Entrepreneurship Educator's Network
www.ae2n.net

Cutler's book reminds us that we have to bring audience members into the creative process. Without fulfilling a real need, our art has little chance of success. *The Savvy Musician* unveils a vision for a healthy musical future, articulating 99% of what we need to do. The missing percentage is YOU, the reader.

Ranaan Meyer
Bassist and composer, Time for Three
www.tf3.com

This is a fantastic book, and should be required reading for every music school student as well as their teachers, professors, and deans. Cutler writes clearly and accessibly, and includes an impressive assortment of real world examples (with their web addresses!). I plan on making *The Savvy Musician* a part of my conferences, seminars, and core curriculum.

Michael Drapkin
Executive Director, Puerto Rico Conference on Music Entrepreneurship
www.prcome.org

The Savvy Musician is compulsory reading, relevant and valuable to anyone connected with the music business, regardless of avenue or experience level. All serious musicians must address the realities of the 'business aspect' as vigorously as they practice their instruments—the two simply go hand in hand. This text makes it quite clear that it's YOUR business and YOUR career. My advice: *Not* reading this book is an enormous risk.

Dame Evelyn Glennie
Solo percussionist, composer, motivational speaker, jewelry designer
Grammy Award Winner
www.evelyn.co.uk

The Savvy Musician is like having a professional consultant at your disposal for just about every aspect of your career, from preparing a photo shoot to setting up a nonprofit. As someone who spends the majority of his time consulting with musicians on how to best utilize the ArtistShare fan-funding model, I will definitely recommend this book to artists for learning about today's music business realities.

Brian Camelio
Founder and CEO, ArtistShare
www.artistshare.com

Cutler succinctly outlines the skill sets necessary for the entrepreneurial musician to thrive in the 21st Century...A must read for any musician contemplating a career in music's new world order!

Dr. Robert Thompson
Dean, Conservatory of Music, Purchase College SUNY
Kauffman Advisor, Entrepreneurship in Music Program, Eastman School of Music

Wow, I can't believe how much helpful information is packed into this book about a challenging career path—music! As a performer on an instrument that is unfamiliar to many, I know firsthand the importance of being savvy. *The Savvy Musician* will help you realize your dreams.

Wu Man
Pipa (Chinese lute-like instrument) virtuoso
Principal member, Yo-Yo Ma's Silk Road Project
www.wumanpipa.org

Cutler well understands both the incredible power of music and the fact that our current collegiate music curricula, which attracts fine students to America from all over the world, do not adequately prepare young musicians for the challenges they face in the new millennium. *The Savvy Musician* represents a giant leap forward in this important domain.

Robert Freeman
Regents Professor of Fine Arts, University of Texas at Austin
Director, Eastman School of Music (1973-96)

Cutler furnishes a common-sense, resource-rich guide that'll help musicians turn their passions into profits.

Peter Spellman
Director of Career Development, Berklee College of Music
Author, *The Musician's Internet* and *The Self-Promoting Musician*
www.mbsolutions.com

As I read *The Savvy Musician*, I kept nodding my head "yes," and saying "that's right." I've been in this business for over 20 years, and each chapter affirmed my past, confirmed my present, and inspired my future. The world will be a better place if we all aspire to the goals set in this book—a new credo for musicians.

Kim Nazarian
Jazz vocalist, New York Voices
Grammy Award Winner
www.newyorkvoices.com

An inspiring book, with an education on every page. The case studies alone are worth the price! Classical music needs entrepreneurs, and this book shows artists how to succeed.

Greg Sandow
Composer and consultant for classical music institutions
Veteran critic for the Wall Street Journal
Blogger on the future of classical music
www.artsjournal.com/sandow

The Savvy Musician is among the most comprehensive sources of self-help available for professional musicians and students. Cutler deals beautifully with every dimension of a musical career—visioning, missioning, marketing, financing, and most importantly, musicing—weaving them together in a well-presented mosaic.

Tayloe Harding
Dean, School of Music, University of South Carolina
President, College Music Society (2005-07)

Hands down, this is the most valuable resource available for aspiring musicians! It addresses all of the questions and concerns that the current generation of emerging artists faces in this ever changing profession. Cutler approaches his topic backed by thorough research in addition to a solid knowledge base that only a musician could have learned through his own experience.

Jeffrey Zeigler
Cellist, Kronos Quartet
www.kronosquartet.org

THE *Savvy* MUSICIAN

THE *Savvy* MUSICIAN

BUILDING A CAREER, EARNING A LIVING
& MAKING A DIFFERENCE

DAVID CUTLER

Published by Helius Press
11632 Frankstown Road, #124
Pittsburgh, PA 15235
(412) 242-7480
info@heliuspress.com

Photography by Ben Bullins | www.thebenjamincollection.com
Designed by *the*BookDesigners | www.bookdesigners.com
Printed and bound in the United States of America

LCCN: 2009921293
ISBN-13: 978-0-9823075-0-2
ISBN-10: 0-9823075-0-0

Includes index

1. Music trade—Vocational guidance.
I. Cutler, David. II. Title.

Acknowledgements

Ideas presented in *The Savvy Musician* have been profoundly influenced by friends, teachers, students, colleagues, and heroes inside and outside the music world. Thank you for touching my life. This publication is meant to give back some of the generous gifts you have bestowed upon me.

One of the great pleasures of working on this project was interviewing the 165 featured artists, in addition to scores of others who were not ultimately included. They were incredibly generous in sharing their stories, experiences, and ideas. Their involvement not only transformed the book, but I made many friends along the way.

Special thanks to those who made *The Savvy Musician* look great. Sculptor and photographer Ben Bullins went beyond the call of duty preparing images for the cover and chapters. The Book Designers team did an incredible job designing the book cover and interior. Justin Winslow created the amazing Savvy Musician website.

I am grateful to the individuals who so generously shared their time and feedback during the preparation phase of this text: Gary Beckman, Lisa Canning, Tom Cantrell, Mary Ellen Childs, Rosa Colucci, Joe DeFazio, Jo Faulmann, James Houlik, Aaron Kablack, Tom Kikta, Edward Kocher, Lance LaDuke, Ted Masur, Mary McKinney, Brian Pertyl, Stephen Pollock, Gary Potter, Sharon Roffman, Jessie Schalles, Alex Shapiro, Adam Silverman, Melissa Snoza, Lewis Steele, David Stock, Fred Sturm, Brandon VanWaeyenberghe, Stephen Wilde, Aron Zelkowicz. The book you now hold is unquestionably stronger as a result of their efforts.

Two individuals deserving special acknowledgement are my wife Erika Cutler and mother Tina Cantrell. They each spent countless hours proofreading and acting as a sounding board for my often crazy and eccentric flow of ideas. I can't thank them enough for their constant support.

Finally, I'd like to express gratitude to you for reading this book. It is my sincere hope that you discover a prosperous life in music that is personally fulfilling and adds something of true value to society. Please let me know when your savvy pursuits result in success: cutler@savvymusician.com.

Introduction

SO YOU WANT TO BE A MUSICIAN?

If you're like me, the decision to become a musician was a natural one. Sure, you had many interests, but music somehow carried an air of excitement like nothing else. People who witnessed your musical abilities trumpeted how talented you were. Somehow, pursuing anything else began to seem like a crime. So you composed a to-do list:

1. Attend music school
2. Become a "pro"

The roadmap begins well enough. You choose a school carefully and work hard. Though that environment is certainly more competitive than your pre-college life, impressive triumphs validate your decision: scholarships, steady improvement, glowing commentaries, good grades, successful projects, support from classmates and professors. Of course, the challenges are substantial, but as each semester draws to a close it becomes clear just how much you have grown. You are learning what it takes to succeed as a professional musician.

As graduation approaches, the first fright strikes. Schooling will soon be over, forcing you to enter the workforce. What exactly should you do? Despite the many wonderful skills developed during your training phase, you have little idea how to leap into the "real" world. (By pursuing advanced degrees, many musicians postpone this inevitable moment of truth.)

It's not that you're lazy. In music school your work ethic was on overdrive, and you are perfectly willing to invest time, energy, and discipline in order to ensure a successful career. You don't need to be rich either. From the beginning, you understood that most musicians did not earn six-figure salaries, and that's OK. But your preference is to avoid food stamps and homeless shelters. After all, you have to pay off student loans, buy new equipment, and cover living expenses. Someday you might even want to raise a family, and then there is saving for retirement. That all costs a lot of money!

What terrifies you most are the statistics. You've heard about orchestras struggling—several declaring bankruptcy—and when there are job postings, the competition is staggering. You are aware of public school districts cutting funding from music programs, and others that are skeptical about the value of music classes during a time when standardized testing and "No Child Left Behind" dominate educational philosophy. You know about the collapse of major record companies, and fear that most of the population could care less about the quality music you've spent your life pursuing.

How can you possibly survive? Do you really have the skills necessary to compete for the limited work available? Are you even good enough? Was your decision to study music in the first place a complete and total misjudgment?

Now that I have you hyperventilating, take a deep breath. There is no doubt that making a livelihood as a musician is challenging, but is this not the case with almost any line of work? And while the details of our circumstances may be new, musicians from every era have confronted significant obstacles.

Truth be told, many musicians today make good, solid, middle-class livings. Some even retire rich. Equally important, they pursue a vibrant and varied line of work that provides personal satisfaction while adding something of value to society. The early twenty-first century is an exciting time to be a professional musician, at least for those passionate about their art. And with your talent, schooling, and skill sets, success is possible. However, it will not happen automatically. That usually requires a clear but flexible vision, pro-activity, and the wisdom to understand that career paths today look significantly different than those even a generation ago.

Are there Too Many Musicians?

Are there too many musicians? No…Emphatically NO! On the contrary, there are not nearly enough musicians. Music affects our mind, soul, and psyche in a way that few other things can. It brings communities together and provides relief for the many stresses, large and small, that face humanity. In today's culture of workaholics and high-pressure negotiations, where the bottom line often takes precedence over inner peace and happiness, music making has the potential of providing a better life.

Consider the contrasting archetype of many African cultures, where everyone is a musician to some degree. Music is interwoven into their cultural fabric. Partly as a result, there is a strong emphasis on community, cooperation, and the human spirit. Many serious issues threaten these societies, yet music provides an outlet that yields empowerment and liberation. Anyone who has experienced African music rituals will surely attest to the divine energy it unleashes. When music is all-inclusive, it adds significant quality to existence. Yes, our society would be a better place if there were many, many more musicians.

Are there too many professional musicians? This question is far more complex. Unfortunately, we are now forced to confront a workplace reality that is over-saturated with well-trained, outstanding candidates vying for a shrinking pool of traditional positions. In the years ahead, these trends will likely intensify. It's the age old equation of supply and demand.

But the ways in which people receive their music is changing, as are the types of experiences they seek, and that provides an exciting opportunity. Musicians who broaden their outlook and approach have distinct advantages. As argued by Robert Freeman, former Director of the Eastman School of Music, "There are not too many professional musicians. There are, however, too many of the wrong *kind* of musician."

ATTENTION: WE NEED LEADERS!!!

The music world is in need of creative artists who understand current realities and are brave enough to experiment with new solutions. There are opportunities waiting to be discovered by performers who bring great music to new settings, educators who instill its transcendent and spiritual values to students, and administrators who foster new audiences while insisting that artistic integrity remain high. There is a shortage of music leaders unveiling new models for success, and artist-citizens leading the crusade to keep meaningful musical experiences vibrant.

Three Questions & a Smart Move

1. Are you passionate about music?
2. Do you have strong musical skills?
3. Can you sustain a career as a result of these abilities?

If your answer to the first question is anything but a resounding "affirmative," you are definitely in the wrong field. The life of a musician may not be an easy one, but it can be incredibly gratifying for those who love what they do. If music is less than an obsession, put down this book and start contemplating alternative career options!

To the second question, I'm quite sure you realize that the music industry requires skilled labor. Isn't that the reason you signed up for music school in the first place? Outstanding performance alone does not guarantee a successful career, but it's certainly an important component. On the flip side, it is absolutely possible to thrive as a professional even if you aren't in the top .23% of your field. Your level of proficiency is one of many contributing factors. This book, however, assumes you are taking steps to develop into the strongest musician possible.

To the final point: In order to sustain a career, as opposed to hobby, you must find ways to earn income from your talents. This is where so many musicians draw a blank. They have the passion and musical knowhow, but can't seem to envision a realistic way to make their living. So they cross their fingers and pray that life hands them the magical potion. If things don't work out neatly—and they rarely do—they have little idea where to turn.

In many cases, what these individuals lack is not musical ability, but imagination. The unfortunate irony is that they often have the potential to create a career that is not only prosperous, but also deeply meaningful. If you are willing to do whatever it takes to develop a fulfilling life in music, but need some help figuring out the roadmap, reading this book may just be one of the smartest moves you make.

From Talented to Savvy

Being talented is wonderful, but technical skills alone do not assure a successful life in this business! *Savvy musicians* have a huge advantage, and it's no mystery why. They work pro-actively to build their career, making smart choices that allow them to earn a good living and make a positive difference. In addition to outstanding musical ability, the savviest musicians:

1. Dream big
2. Think creatively
3. Take the initiative
4. Follow through
5. Take risks and are willing to fail (or even succeed!)
6. Create opportunities
7. Understand business realities
8. Invent remarkable products
9. Distinguish their work
10. Build a strong brand
11. Prioritize both content AND presentation
12. Market extraordinarily
13. Are financially literate
14. Fundraise effectively
15. Educate powerfully
16. Embrace technology
17. Excel with people skills
18. Maintain a strong network
19. Assemble an outstanding team
20. Leave a legacy

About This Book

The Savvy Musician was written to help musicians build a career, earn a living, and make a difference. It breaks down challenges in detail, but doesn't dwell upon them. Instead, it focuses on strategies for success, addressing the kinds of issues outlined above. Why waste energy on negativity when a world of possibility awaits you?

Whether you're a student, breaking into the scene, or an established professional, take control of your life. Embrace a holistic approach to your livelihood and art. Consider even the most unusual solutions. *Allow yourself to become a truly savvy musician.*

Vignettes

One hundred sixty-five stories of real musicians are cited throughout this book, representing a broad cross-section of instruments, ensemble types, genres, geographical regions, and experiences. (Though many feature classical and jazz artists, techniques can be applied to any musical path.) In most cases, they aren't famous superstars, but rather pro-active artists working to create a meaningful and prosperous career. Interviewing them has been truly inspirational.

When available, web addresses are noted. For updated links, visit *The Savvy Musician* (www.savvymusician.com). I encourage you to learn more about these creative artists, as all have many interesting stories, contributions, and ideas beyond that which is included here.

Chapter One

THE ENTREPRENEURIAL MINDSET

Chapter 1

THE ENTREPRENEURIAL MINDSET

How do you know if you've really made it as a musician? When someone reads your resume, bio, or obituary, how will they tell if your career constitutes one of success? When reading a few lines from the bio of fictional character Elvin Schlottsworthy, most readers will immediately concede that his story is one of respectable achievement.

Elvin Schlottsworthy is an international sensation. Stunning audiences with his dizzying technique and sensitive phrasing, he has performed more than 3,000 concerts worldwide. His 150 recording credits and appearances as a soloist with virtually every major symphony orchestra have earned a host of prestigious awards.

Wow! This guy is hot!

Each career path has its own hierarchy of triumphs. For performers, landing a major orchestral job, winning an international competition, establishing prominence in New York, maintaining an international touring schedule, or having an album go platinum are all accepted signs of prestige. For educators, a teaching job at a top college sounds more impressive than working at an elementary daycare center. Instrument makers who craft high-end cellos appear more noteworthy than one who manufactures trombones for kids, and a recording contract with Sony is more prestigious than self-releasing.

But bios tell only part of the tale. Consider the next paragraph of Schlottsworthy's story, one that is never included in his press kit.

Due to the demand for Dr. Schlottsworthy's playing, he tours non-stop. Spending precious few days with his three children, the oldest now refuses to acknowledge his existence. Two years ago, his wife left him for a restaurant employee who treats her and the kids extremely well. Most of Schlottsworthy's friends have written him off, aside from the few who exploit his connections. Gradually, this musician's predilection for alcohol consumption has gotten out of control. Last year he was arrested for driving drunk and spent a week in jail.

Oh my, how depressing! This is no success story, but one of utter, miserable failure!

It's easy to buy into the myth that there are absolute determinants of success. We convince ourselves that a clarinet prodigy who winds up a general music teacher or stockbroker is an embarrassment, and that winning that special competition, getting that special job, or making that special connection would put a stamp of approval on our lives. Many musicians worry obsessively about how they will be judged, constantly comparing personal accomplishments with that of their peers and superstars of the industry.

In truth, many variables contribute to our level of success, as both artist and human being. *Savvy musicians understand that finding a lifestyle that works is much more important than fulfilling traditional benchmarks of accomplishment.* The ideal solution for one person might be the worst possible scenario for someone else. So stop worrying about how the world views you and which accolades will be boast-worthy at your 25-year reunion. Instead, discover a path that complements your dreams, skills, and goals. In other words...think like an entrepreneur.

Doing the "Wrong" Thing

Lisa Canning (www.entrepreneurthearts.net) was on the fast track to becoming an orchestral musician. Studying with one of the world's great clarinet instructors, she locked herself in the practice room 8 hours per day, eventually becoming the studio's top performer. Then a shocking and unexpected revelation struck–perhaps this vocation is not a good fit. The demands of orchestral playing somehow didn't inspire her. Classmates and teachers balked at her idea of changing course, insisting that all other roads were indicative of giving up, selling out, and failure. Besides, with her limited skill sets, what else was possible?

Lisa began operating a business from her dorm room focused around the thing she knew best: clarinets. Serving as a matchmaker, she identified the best possible instruments for players based on their unique abilities and personality. Her company eventually expanded into a twelve million dollar enterprise incorporating a range of instruments, fifty full-time artist-educators, a mail order component, and four retail centers.

Among other activities, Lisa coaches artists across disciplines, helping them tap into creative impulses that lead to successful careers through entrepreneurship. Without ever joining a major orchestra, she has impacted the lives of numerous others. Better yet, she maintains a passion for music making.

THINKING LIKE AN ENTREPRENEUR

Why Be Entrepreneurial?

There are many definitions for the word "entrepreneur." For some, it is strictly a business term, representing an individual who starts and runs her own enterprise, as opposed to working for someone else. However, the expression is used here rather liberally, referring to any individual who creates opportunities, thinks outside the box, gets the "big picture," and is not afraid to question conventional wisdom. Under this definition, entrepreneurial inclinations can also influence artistic, educational, or personal decisions, even when no finances are involved. Entrepreneurship equals creativity—as much an attitude as it is a business practice. There are many rationales for gravitating towards this kind of disposition:

1. TO ENHANCE FINANCIAL GAIN. Entrepreneurs discover and create opportunities for earning income, regardless of the environment. Even musicians with traditional jobs can benefit by generating additional work.

2. TO CREATE FREEDOM AND GRATIFICATION. Entrepreneurship means taking control of your own destiny. Though there are significant challenges that accompany this model, efforts can be focused around personally fulfilling pursuits since you make the rules. Most music entrepreneurs proudly pursue "labors of love."

3. TO STAND OUT. Many music opportunities are extremely competitive, with the number of accomplished applicants far outweighing positions available. Musicians with a unique history and vision stand out from the rest. Entrepreneurs have an edge on those who have simply done the "normal thing."

4. TO ADDRESS JOB DEMANDS. Aspects of many music jobs, even traditional ones, require entrepreneurial solutions (recruiting students, attracting audiences, etc.).

5. TO INCREASE RELEVANCY. It will take entrepreneurial efforts to ensure that quality, sophisticated music maintains an important and active voice in society for years to come.

6. TO ENSURE A LEGACY. Most musicians hope to make some sort of meaningful, positive difference. Entrepreneurial actions can result in powerful legacies.

As a result of their inventive approaches, entrepreneurs often enjoy exciting successes. By employing innovative solutions, they create a demand for their art, pack concert halls, attract media attention, grow new consumers, and earn respectable livings. Consequently, entrepreneurs are often revered and rewarded in ways that most other musicians envy.

There are many levels of entrepreneurship. Whether hoping to augment income, stand out from a competitive field, add variety to activities, or erect a musical empire, realize that your chance of success increases exponentially when taking control of your own destiny.

BUT WHAT IF I JUST WANT A JOB?

While most music-oriented career paths clearly benefit from entrepreneurial foresight, there are possible exceptions. For example, suppose you aspire to win a top orchestra job. After landing this impressive, high paying position, the contract simply compels you to show up on time and be prepared. The literature is chosen by others, events are scheduled years in advance, and administration is responsible for marketing efforts. No entrepreneurial thought required!

Though there is logic to the argument, it comes with shortfalls. First, what if things don't work out and you're unable to land this dream job? Is there a Plan B? Few orchestras pay well enough to constitute a full-time living, and not every deserving candidate can obtain this kind of employment. Additionally, even if plans do come to fruition, you may want supplementary work in order to augment income, variety, and artistic fulfillment.

And, most interestingly, perhaps relinquishing responsibility for an organization's commercial success from its employees is a flawed notion. If orchestras are truly in dire straits, struggling to survive, wouldn't they be well-served if members actively promoted activities?

Imagine a hypothetical model where great playing alone is not enough to land a "gig." Finalists are required to face an interview round. "How can we attract new audiences? What educational/advocacy initiatives interest you? Which musical and non-musical skills do you offer besides your primary instrument?" Each employee is then responsible for fulfilling some role that helps the group thrive commercially as well as artistically.

Not only does this policy adjustment favor a new kind of player, but it might provide the foundation for an entirely different enterprise. Many performers would take more ownership in their professional community, and this inspired energy would benefit the ensemble. An entrepreneurial structure might revolutionize even the orchestral world.

An Entrepreneurial Existence

Savvy musicians follow a huge variety of paths. Some maintain a singular, traditional source of employment, but tinker with occasional business or creative ventures on their own time. Others juggle complex careers combining their own personal business, full- or part-time music jobs, freelance work, semi-regular residencies, or even labor in fields far outside the scope of music. Many balance a number of artistic interests: playing, composing, arranging, educating, recording, writing, engineering...you name it. All are willing to take chances, at least occasionally, and find potential where others see roadblocks.

Now, having a vision and bringing it to fruition are different animals. Much of life is out of our control, making some ambitions impossible to fulfill regardless of preparation, diligence, or wishful thinking. But an entrepreneur is not simply someone blessed with the mystifying ability to concoct one perfect, magical revelation. On the contrary, they are constantly cooking up hundreds of exotic recipes, many of which fail. But they continue baking until something delicious emerges and, after enjoying their riches, they quickly return to the kitchen.

Being an entrepreneur doesn't mean you have to constantly reinvent the wheel! Take advantage of available resources, many of which are free. Learn from others, and adopt lessons to your own situation.

Dreaming the Dream

While earning a living that allows you to put food on the table and a roof over your head is obviously important, savvy musicians have a higher calling. Think big, and never forget what is truly important to you. When pondering the following questions, dream like an entrepreneur. Don't allow yourself to put up roadblocks, making excuses why these things can't happen. At least for the moment, imagine the ideal. How would you approach your career if anything were possible?

1. What types of work do you enjoy the most?
2. What working conditions are optimal?
3. What are your overriding artistic goals?
4. What kind of impact do you hope to make?
5. What single project, above all others, do you want to accomplish in your lifetime?
6. What sort of legacy do you hope to leave?
7. To what lengths are you willing to go in pursuit of these dreams?

Evaluating your Skills

Savvy musicians are known for designing diverse, entrepreneurial career profiles that incorporate their full range of abilities. *Every skill you possess can contribute to your professional life.* Take a moment to brainstorm your full range of aptitudes.

- **PRIMARY MUSICAL SKILL.** Obviously important. Many musicians, however, limit their work largely to this category, failing to take full advantage of other aptitudes.

- **SECONDARY MUSICAL SKILLS.** Do you play a second instrument? Arrange a little? Have a good ear? All of these competencies can help earn income. You may not think you are "good enough," but others may see it differently. Believe it or not, secondary skills often morph into primary ones over time.

- **NON-MUSICAL SKILLS.** Outside of music, what aptitudes do you possess? Consider artistic, physical, cognitive, specialized, and business-oriented directions. With creativity, there are probably many ways to use these abilities to enhance your career in music.

- **UNIQUE SKILLS.** A challenge for musicians is that so many people doing the same thing compete for the same work: twenty-three teachers vie for piano students, 250 violinists audition for one orchestral spot, etc. Consider which unique skills you possess. Perhaps this individuality emerges when combining a number of areas. For example, suppose you are a pretty good pianist who also sings well. Individually, neither talent can win international competitions, but combining them unlocks fascinating possibilities.

Musical Skills		Non-Musical Skills	
Analyzing	Orchestrating	Accounting	Photography
Arranging	Performing	Art	Problem Solving
Composing	Primary Instrument	Bookkeeping	Psychology
Conducting	Producing	Communication	Public Speaking
Digital Audio	Synth Programming	Computers Skills	Sales
Engineering	Recording	Dancing	Schmoozing
Improvising	Score Reading	Fixing Things	Supervising
Interpreting	Secondary Instrument	Graphic Design	Teaching
Hearing	Sequencing	Leading	Video
Music Business	Sight Reading	Marketing	Web Design
Music History	Singing	Money	Working with Adults
Music Literature	Transcription	Management	Working with Kids
Notating		Networking	Writing
		Organization	

Multiplicity

Caleb Burhans (www.calebburhans.com) employs a wide range of skills in his professional life. While the bulk of his income is generated through singing with church choirs, he also composes chamber music commissions, plays electric violin in an improvisational "ambient, post-rock, minimalist" duo, and does studio work on violin and viola. Additionally, Caleb has gigged on an array of other instruments: piano, guitar, electric bass, mandolin, banjo, slide whistle, harmonica, and percussion. Every aptitude he possesses has literally been put to work.

Mapping Your Goals

Unlike non-entrepreneurs, who see few possibilities for themselves, savvy musicians seem to continually produce ideas for meaningful, profitable projects. In fact, after granting yourself permission to be creative with your future, the problem may be that too many possibilities compete for attention. Where do you even begin?

Study after study has shown that people who map goals in writing are much more likely to accomplish them than those who don't. Although it is possible to organize these thoughts mentally, writing down aspirations somehow makes them feel more real and urgent, greatly increasing the odds they will be realized.

Take a moment to jot down your long-term ambitions. In an ideal world, how will your career profile look like in 5-10 years? Limit this list to seven major points, helping you focus on what is truly important. Mix grand fantasies with a sense of realism. Though it is quite likely these objectives will shift over time, setting the compass helps plot a course, even if your journey eventually takes radically unexpected turns. In fact, successful entrepreneurs are flexible, always open to new opportunities and course changing. But they begin with a destination in mind.

For active dreamers, this list is probably both exciting and intimidating. Sure, it would be amazing if everything worked out, but proposals may seem huge and out of reach. At this point, some entrepreneurs get stuck—ideas *ad infinitum*, but no clear path forward. The next step is breaking down aspirations into reasonably manageable tasks. Continue by recording medium-term goals. What steps should be completed within the next 12 months to advance your cause? Be realistic. You may even want to architect a timeline. Over the next year, check this often to ensure you are staying on track and true to your priorities.

Finally, produce your short-term statement. What specific, concrete actions *must* be taken this week? Perhaps your first commitment should be to complete long-, medium-, and short-term goal lists. Force yourself to follow through, and don't permit excuses. Anyone can come up with a great idea, but only those with a clear plan and determination to act will see it to fruition. In summary: 1) dream big; 2) break it down into reasonable chunks; 3) get to work.

Life Map

Jeff Nelsen (www.jeffnelsen.com), hornist with the Canadian Brass, is obsessive about mapping goals. His "Master To Do List," a Google Document that may be accessed from any computer, currently catalogues 950 life ambitions. The "To Do Now List" contains non-urgent but time sensitive objectives, and is stored in a word processing document on his desktop. Finally, he e-mails himself the "To Do ASAP List" each evening, outlining tasks that should be completed the next day.

Yet even with this meticulous planning, Jeff is always open to unexpected opportunities, even if it means a radical change in direction (he grew up a pig farmer!). However, when pondering how he has done with the pursuit of goals, he asks two questions: "1) did I learn, and 2) did I love well?" Coupled with, "will this matter a year from now?" these inquiries help him focus on what is truly important, and which steps to take next.

AN ENTREPRENEUR'S "HOW-TO" GUIDE

How To Create Opportunity

Picture the music world as a high-rise building. The goal, called "Musical Success," is located on the top floor veranda. There is no elevator, only a narrow staircase. Thousands of individuals compete to make it there. Let's call them "The Musicians."

The Musicians pack themselves into the staircase, trying to get ahead of the rat race. Each player pushes and pulls, hoping to progress upwards. Some fall, some get trampled, others get stuck, and still others choose to stop before reaching their goal. And every once in a while, someone new makes it to the top.

Introducing character: *"You."* You have a choice to make. Of course, You can join the rat race, take the same stairs, pass the same floors, and face the same challenges. Or...You can take a different approach. Maybe You can crawl up the fire escape ladder to the desired floor. A friend has a helicopter—perhaps he could help deliver You—or You could work out an agreement with the window washer to see if she will bring You along for the ride up. And there is a less crowded structure almost kissing this one. Wouldn't it be possible to ascend in that building and create some sort of a bridge across? Finally, maybe You could find your own Musical Success somewhere else. After all, don't we define our own victories?

All of these alternate solutions introduce an element of risk and challenge. However, isn't there also significant risk involved in trying to make it up the heavily trafficked staircase? Many of The Musicians decided to take these steps without even considering other options. In fact, they believe there is only one way to Musical Success. The sad irony is that many of them will never make it there. Believe it or not, the staircase may just be the most difficult route.

Make no mistake; pro-active musicians are constantly in search of existing opportunities. If something presents itself that helps fulfill your goals, *please* take it. Pursue all leads vigorously! Competitions, jobs, advertised gigs, work from friends, and other prospective breaks play a huge role in the livelihood of even the most entrepreneurial artists. Just understand that many pre-established "goldmines" are quite competitive. There is a surplus of great musicians, and if something looks good to you, chances are that others are drooling over it as well. When something doesn't go your way, that doesn't mean you are unqualified to be a musician. There are just a lot of people in the staircase.

For those who desire more, but the stairwell is too clogged, here's a valuable secret: *look for opportunities where they don't currently exist.* Sound crazy? Consider this: With existing opportunities, there may be dozens or even hundreds of competitors. On the other hand, you are the only one in the running when proposing something completely new. True, a compelling argument must be made, but you have an "attention monopoly." Invent ways to create new markets and reap the rewards.

There are vast audiences for every kind of music, only many potential enthusiasts may not know it yet. Art-funding prospects do exist for those creative enough to find them. A place for you to shine in the music industry is absolutely realistic. You just have to figure out a solution, like working through a puzzle. There may not be formulas in the music world, but there are many roads that lead to prosperity. And, ironically, people who take charge of their own destiny often find themselves courted by pre-existing opportunities!

You Have One Minute

Rob Voisey (www.voxnovus.com) was discouraged by the lack of attention his music was receiving, as well as the underexposure of even the most well-known contemporary composers. So he decided to do something about it. He founded the 60x60 Project, an initiative brilliant in its simplicity: present recorded, hour-long concerts compiled of 60 recorded pieces, all one minute or less in duration. These shows are easy to host—only a CD player and clock with a second hand are necessary—and audiences are quickly introduced to a slew of new composers through the ultimate post-modern presentation.

The idea exploded. To date, 60x60 Projects have received 100+ performances internationally, presenting works by more than 1000 composers from 30 countries. Several mixes are created each year, and some compilations are produced in collaboration with video artists or dancers. As a result of his work, Voisey has connected with untapped audiences and hundreds of composers from across the globe. Here's an artist who knows how to create opportunities where they don't exist!

How To Become "Famous"

A teacher of mine once claimed that "everyone wants to be around a famous person." There's a lot of truth to that statement. People like to be associated with others who are successful. They believe it looks good, making them more impressive as well. Getting famous here does not necessarily mean becoming a household icon or an international sensation. For most musicians, fame of this caliber is out of the question. But within every community, there are people who are revered for their work, accolades, and legacy.

People are more likely to boast about well-known personalities with whom they've worked than unfamiliar ones. To team up with a celebrity, even once, somehow *sounds* more impressive than an ongoing collaboration with an unknown, even if the latter situation resulted in more substantive output. Another example of this phenomenon occurs when someone asks for a raise at work. Employers are much more likely to consider this request if another job offer is on the table, not only because they don't want to lose the employee, but also because *perceived value rises when one is desired elsewhere* (analogous to dating!). Of course, the employee's talent and potential is identical whether there is an outstanding job offer or not.

There may be little correlation between ability and perceived success. Some superstars have little to offer in the way of talent, while there are first-rate artists who live in complete obscurity. No qualitative value judgment is being offered. However, those with a track record of triumphs are more likely to be recognized.

When things go well, everyone wants a slice of that pie, and opportunities seem to appear out of nowhere. Success begets success. On the other hand, someone with less kudos may have difficulty locking in coveted opportunities. Some awards require prior honors, and some jobs favor applicants with previous experience. But how do you get your foot in the door?

Fair or not, this reality places many individuals in a "Catch 22." Your lucky break may seem out of sight because the good gigs are directed to the same handful of "celebrities" in a cycle that is difficult to infiltrate. Joining their prestige and rank can seem hopeless. So how does one advance on the professional ladder of success?

The Irony of Fame

Tim Adams, timpanist with the Pittsburgh Symphony Orchestra, recalls how he always had to pay top dollar for percussion equipment when he was a struggling artist with little cash to his name. Now, with the prestige of his current position, companies give him free or heavily discounted instruments on a regular basis, despite the fact that he has significantly more financial resources than before. With his current "fame," companies want to be associated with *him*. What an interesting role reversal!

Let's say you are a performer seeking to present solo recitals. Despite an intense campaign of press kit mailings, no one is biting. Instead they favor artists with more dazzling histories than yours. Though your playing is as strong as the others, they have more experience and stronger reputations. What can you do to jumpstart your career, making yourself seem more "famous," and thus desirable?

Why not plan a 5-state tour? Sounds impressive, no? It can actually be relatively easy to set up. This simply means that you perform in five locations. They can be held in homes, schools, libraries, churches, bookstores, or anywhere else you dream up. Call relatives, friends of friends, old classmates, and others you know who could help organize a performance of great music. Even if you don't get paid much—or anything—this experience may prove worthwhile. Perhaps your liaisons can help arrange home-stays or subsidize travel to minimize expenses. Then take off two weeks, get in your car, and drive to the locations of your solo tour.

Remember, fame is perceived, not concrete. People reading your updated bio will no doubt be impressed when learning about your recent tour. Someone performing around the country *must* be outstanding. Very few people care where the concerts were held. The fact that you are active may be enough to convince them of your worth. Of course, your claim is true, so there is no ethical contradiction here. In addition to resume building, consider a few of the many other advantages gained:

- The opportunity to perform a recital in front of new audiences, solidifying your presentation. Your confidence may be boosted as a result.

- The experience of meeting and interacting with many people from different communities. Your name is getting out there, and chances are that at least one person in attendance will offer you something in the future.
- The opportunity for word of mouth to spread your fame ("I saw this amazing performer..."), increasing exposure and possibly leading to additional work.
- The learning that comes with booking and performing tours. Many lessons will be gained about marketing, interacting with audiences, and staying on top of logistics.
- The advocacy that happens by organizing concerts where none exist. You are positively contributing towards opening up the music market.
- The perception that you are an entrepreneurial musician. People who learn about the tour will likely be impressed with your self-starting initiatives.
- The trip will undoubtedly result in interesting encounters and fun tales. It may provide memories for a lifetime.

By the end of your tour, you will have gained a tremendous amount. In addition to earning a certain number of "fame points," which will probably open doors in the future, there will also be significant richness added to your life and art.

How To "Get Lucky"

All successful people have at least one thing in common—they are lucky. They have all experienced fortunate breaks, partially or completely out of their control. Their lucky moment may have been getting a job offer (no one better for the position happened to apply), winning a composition award (their aesthetic happened to suit the judges), or being signed by a recording label (a talent scout happened to listen to their demo). The recipient may fully deserve these honors, but issues far beyond their control play an enormous role.

The contention has been expressed that some people are just born lucky, while others don't get any breaks. Certainly where and when we are born, the kind of parents we inherit, some health matters, and many other issues are completely out of our control.

Yet there seems to be a science to getting lucky. Some people find treasure no matter what obstacles life throws. Keep in mind that most successful musicians do not get where they are based on a single stroke of fortune. They somehow manage to attract repeated blessings. Anyone can get lucky once. For it to happen repeatedly requires something else.

Perhaps luck is a skill. You don't just have to be in the right place at the right time—you must make good decisions that place you there. When "luck" does display its pretty face, it often appears as the result of hard work, clear planning, dedicated follow through, and smart choices. Here are some suggestions that increase your odds of "getting lucky:"

1. **BE GOOD AT WHAT YOU DO.** When you excel, word spreads and luck may come your way. If, on the other hand, you do not perform satisfactorily, the aftermath can be harmful.

2. **HAVE A PLAN.** Take control of your life, define goals, and construct a plan to accomplish them. Cycle through these steps on a regular basis.

3. **SCHEDULE "LUCK TIME."** Regularly arrange time to evaluate how you are doing and work proactively towards promoting your career.

4. **MAKE "LUCK" HAPPEN.** Aggressively pursue opportunities. Luck may be random, but lucky people usually only appear that way after they've spent years working diligently.

5. **BUILD YOUR NETWORK.** The more people who know and like you, the more probable it is that one of them will pass some luck in your direction.

6. **INCREASE YOUR LEVEL OF "FAME."** The perception of success attracts new opportunities.

7. **BE FLEXIBLE.** When an opportunity falls outside of your master plan, consider changing the plan. In other words, don't look a gift horse in the mouth. Lucky people know the difference between a blessing and a distraction.

8. PLANT A LOT OF SEEDS, AND SEE WHICH ONES GROW. Since only a small percentage of projects are likely to pan out, investigating more opportunities increases your chances of finding a four-leaf clover. If you apply for a twenty grants, you have twenty shots at getting lucky. When applying for just one, odds are greatly diminished.

9. PLANT BETTER SEEDS. As you become familiar with the industry, learn which kinds of initiatives are most likely to come to fruition, and focus efforts on these.

10. TURN NEGATIVES INTO POSITIVES. Luck is often a matter of perception. When obstacles appear, find ways to turn them around, using the results to your advantage.

A Lucky Star

James Houlik (www.jameshoulik.com) is the world's leading classical tenor saxophonist. At this point, you may be rereading the previous sentence, stunned to learn that there are, in fact, classical tenor saxophonists. Though few opportunities are earmarked specifically for this specialty (approximately zero), Jim knows how to tempt fate. As a result, he has created a thriving, varied, and exciting career.

Constantly concocting projects, applying for grants, networking, and opening new worlds of possibility, no idea is too outlandish. He has commissioned over 80 works, soloed with many of the world's great orchestras, and frequently tours the globe. In addition to performing, James holds a university teaching position and runs a saxophone retreat each summer. He is working with a Chinese company to develop a line of saxophones. Finding work is never a problem for this entrepreneur—only creating enough time in the day to balance his many pursuits.

How to Make Your Work Stand Out

Whether composing, performing, teaching, booking a band, engineering a recording, or building an instrument, the level of your workmanship should always be high. This is a given. The minimum expectation is not simply to complete the job, but to do it well.

While outstanding quality may be enough to make your work stand out, it often requires more, especially in situations where the employer deals with a large number of professionals in your area. So how can you differentiate your services? *Fulfill at least one special element above and beyond the job's requirements.* This practice adds icing to the cake, increasing the probability of your getting the call the next time an expert is sought. A few examples:

- Completing work significantly BEFORE the deadline
- Adding an unexpected perk, free of charge
- Self-initiating a small but helpful undertaking outside the scope of your hire
- Offering a unique and personalized gift
- Sending holiday cards or other niceties
- Keeping in touch even when no work is in sight

How to Build an Empire

Here's one strategy:

STEP 1: BECOME AN EXPERT. Identify something you enjoy, and become a leading authority in that area. If you love tangos, do not merely tackle a few transcriptions. Instead, research every aspect of this genre: sociology, major figures, stylistic traditions, artists it has influenced, etc. Take up *bandoneón* and study the dance moves. In fact, go even further by travelling to Argentina, mastering Spanish, and learning to cook traditional foods. When it comes to any aspect surrounding the tango, curious people can simply consult Encyclopedia You.

Please note that you will only be able to build a sizable empire if a significant chuck of people share your interest. Becoming the world's leading scholar on Claudio Merulo's (1533-1604) Venetian polychoral stylings might be fascinating, but this niche is far too obscure to generate much of a following unless you do a great sales job!

STEP 2: CREATE YOUR EMPIRE. Dream big, spinning as many projects from your expertise as possible. Organize a band. Make recordings. Speak at conferences. Write a book. Start an organization, post a website, offer educational programs, do consultant work. Be creative in the proposals you generate. Before you know it, you may just have your own little empire.

It All Started with a Book

After reading an account of the vibrant artistic culture in Terezín, the horrific Holocaust concentration camp, violist Mark Ludwig was intrigued to learn more. He traveled to the Czech Republic, researched the role music played in maintaining morale, and interviewed Holocaust survivors. Since then, he has established himself as a leading authority in this area.

Mark founded the *Terezín Chamber Music Foundation* (www.terezinmusic.org). This organization, devoted to the music and memory of composers who perished at the hands of the Nazis, sponsors commissions of chamber works that will serve as agents of inspiration, healing, and transformation. His curriculum *Finding a Voice: Musicians in Terezín*, which examines the Holocaust through the lens of today's social context, has been presented to millions of children. Mark has recorded CDs, written liner notes, edited scores, drafted essays, taught college level courses, appeared in documentaries, and served as a film music consultant for projects that relate to his expertise. In addition to generating professional opportunities, activities have allowed him to pursue a passion that is deeply meaningful.

How to Change the World

To start with, take an interest. Educate yourself about social, political, economic, educational, and cultural issues on both micro- and macrocosmic levels. Get involved in your community. Bring music to places where its impact isn't normally felt and go beyond producing high-quality events—make work relevant and meaningful. When imagining projects, consider the ways in which they solve problems, address needs, or break down barriers.

Music in the Kitchen

When violinist Kelly Hall-Tompkins (www.musickitchennyc.org) wanted to run through a concerto for colleagues, but no one was available, her husband suggested she play at a homeless shelter operated through their church. Hesitant at first, she eventually gave it a shot, and the response was amazing. Though most audience members had never previously experienced classical music, they cherished every second—despite personal tragedies, somebody actually cared enough to share beauty with them.

As an outgrowth of this powerful experience, Kelly founded *Music Kitchen*, which presents around 10 shelter events per year. To date, over 50 musicians have been featured. Almost all artists feel it has been a personally transformative experience, and many claim the MK audiences are more receptive than most ticket buying ones. Not only have these efforts provided hope and happiness to the lives of many who desperately needed it, but love and appreciation emanating from audience members have changed Kelly forever.

How To Deal with Rejection

When reading the biography of a thriving musician, it is easy to be humbled by the weight and amount of accomplishments they have achieved. Yet any successful artist can produce an alternative set of accounts detailing failed ventures and dreams shot down. In almost all cases, this volume is exponentially thicker than the "Success Showcase." Rejection plays a major role in the life of all entrepreneurs. Musicians who have not experienced a substantial list of negative responses are undoubtedly playing it too safe.

Nobody likes to feel rejected, and the pain inflicted when a meaningful musical project or proposal is denied can be particularly agonizing. In the mind of some people, being turned down equates to a direct attack on the ego and soul. It causes them to question their art, talent, and direction in life. Rejection has the potential of triggering depression, low self-esteem, and angst.

A crucial attribute for entrepreneurs is the development of thick skin. In fact, individuals with fragile self-identities that crumble at the hint of criticism or rejection, dependent instead on constant affirmation, are probably not healthy contenders to become professional musicians.

Please realize that when a decision is made to accept or deny a proposal of any sort, the choice often says as much or more about external factors and the people judging than the quality of your product. *All decisions are biased,* based on the unique dispositions and history of evaluators. There may be internal candidates, aesthetic preferences (i.e. a concerto competition judge makes a choice based on literature rather than performance quality), too many applicants to reward all qualified contenders, or a host of other issues. The same set of five applications in the hands of five separate jurors could be ranked in five unique orderings. Acceptance or rejection, in many cases, is largely a matter of luck.

EXPERT OPINIONS

A judge at a major piano competition was struck by one of the competitor's exquisite use of pedaling. This said, she was surprised that a fellow judge felt the pianist used too little pedaling. To solve this disagreement, they approached juror number three. Scanning his comment sheet they happened upon the most shocking of comments: "Far too much pedal!" Acceptance or rejection is often based, at least partially, on subjective aspects out of your control.

Nonetheless, some rejections are in fact the result of a flawed or weak submission. After receiving a rejection, try to detach your ego and search for ways to benefit from the experience. Consider which aspects can be improved in the future. Sometimes rejection has little to do with content or potential, but is instead the result of shortcomings in presentation. Try to obtain feedback about the decision. Some sources refuse to provide clarification, but others are forthcoming. What you learn may be surprising.

Some entrepreneurs ease the sting of rejection by adopting an interesting perspective. They believe that with each denial comes bragging rights, and proudly display rejection letters for all to enjoy. Such artists understand that dismissals are healthy and real parts of the music industry game. Rather than staying hidden, avoiding any element of risk while praying for the occasional break, they are proud to be artists actively seeking opportunity.

Rejections and Successes

Fresh out of college, composer Eve Beglarian (www.evbvd.com) did all the "right" things to promote her career. She met everyone involved with New York's uptown music scene, gave scores away, served on music ensemble boards, produced recordings, and organized concerts. Yet something wasn't clicking professionally; composition opportunities were few and far between. After 7 years of struggle, she began listening to her inner dissatisfaction and decided to purse an alternative approach.

Eve moved downtown, meeting a set of artists with different priorities. She started writing music for theater and dance, and performed her own compositions. Each step was accompanied with new successes. These experiences taught her the importance of working within appropriate environments, getting involved with the right people, and not trying to force things when signs seem to point in another direction.

Even now, Eve's professional life is not linear. During some periods—after a fabulous premier, great review, or high paying commission—she imagines that things will run smoothly from that point forward. Six months later, she may be struggling once again, wondering how to pay the rent. Yet even with so much uncertainly, the decision to pursue such a challenging career path is deliberate. "If I wanted to write jingles, score nature documentaries, or teach at a university, that economic instability would disappear pretty quickly! It's because I really, really, really want to do particular work that I find myself in risky places now and again."

How To Become Excellent

There are more resources available than ever to guide you towards excellence. Music schools are renowned for developing efficient and effective ways to advance towards outstanding performance. The number of how-to publications on every topic under the sun is staggering, and the world is at your fingertips thanks to the Internet. The "Age of Answers" is upon us. Learn which tools are available, and take full advantage of them.

But to become excellent, all the reading, studying, and theorizing in the world is simply not enough. The key? *Just do it.* Jump in, get your hands wet, be willing to make some mistakes along the way, and stick with it. Many musicians become so obsessed with the idea of excellence, they refuse to even try anything that doesn't guarantee 100% success. As a result, ironically, their growth is stunted. So live your life, take chances, work hard but don't judge, and love every minute. Excellence will come when it's nice and ready!

Chapter Two

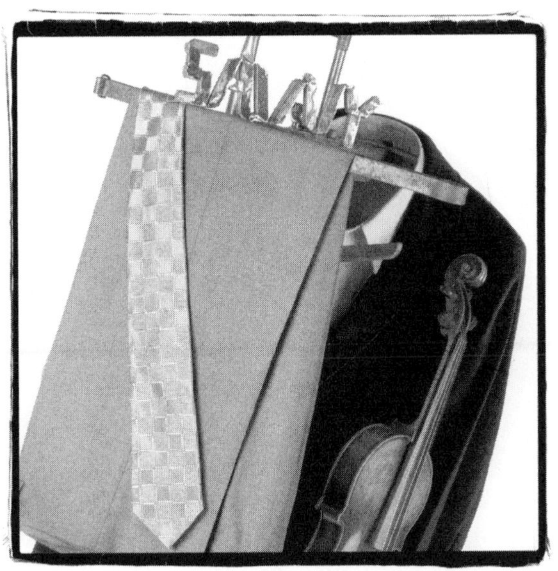

MINDING YOUR BUSINESS

Chapter 2

MINDING YOUR BUSINESS

"I am one of the best musicians around" exclaimed Sandra, "but have a hard time getting work. What am I doing wrong?" As she explained her dilemma, the problem quickly became apparent. "What kind of opportunities do you want?" I inquired. Her response: "I don't know—anything." There was the red flag. You see, nobody is simply looking to hire *talent*.

Upon deeper probing, Sandra eventually identified several areas of professional interest. Towards the top of her list was a desire to concertize. "So what next? Should I contact presenters?" she asked naively. Slow down, Sandra. The articulation of a precise career goal is helpful, but no employer in their right mind employs someone who just has an *idea*.

"Go home and dream up a concert. Identify the title, literature, collaborators, and cost, while determining what is appealing about your project." A few weeks later, Sandra enthusiastically described an intriguing program. Eager colleagues were already rehearsing! I congratulated her on this impressive progress, but sensed she was growing impatient to get some bookings. Once again, there was no option but to deliver the bad news: imagining an inspired, creative venture is exhilarating, but it is nearly impossible to sell a *concept*.

Only a *product*, I explained, has the chance of thriving professionally. *The metamorphosis of an idea or concept into a product occurs only when it is represented in tangible form.* Physical documentation is necessary to substantiate the vision. True, it is possible to get limited work through friends and word of mouth alone, but if serious about promoting a music career, start thinking like a businessperson. Turn ideas into "appealing merchandise," and approach audience members as if they are "valued clients." Without sacrificing artistic integrity, embrace the commercial aspects of being a savvy musician.

Sandra did just that. She created a written proposal, website, demo recording, press kit, and business cards. When we met months later, I felt she was a true professional with a strong concrete product to pedal. Now was the time to pursue leads. And at that moment, it struck me…Sandra is really talented!

INVENTING PRODUCTS THAT SUCCEED

Sample Products

Any kind of service, skill, resource, or good can function as a product. Savvy musicians typically offer an array, whether closely related items or a wide variety of categories.

PRODUCT TYPE	MARKETED TO
Compositions	conductors, performers, ensembles, recording artists, film directors, educational groups, teachers, competitions
Concertizing Ensembles	presenters, agents, record labels, media, educational organizations
Gigging Ensembles	party planners, booking agencies, restaurant owners, cruise ship entertainment directors

Music Lessons	students, parents, schools
Performances	audience members, financial backers, media
Projects	financial backers, grant committees, potential participants
Recordings	fan base, radio stations, critics, web-based audiences
Recording Studios	musicians, concert halls, businesses that create material for broadcast media (commercials, shows, etc.)
Yourself	employers, contractors, managers, music businesses, media

Identifying Your Audience

When creating a new product, consider the types of consumers you aim to attract. What interests do they have? Where do they spend time? What is their age range and financial profile? Brainstorm without editing, and be creative. Later you can trim down the list.

Musicians often lack vision when it comes to identifying audience groups. They limit their scope to the usual suspects, giving little thought to new kinds of clients. While a proven patron is certainly a likely candidate for your product, many similar "companies" may be vying for attention. By neglecting to engage new demographics, you may close doors on prospective customers who have a "need" for what you offer but just don't know it yet. Generating fresh music lovers not only serves your interests, but also benefits the artistic community.

SHOPPING FOR FANS

Here are some groups that might be interested in a chamber music concert. As the list progresses, less conventional possibilities are explored.

- **College music majors.** An obvious choice.
- **Professional musicians.** Also obvious.
- **Established music buffs.** They already have a recognized interest.
- **School-aged musicians and their families.** Not only are school-aged musicians often super-enthusiastic and impressionable, but bringing them to inspiring concerts helps build audiences for the future.
- **Fans for other performing arts.** Tremendous potential exists among theatre and dance patrons. Many eagerly approach new artistic experiences.
- **Independent, foreign, and experimental film fans.** Similar to the point above. In addition, they have probably watched films employing interesting music, so attending a concert is a logical extension.
- **Visual art and museum aficionados.** In fact, perhaps you can host your performance in a museum or other visually stimulating venue.
- **Businesses.** A good shared concert experience boosts morale and pride in the company. Offer a discount when companies purchase blocks of tickets.
- **Organizations/individuals connected to "theme" of concert.** The stronger the theme, the more interest you can drum up.
- **Singles groups.** Perhaps the event can double as a singles mixer.
- **Other organizations.** Historical societies, political associations, book clubs, fraternities, religious groups, etc.
- **Senior citizens.** Retirees often have the time and means to visit concerts.
- **Punks.** You know, with tattoos and body piercings. These individuals are actively seeking alternative experiences. Why not a chamber music event?

After considering potential population segments, narrow down your options. Do not make the mistake of trying to appeal to everyone, as reaching each constituency requires additional resources. Unique tactics are necessary to engage business professionals, baby-boomers with an artistic flair, wealthy patrons of the arts, college-aged singles, or high school musicians. (Of course, if people from outside the chosen factions employ your services, consider it a blessing.)

Concentrating efforts has other advantages. Let's say your teaching studio targets retirees. Not only does this specialty give you an edge over competitors when golden-agers look to take lessons, but it might intrigue people who hadn't previously considered music study. After all, you cater specifically to their kind of people. And there are excellent forums for reaching this group: retirement communities, centers that appeal to seniors, newsletters for retirees, etc.

Expanding the Base

The slogan of the Marian Anderson String Quartet (www.mariandersonstringquartet.com), an ensemble comprised of African-American women, is "Creating New and Diverse Audiences." As a result of their efforts, they often attract full houses with a high concentration of minorities, blue collar workers, and other persons lacking prior classical music exposure.

Whenever possible, the group schedules 3-4 days in a specific location before each concert. During this time, they offer inviting informative presentations in libraries, churches, schools, colleges, and other settings. By providing exhilarating experiences, observers often decide to attend the featured MASQ event.

Another way they have built audiences is through the *Marian Anderson String Quartet Chamber Music Institute*, which focuses on sharing the joy of chamber music making with amateur musicians. Participants have ranged from 7-76 years of age.

Focus on Benefits

Consumers are only interested in purchases that benefit them directly. If your talents and passions are all that is offered, your product will be doomed. After identifying the target audience(s), consider their needs and priorities. Find ways to solve their problems.

The more specific you can be, the better. For example, hopefully a private music instructor helps students improve, but why is this useful? Does it provide personal joy? Build self-confidence? Develop creativity in ways that apply to other areas of life? After identifying aspects that are truly beneficial and in need, create a product that actively addresses these issues.

Distinguishing your Product

Most music markets fall somewhere between competitive and cutthroat. You're probably not the only "company in town" presenting your type of "commodity." Though many musicians spend a lot of time trying to be alike (i.e. playing standard repertoire in standard venues with standard ensembles in standard ways), only better, simply offering high quality products rarely leads to widespread success.

Savvy musicians understand the importance of standing out. They focus energy on inventing remarkable products with the potential of attracting an audience. There may be a hundred great cellists in town, but those with the strongest and most unique identities will probably grab the most attention. Which features set your work apart?

OUTSTANDING PERFORMANCE. Of course, outstanding performance can distinguish a product, and you should strive for nothing less. However, attracting first time customers typically requires a different set of talking points than returning clients. Repeat business often comes as the result of a job well done. First time patronage, however, usually requires something else. Your actual abilities only become a primary consideration after you have an audience's attention.

ATYPICAL ASPECT. What differentiates your product from the competition? Is there a fresh angle, bonus feature, or special approach? Unusual presentations, distinctive offerings, and other oddities can intrigue and attract business.

Let's suppose your chamber group specializes in private parties, but a hundred groups are competing for attention. Below are some bonus features that could separate you from the pack. Naturally, these distinctions should be prominently emphasized in promotional materials. You may want to charge extra or include them as part of a "package deal."

- If a good dancer is in the group, offer instruction.
- A personalized composition tailored to the occasion makes a huge impression. This doesn't need to be elaborate or take long to compose.
- Fun, interactive games can liven up the merrymaking.
- Some groups wear costumes—one drummer's sticks burst into flames on request.

- A souvenir CD-Rom for guests can include photographs provided by the host along with several tracks from your demo (providing free publicity!).

For thoughts on producing remarkable performance experiences, see chapters 12 and 13.

NICHE. A *niche* may clearly present itself or require some soul searching. By framing your product in such a way that highlights a unique area of expertise, you become the obvious choice when someone seeks that specialty. Of course, the flip side is that this can typecast you, with people expecting the same kind of output over and over again. Examples include:

- Performing Bach
- Accompanying saxophonists
- Composing comical numbers
- Recording folk singers
- Producing outlandish concerts
- Offering world music seminars
- Teaching adults
- Selling/repairing string products
- Playing weddings
- Publishing sacred music

The Saw Lady

Natalia Paruz (www.sawlady.com), aka the "Saw Lady," built her entire career around playing unusual instruments: musical saw, Austrian pitched cowbells, English handbells, glass harp, and theremin. Her unusual niche has led to opportunities ranging from solo engagements to featured performances with ensembles such as the Israel Philharmonic Orchestra.

CUSTOMER SERVICE & REPUTATION. Customers want to do business with those they like and trust, even if it means paying a little more for that privilege. Elicit passion, positivity, and a willingness to go the extra mile in all interactions. Make exceeding expectations central to your identity. At the least, be punctual, professional, and pleasant.

An extraordinary reputation earns referrals and prestige. Building one requires considerable time, but it can be damaged or destroyed instantaneously. People are much more forgiving about wrong notes than problematic episodes, so don't mess up! And if you do, work vigorously to fix things.

FEE & MARKETING. When charging more or less than competitors, the price differentiates your work. However, always offer additional benefits besides the fee.

A strong and unusual marketing campaign is a powerful way to distinguish your business and hook customers. Chapters 3-7 deal extensively with marketing strategies.

Content vs. Presentation

With every product you offer, and all marketing materials for that matter, two overriding elements must be balanced: content and presentation. Content involves the product itself and its quality. Presentation entails the way in which it's packaged and delivered. In almost all cases, both content and presentation play an integral role in determining ultimate success.

Many musicians employ a ratio of approximately 99:1 when it comes to content vs. presentation. With your own activities, aim for 50:50. This doesn't mean that the same amount of minutes must be spent preparing each aspect. It may take weeks to organize the details of a resume and just hours to adjust the look, or months to learn a program and 10 minutes to select a special outfit. But the final product should be strong in every respect.

ITEM	EXAMPLES OF CONTENT	EXAMPLES OF PRESENTATION
Cover Letter	points conveyed	clarity & organization, writing quality, overall look, grade of paper
Resume	specific accomplishments, thoroughness, honesty of claims, quality and quantity of entries	layout & design, organization, use of fonts, grade of paper
Website	text/information, photographs, audio and video clips	ease of navigation, interactivity, visual interest, aesthetic appeal, upload speed, amount of text per page
Concert	pieces performed, quality of performance	venue, audience interaction, visual elements, use of hall, amplification, program order, stage presence
Lecture	information covered	charisma, attire, use of humor & drama, teaching aids (board, computer, etc.) interactivity, enthusiasm
CD Recording	pieces recorded, quality of recording, program notes	cover and graphic design, order of tunes, casing type
Teaching	thoroughness of concepts taught, methodologies employed	level of formality, interactivity, variety of activities

Many observers take little from a poorly delivered lecture, regardless of its profundity. Grant committees dismiss poorly written applications from the most qualified of candidates. World-renowned conductors veto powerful compositions solely because of sloppy notation. Though these examples may not be "fair" in a perfect world, they represent reality.

A flashy product with limited depth might eventually be dropped under the pretext of superficiality, but something without an acceptable appearance may never be given a fighting chance. Presentation is often the first test that must be passed. People often assume that stunning visual appeal equates to valuable content, while sloppy presentation means substandard quality. This isn't necessarily true, but the belief exists overwhelmingly, on subconscious if not conscious levels.

To be perfectly clear: accept nothing less than a product of the highest caliber. However, when poorly packaged, it will likely be doomed to failure before being given a chance. Keep this reality in mind for each aspect of your professional life. Everything matters!

BUILDING YOUR BRAND

McDonald's, Nike, Obama, Trump, Juilliard, Steinway, Marsalis, Yo-Yo. After hearing each name, a distinctive connotation probably arises, thanks to their strong *brand identity*. As a result of unique products and/or marketing, you have a well-defined idea about what each stands for. When someone hears your name, what comes to mind?

The art of branding is more than creating products with a catchy name and logo. It is the sum total of what you do, how it is presented, and most importantly, how others perceive your offerings. According to Neil Burns, professor of advertising at the University of Texas at Austin, "Not building a brand is much more costly than building one."

Choosing a Name

What's in a name? A lot. Without a title, you simply don't have a product, and certainly not one that can be marketed effectively. Yet there are numerous composers who reference pieces as "untitled" and performers who do not name concerts. Can you imagine trying to advertise an anonymous movie, restaurant, or amusement park? The notion is absurd. For every product, prioritize finding a high-quality title.

For prospective customers, the name creates a first impression. Just as people often decide whether or not to purchase a book based on the title, yours may be enough to attract their curiosity or turn them off. Not all names are equal, at least not in the music business. One that is too complicated renders your product unmemorable, while something too generic has little chance of making an impact. Names project an image, whether intentional or not, so reflect upon these implications. Creating a catchy name may require some effort, but consider it a critical aspect of your product development!

WHAT'S IN A NAME?

Let's say you are considering naming a professional ensemble the *Southwest Iowa Euphonium Quartet.* On one hand, it tells exactly who you are: four players of one instrument from a particular location. People interested in euphonium music (low brass players and maybe their moms) and those connected to Iowa might decide to check out a performance as a result of the name. But it would render most others apathetic. Euphonium music doesn't exactly have a large following (sorry), and the designation of Southwest Iowa makes it sound like a regional amateur group. With such a title, this band may have a difficulty attracting attention even if shows are inspiring and entertaining.

Though this is a rather obscure ensemble, similar logic can be argued for other products. Could you imagine the rock group *Phoenix Guitar Band* trying to make the big time? Preposterous! Fashioning a memorable and intriguing name is a crucial step towards creating strong brand identity.

Slogan & Logo

A slogan is a short, memorable phrase used for advertising and branding a business. It can describe the benefit of your product, spirit of the company, or what differentiates your work. The fast food chain Wendy's began running ads with the slogan *It's waaay better than fast food.* ™ Whether or not you agree, they are trying to distinguish themselves from the competition. The best taglines are concise, usually 7 words or less, and easy to recall. Coming up with a catchy slogan is a bit like writing poetry.

Catchy Taglines

- Musica Viva (www.musicaviva-swva.com), chamber music presenter: *World Class Music. Small Town Touch.*
- River City Brass Band (www.rcbb.com), brass ensemble: *Serious Music is Fun.*
- Ludwin Music (www.ludwinmusic.com), independent publishing company of double bass music: *Music with Bass in Mind.*
- Violinnovation (www.violinnovation.com), private violin studio: *Where Violin and Innovation Connect.*
- Wes Funderburk (www.funderbone.com), trombonist: *Knick, Knack, Paddy Whack, Give the Gig a Bone!*

A logo is a visual element that represents your product. At the least, it is a presentation of your name written with a special font, design, and color. But to make logos more memorable, it is helpful to include a graphic element that somehow conveys your mission, suggests the services offered, or describes the "attitude" of your business. Once a slogan and logo have been devised, they should appear on all appropriate materials, including business cards, letterheads, posters, brochures, contracts, and websites.

Unpack Your Musical Parade

David Cutler (www.trunkmusic.org) is a jazz and classically trained composer/pianist. His brand is built around the concept of extreme eclecticism: borrowing freely from an array of musical languages (jazz, classical, world, pop, folk), collaborating interdisciplinarily (with dancers, visual artists, actors, filmmakers, circus performers), and encompassing a wide range of emotive qualities (from tragedy to comedic hilarity).

Brand name: Trunk Music

Slogan: *Unpack Your Musical Parade*

Graphic:

Description: "In a trunk, seemingly unrelated items find themselves side by side—sometimes harmoniously, other times with agitation. Thus emerges the wildly varied music of David Cutler."

Conveying an Image

Whether applying for a job, promoting a product, or advertising an event, it is essential to consider the image you wish to communicate. "Hip and modern," or "traditional and sophisticated?" "Professional but personable," or "fun and user-friendly?" Brainstorm adjectives that illustrate the essence of your work, and figure out ways to reinforce that aura. Decisions should affect everything from product name to marketing campaign, look and content of promotional materials, and the atmosphere of events.

Whichever direction you decide to go, there is one trait that should be included on every list: *success*. People want to be associated with winners. They crave being in the presence of greatness and prosperity, not mediocrity. As trained musicians, we understand that all products are flawed—there is no such thing as the perfect performance. As a result, we sometimes project a bashful or even self-deprecating persona. This is not a healthy business practice. Without bending the truth or portraying arrogance, radiate success at every turn. Consumers, colleagues, and competitors will take note.

People may already have a general image etched in their mind about what you do based on their past experiences. Parents in some school communities consider music lessons for their children essential, while others view this undertaking as an unnecessary frill. When hearing the words *classical music*, some groups immediately imagine "beauty and passion," while others assume "boring and unhip."

Classical Blue Jeans

Edward Klorman, violist and co-artistic director of the Canandaigua LakeMusic Festival (www.lakemusicfestival.org), has thought a lot about branding. Hoping to offer sophisticated, high-level concerts to a community with little-to-no previous classical music background, he created a series called *Classical Blue Jeans*. Concerts take place in familiar local venues, and everyone is encouraged to wear jeans. After a barbeque dinner, the evening continues with a highly interactive presentation, inviting audience members to coach the musicians, compose melodies, or participate in other ways. The name alone sells the concert, and visitors leave with one idea: classical music is fun!

In both instances, the first group will not need much convincing in terms of the value of your field. Simply persuade them that your company is the best vendor. For the second group, you must work to create an image that challenges preconceptions. This may be difficult, but by pulling it off you can strike gold and energize a new customer base.

WRITING THE BUSINESS PLAN

Rationale

The most successful music entities invent remarkable products, build a strong brand, and market effectively (as shown in the next several chapters). With so many elements to consider, a written business plan increases your chances of success exponentially, whether focusing on a single event, ongoing enterprise, or your career in general. The act of writing this document helps you pinpoint priorities, identify opportunities/challenges, and solidify a course of action. Additionally, you may choose to share it with colleagues, employees, clients, grant committees, or donors for input.

Some otherwise savvy musicians skip this step, either because they're "too busy," "too lazy," or "intuitive enough to succeed without one." But this decision may compromise effectiveness. In fact, many veteran musicians openly admit they would have been better off if a written plan had been created early on. Solidifying details on paper forces you to grapple with pertinent issues easily overlooked when ideas exist solely in the mind.

Drafting an Effective Plan

Business plans range from basic outlines to comprehensive reports. At the very least, draft a single sheet overview. This brief statement forces you to focus on what is truly at the heart of your operation. For greater detail, expand the plan, but limit it to 10-pages unless the enterprise is extremely complex.

Regardless of length, the writing style should be specific and concise. Make it easy to comb through and identify primary points, employing bullets, charts, and graphs when appropriate. Be idealistic but realistic, and clearly address vision, mission, objectives, and strategy. Business plan excerpts from the fictional group Ensemble Amazing are in italics below.

1. VISION. What are your hopes for the future?
The reputation of Ensemble Amazing will grow nationally. Earnings will provide $35,000+ annually to each member in addition to covering expenses and funding a bi-annual recording project. Sources of revenue will include concerts, educational events, recordings, and publications of our arrangements for high school musicians.

2. MISSION. What is the purpose of your business?
Ensemble Amazing specializes in performing, recording, and publishing music based on folk traditions from around the world. Featuring friendly and outstanding musicians, all of our offerings are high quality and easily accessible.

3. OBJECTIVES. What specific achievements do you hope to accomplish in the near future?

This year, Ensemble Amazing will a) double the amount of bookings from last year, b) create and market an educational event, and c) begin a publishing wing of our business. In addition, we will continue previous activities such as...

4. STRATEGY. What specific steps must be taken to accomplish these objectives?

a) To increase bookings, we will implement the marketing plan detailed in this document's appendix. The most pressing need is creating a new, savvier website.

b) Member X will arrange music for our educational event by March 1. The following week, we will rehearse, write a script, and film a run-through for marketing purposes.

c) We already have twelve rough arrangements appropriate for high school students. Member Y will edit the scores and write accompanying blurbs about the origins of each piece. Member Z will obtain a business license and work on promotional aspects.

Be sure to address the following issues somewhere in the business plan, either within the categories above or in independent sections or appendices.

- **PRODUCT DESCRIPTION.** Which products are offered and what makes them unique?
- **AUDIENCE.** Who are the primary and secondary demographics to be targeted?
- **MARKETING.** What kind of marketing campaign will you run?
- **MONEY MATTERS.** What are your financial goals, and how will they be accomplished? A detailed budget should be included.

Consider incorporating a *SWOT analysis* (Strengths, Weaknesses, Opportunities, and Threats). The first two areas deal with issues internal to the business, while the latter pair focuses on external considerations out of your control. After completing this breakdown, find ways to exploit strengths, resolve weaknesses, seize opportunities, and circumvent threats or turn them to your advantage. Below is a SWOT analysis for Ensemble Amazing:

S	W	O	T
Great players	Not enough products	Publishing	Economic downturn
Great music	Fan base too small	Educational market	Arts funding cuts
Entertaining shows	Need new website	News item: Olympics	Competition is fierce
Strong brand identity	Not enough East Coast connections	Growing interest in multiculturalism	Competition has more marketing $

Tom Davis Music Publications

Tactical Marketing Plan (2006-07)

PRODUCT

- Quality jazz ensemble compositions for intermediate to advanced high school and college jazz ensembles
- The opportunity to commission a new work for your ensemble
- Guest artist, guest conducting opportunities, artist in residence, clinician

COMPETITIVE ADVANTAGE

- Composer's desire to connect with those that plays his music
- Composer is available for consultation and advice
- On-line tips and advice for each piece
- On-line practice tracks
- The printed music comes with "customer support" including
    - Transcribed Solos
    - Composer led interviews of soloists and rhythm section
    - Composer lectures on rehearsal techniques and important points for each composition
    - High quality audio of each composition
    - Practice tracks for each composition
    - "Top ten" lists for successful performance for each chart
    - Video of rehearsal and recording session of each chart
    - Video of soloists performing transcribed solos
    - Access to the composer for questions and comments
- The music is colorful, fresh, more through composed than most publications. Structured as compositions rather formula arrangements

PURPOSE IN DEVELOPING THIS MARKETING PLAN

- Organizing marketing strategy
- Efficient use of advertising dollars
- Monitor successful/unsuccessful strategies
- Reach target customers – those that look carefully at the site are impressed. People who have played my music like it very much
- Focus goals and message of this business
- Currently not reaching targets
- Have heretofore employed a "hit or miss" strategy
- Develop a "Brand"-like message
- Clarify the message I am sending about the product
- Perhaps create sub-targets groups and market differently

TIME AND MONEY FOR IMPLEMENTATION OF THIS PLAN

- $1- 2000? Not a lot, but I'd be willing to take out a loan if confident of the plan
- Time - I am a full time K-12 music supervisor in a Public School District
    - I have evenings, weekends and summer to work on this
    - I spend a great deal of my "spare" time on this project

CURRENT APPROACH TO MARKETING THIS PRODUCT

- Demo CD produced in August 2004 of current tunes
- E-mailed closest colleagues and acquaintances about its release
- Sent product to NYSSMA News reviewer
- 500 CDs with order forms sent to IAJE members (my own list from the publication – my guess as to those most likely to be interested)
- 500 post cards sent to similar targets
- NYSSMA news review February 2006
- Joined and posted on ArtistShare site May 2005
- Sent product for review to IAJE Journal
- Monthly newsletters to website subscribers (only 67 since May). Many are not potential customers
- Began to send newsletters to 1000 musician emails in my address book
- I have tried to generate interest when I guest conduct and perform
- "Cool" stickers with web address. Target students, not directors.
- Coupons for some free material on the site to people that I meet at residencies—not successful
- There will be an IAJE review of the charts in April

RECENT ACCOMPLISHMENTS IN THE MARKETING AREA

- Charts sent to NYSSMA reviewer yielded a guest appearance– 11 free charts set up a $1300 residency. Took 1 year+ to materialize, but good strategy
- Guest conducting gigs have seen a bubble of 15 additional e-mail log-ons to the site however not many can be defined as potential customers

CURRENT CHALLENGES IN THE SALES OR MARKETING ARENA

- Advertising power of large educational publishers & catalogue dealers
- Above send CD's or catalogues to all 10,000 US high schools
- Most high school directors seem to have limited knowledge ort ability to want to play advanced material
- Many high school programs have limited rehearsal time
- Major publishers will publish popular big band music that may not be as accessible, but have great "star" power
- Many directors' are looking for quick solutions and not willing to push the "boundaries" of their skills

INITIAL IDEAS TO EXPAND MARKETING EFFORT

- Need for a "Brand" focus so that the message is focused
- Include a recognizable logo and slogan
- Networking e-mails - personalized may be more effective
- Send all charts to each states music ed magazine reviewer
- Multiple postcard "touches to potential customers with sequential messages highlighting benefits.

Update your business plan at least every two to five years. Doing so will provide an opportunity to assess your progress and reevaluate goals.

Seeing the Trees

Jazz composer/educator Tom Davis (www.tomdavismusic.com) believes his personal career is every bit as important as that of a large business. To address relevant concerns, he created a detailed eight-page business plan. This document has proven extremely helpful, articulating purpose, limiting career choices, evaluating time and money spent, and ensuring core values are realized. "To view the forest, you need to see the trees."

The previous two pages are excerpted from his plan. It continues with a number of charts assessing potential target groups, why they are attractive, customer needs, and specific strategies for moving forward. After completing the plan, Tom was disciplined about keeping notes on actions taken and their results.

Split Personality

In order to thrive, musicians must have a split personality. In some moments, artistic concerns take center stage as you work to craft the quintessential musical statement. Other times, you must operate as a businessperson: marketing a product, building a brand, attracting an audience. Yet the two personas have much in common. They both require discipline, vision, and creativity. And when an artistic/business venture succeeds, the results can be extraordinarily gratifying.

Chapter Three

MINDING YOUR BUSINESS

Chapter 3

MARKETING IS EVERYTHING

Many musicians are totally disinterested in the notion of marketing. They'd rather be practicing, or composing, or fishing...or anything else. In fact, they long for the day when a record label, publishing company, artist manager, or some other noble third party will do it for them.

Reality check—that's not how the game is played! True, some sources may assist with promotional efforts, but the ultimate success of every artist is in their own hands. No matter how famous you become or how many helpers are on your side, savvy musicians understand that they alone drive their marketing campaign...even if a great deal of labor is fulfilled by others.

Don't fool yourself into believing that marketing is simply advertisements, business cards, and websites. These are critical, but it's much more than that. Marketing is an attitude—a way of life. It encompasses everything from brand name to customer satisfaction. Your interactions, passion, punctuality, "phone presence," and thank-you cards are vital. So is the uniqueness of your vision. All of these things contribute to whether a product thrives, placing marketing at the core of each business. *Marketing is everything, and everything is marketing.*

Marketing shapes the way people think by directing their priorities and perceptions. Used to increase sales (get more gigs, more clients, more notoriety), it has three overriding goals:

1. **KEEP PAST CUSTOMERS ENGAGED.** It is infinitely easier to attract repeat clients than earn new business. Stay current with past patrons, keeping them posted on new products (upcoming concerts, your latest service, etc.) while reminding them that you still exist.

2. **ATTRACT NEW CLIENTS.** Whatever type of operation you manage, you will want an ever-expanding list of customers.

3. **INCREASE NAME RECOGNITION.** Name recognition is the primary goal of many marketing campaigns. The theory: the mind registers a product's name subconsciously each time it is heard. At a certain point, people begin to assume that familiarity equates to value. Why else would the name be floating around? Even when ignorant about specifics, most people favor businesses with a recognizable brand identity.

MARKETING OVERVIEW

Reaching Your Audience

Hopefully you identified specific audiences to target when designing your product. In order to be successful, your marketing messages must reach them directly and effectively. To do this, it is imperative to understand their lifestyle. How do they spend time? Where do they obtain information (blogs, magazines, organizations, friends, etc.)? What kinds of messages resonate with them? If necessary, interview a representative sampling. *An effective marketing campaign is one that meets constituents on their terms.*

Multiple Streams

There have been instances of people attending concerts due to one newspaper listing, or hiring a band simply because of a phone book entry, but that is the rare exception. Just think about it. When was the last time you bought event tickets based on a single promotional item? More likely:

You received an e-mail, noticed several posters, heard a radio interview, witnessed friends buzzing, visited the website, and finally decided to give it a shot.

Don't expect a simple poster campaign to produce extraordinary results. Repetition and multiple marketing streams are necessary. An old business adage claims that it requires seven marketing encounters before a message begins to stick, let alone sell the product. In today's world of consistent marketing bombardment, it may require even more.

Redundancy is the Key

Each year, the clarinet quintet Orion Ensemble (www.orionensemble.org) performs four individual programs three times apiece. The challenge is not only attracting guests to individual events, but also cultivating long-term patrons. They have always hired a publicist; in fact, early on, this expense was often more than the gross revenue. But it takes time to develop a regular fan base, and their consistent marketing efforts have paid off.

1) **Brochure.** Each year, 4000 season brochures are printed. In early summer, a batch is sent to their mailing list (about 800). Before the first concert, a second mailing is made to those who haven't yet purchased tickets. Brochures are also dispensed by hand.
2) **Newsletter.** Early each spring, an annual newsletter is distributed.
3) **Newspapers/Magazines.** News releases are sent to every local newspaper or magazine that might have a remote interest in running a feature or reviewing their concert.
4) **Radio.** A local classical radio station promotes events through announcements, interviews, and live concert broadcasts.
5) **Website.** Orion's website announces and describes all events. They are currently adding a feature which allows patrons to purchase tickets via PayPal.
6) **E-mail.** Beautiful e-mail communications are sent regularly to their fan list.
7) **Raffle.** In order to beef up their fan list, they tried an unusual tactic during one series: Anyone who reveals their e-mail address is entered into a raffle.
8) **Volunteer committee.** A committee of volunteers actively recruits audience members.
9) **Partnerships.** To expand their fan base, Orion has formed partnerships with other organizations, making cameo appearances on external music series and involving visual artists, poets, or mimes.
10) **House concerts**. They have performed house concerts, inviting only people who haven't previously seen their shows.

Timeline

Though some musicians pray for immediate results, it rarely works that way. People who learn about a great concert the night before will have a difficulty rearranging their schedule, even if they truly want to attend. Recording studios will not suddenly be booked to capacity the day after a new ad is printed, and critics require months of warning. Marketing takes time.

> Many performers have expressed disappointment after an outstanding concert attracted distressingly few audience members. They worked so hard, and the concert was fabulous—why weren't more people interested? Upon deeper investigation, it turns out that that four typed posters were displayed a week before and e-mails sent the previous evening. So what did they expect? People don't "buy music" because they magically understand something great will take place. They do it only after being motivated by effective marketing!

Ongoing businesses will find certain periods of the year more lucrative than others. Learn the high points for your area and ratchet up marketing efforts accordingly. For example, a majority of students commence music lessons when the school year starts, making the end of summer a critical time for teaching studios. Holiday parties make winter (November through December) a gigging high season, so booking agents should increase visibility in months prior. January is quiet for most businesses, as people recover from holiday overspending.

Whether promoting a single happening, ongoing service, or your career in general, make sure to block off sufficient and regular time in your schedule for marketing efforts. Just two or three hours per week makes a tremendous difference. This time can be spent strategizing, working on web development, sending out letters, designing fliers, doing market research, or anything else that helps visibility and contributes to an expanding business.

When promoting an event, here is an approximate timetable to follow:

TIMELINE	ACTIVITIES
3-6 months prior	Draft publicity plan Compile media list Organize and update mailing list of guests to be invited Announce events on your website Mail news releases to quarterly/monthly publications*
2-3 months prior	Mail invitations to critics*
1-2 months prior	Mail news releases to local radio/television producers* Mail news releases to weekly publications* Mail save-the-date invitations (especially to out of town invitees and other critical guests) Register performance information with various calendar listings
3-4 weeks prior	Begin poster/flier campaign Mail news releases to daily publications* Send reminder notice to critics
1-2 weeks prior	Ratchet up poster/flier campaign Mail invitations to invited guests Get people talking about your event (through advertising, word of mouth campaign, news stories, etc.) Employ other promotional strategies
1-3 days prior	Send reminder e-mails
1 week after	Mail thank you notes to critics, helpers, and guests Collect all media coverage for event Finally...sleep

**When appropriate, follow up with phone call to confirm receipt.*

Budget

Some musicians believe they can't afford the expenses associated with marketing. In actuality, the opposite may be true—anyone serious about a music career cannot afford to *not* market.

No formula prescribes the exact percentage of an operational budget that should be spent on promotion, and there is no fixed correlation between dollars spent and business earned. Successful plans eventually recoup all expenses at the minimum. Do not be cheap when it comes to marketing, but spend money wisely and give methods sufficient time to work. If investments do not ultimately yield satisfactory results, reevaluate the approach.

Successful marketing necessitates time, energy, planning, and follow through, but not a second mortgage. Believe it or not, low-cost solutions are often more effective than high-priced ones. A savvy musician with a limited budget may actually be in an ideal position to market because they are forced to invent creative, low-cost solutions that stand out. Many techniques described in this book can be pursued for next to nothing, or even free. It need not take an enormous marketing operation to get noticed; it does, however, require a smart one.

Are There Any Guarantees?

Absolutely. *Musicians who don't effectively market their products sacrifice untold potential, guaranteed.* If interested in expanding visibility, patronage, and earnings, there is no substitute for smart, aggressive, strategic marketing.

Marketing is not simply a matter of luck. Some methods work better than others. Therefore, study the scene, target specific populations, understand their mindset, deliver clear messages, design effective materials, employ multiple streams, and allow the campaign time to work. Differentiate yourself from the competition in ways that encourage consumers to choose you over the other guy. Keep track of the ways people learn about your offerings, and be willing to alter approaches that do not work. Trial and error, as well as an ever evolving marketing mechanism, is a key to building long-term success.

TECHNIQUES & STRATEGIES

Advertising

Advertising opportunities are everywhere if you're open enough to imagine them. Take note of the many ways in which companies try to communicate with you throughout an average day: radio, television, newspapers, magazines, Internet, posters, billboards, merchandising, direct mail, "proselytizing," etc. After observing an effective technique, ask how your business could adopt that approach. And in the rare case you notice something unadorned by advertisements, perhaps this signals an opportunity. (Some companies now place ads on eggs!)

A given neighborhood has endless potential for advertising. Many stores allow approved posters to be displayed in windows, and others have bulletin boards for fliers. Chalking sidewalks, brochure canvassing, and posters in restaurant bathrooms are possible. Don't forget to adorn your home with a banner. Still not creative enough? One promotional team raided a cafeteria, placing fun colorful concert leaflets on trays. Surprised and bored customers waiting in line were grateful for the distraction. Several curious eaters took the bait.

You can learn a great deal about advertising from other businesses, including what not to do. Here's a technique—Examine your rivals and take the opposite approach, venturing into territories foreign to the competition. Recasting someone's slant is risky. Your business may have a difficult time escaping their shadow. Make advertising as distinctive as your product.

When it comes to marketing, some musicians think first and foremost about traditional advertising techniques. Often, that's the only element pursued. Unfortunately, these methods can be costly and there's no guarantee that sales will increase as a result. In fact, because of the vast amount of ads competing for attention, their outcome is often disappointing. Before paying to advertise, weigh the expense against how much work will realistically be generated. And be open to other types of marketing. Many are less expensive and exponentially more effective.

Permission Marketing

In his groundbreaking book "Permission Marketing: Turning Strangers into Friends and Friends into Customers," Seth Godin discounts the efficacy in the early twenty-first century of what he calls *interruption marketing*—a TV show disrupted by a commercial, a print ad disturbing the flow of an article, etc. The problem, he contends, is that we are so overwhelmed with these kinds of messages that consumers tune them out. Instead he argues for *permission marketing*, directed efforts to reach clients who are eager to receive your communication. This is accomplished by building trust and providing messages that are "anticipated, personal, and relevant."

There are many ways for musicians to increase their level of permission. One method is what Godin calls the "opt-in." The idea is that you attract a potential client's attention by offering something of value for free. But this privilege costs their anonymity—they must disclose name and contact information. An effective gift earns you the right to begin a dialogue, which often leads to future purchases and increased trust. Here are a few permission-building incentives that musicians can offer:

- **INFORMATIONAL DVD.** A teacher can distribute a free video discussing the benefits of music instruction.
- **FREE MEETING.** *Call now for a free meeting on how to make your party remarkable.* During the get-together, address a number of personalized elements, including live music. "By the way, we have a band that would be perfect for your event."
- **WEBSITE RESOURCES.** Create a blog or resource guide about relevant topics (practicing tips, local businesses, etc.), available only to those who give permission to be contacted in exchange for a password.

Customer Service

Outstanding customer service should be at the heart of every marketing campaign. When a potential client contacts you, go out of your way to be friendly, positive, flexible, and responsible in *all* interactions. Cultivate personal relationships, return calls and e-mails promptly, and follow through with promises. When possible, arrange face-to-face meetings. Most people ultimately hire the person with whom they connect the most.

Above & Beyond

Flutist Christine Soroka-Greenfield (www.pittsburghmusiclive.com) places outstanding customer service at the heart of her gigging business. "My reputation is built on providing stress-free, personal, enjoyable experiences." This means taking a personal interest in clients. She makes a conscious effort to ask questions, learn about their background and interests, and customize events. Also a good vocalist, she often volunteers to sing at no extra charge.

Christine has a reputation for being unshakably reliable. She typically answers correspondence within an hour—e-mails are forwarded to her cell phone—and certainly never waits more than a day. People often express appreciation for this quick response, as if reliability were an unusual trait. (Having worked with musicians who have not shown the same courtesy, Christine understands how crucial it is to be dependable.) She arrives to all engagements prepared, at least an hour early, and is cheerful, personable, and flexible.

Generating a Buzz

There is no better marketing than word of mouth. When people start chatting about your business, the rewards will surely follow, increasing name recognition and encouraging newcomers to research your activities. But how can you get people talking?

An upcoming event might encourage some chatter on its own merits, but getting hype to spread like an out of control forest fire requires more. Active buzz is generated by the exceptional, the unusual, the newsworthy, the controversial. But beware—once rivals learn of your success, they will likely try to replicate it. At this point, figure out your next move or risk losing the buzz advantage.

Riding the Buzz

In order to generate excitement about an upcoming piano recital, Michael Schneider (www.pianomike.com) pursued an unusual tack. After voluntarily performing for a school district's K-12 teacher retreat, he unveiled the plan: Local citizens were invited to submit requests for pieces they would like him to perform. The winning applicants/compositions would be announced at the concert. Beautifully crafted paperwork was distributed, and teachers were urged to encourage their students to make submissions.

Because of his novel approach, the local newspaper ran a feature article, and Michael was invited to interview with a public radio station. As the concert approached, he had students of several private music teachers sell tickets, awarding a pizza party to the studio that sold the most. These engaging strategies got people in the community chattering with anticipation, and as a result, a full house enthusiastically supported the event.

Referrals

Most often, people looking to hire musicians offer the work to someone they know and like. If no one fits that bill, they then ask trusted friends or colleagues for a referral. Blind Internet searches typically only occur after other options have been exhausted. Therefore, referrals are a coveted form of marketing, not to mention free. Take steps to ensure that your name emerges at that all-important moment.

There are ways to increase the number of referrals you receive. One possibility is simply asking your network to advocate for you. How will they know you're looking for more work if you don't tell them? For a higher success rate, create some kind of incentive system. Offer discounts, prizes, free services, finder's fees, or special benefits to customers who bring in referrals. This marketing tool is extremely cost-effective because you pay only when a new client has been engaged—a 100% success rate!

While everyone you know has the potential to provide referrals, some individuals are particularly valuable. Identify these people, wine and dine them, and become friends. In particular, seek useful alliances that are not regularly courted by the competition, providing you with a monopoly on their loyalty. Some helpful groups are:

- **OTHER MUSICIANS.** Professionals with a complimentary but non-competing line of work. Useful connections for a classical violin teacher are local school string educators, youth symphony conductors, music store employees, and even non-classical violin teachers.
- **NON-MUSIC PROFESSIONALS.** Individuals typically employed by your target demographic. If you play private parties, this group includes wedding planners, caterers, photographers, videographers, florists, bartenders, bakers, and dress/tux shop employees.
- **EVENT VENUE EMPLOYEES.** Staff members from the kinds of sites where you hope to work: concert halls, country clubs, bars, hotels, fancy restaurants, resorts, etc.
- **PUBLIC FIGURES.** People who wield influence over your goal audience such as teachers, religious leaders, business managers, political figures, and social organizers.

Don't Discount Discounts!

Julie Johnson, a piano teacher specializing in beginners, offered a $15 discount to any family in her studio that set up a free consultation between her and a prospective student. Though anyone could have qualified for those meetings, most referrals turned out to be sincerely interested in the possibility of music study. After the face-to-face presentation, many decided to give lessons a shot, and her studio grew quickly. Now Julie has a waiting list. This kind of direct marketing proved extraordinarily effective. In exchange for $15 and a half hour of time, she was able to attract many new students who eventually purchased years of lessons.

Free Services

Offer freebies to first timers. True, they do not generate income directly, but clients drawn to your doorstep are likely to become customers at some point. Complimentary gifts also get people talking, bragging about their acquisition, which in turn circulates your name. Radio giveaways are a great way to earn free publicity.

First-Limers

The Pittsburgh New Music Ensemble (www.pnme.org) implemented an interesting marketing approach. Bring someone new to see a show (called a "first-limer", in tribute to the band's lime-green theme color) and get in for half price. Bring two or more and enter for free. First-limers also receive tickets gratis. The result: concert attendance shot up dramatically. PNME feels confident that people who see one of their innovative productions will be compelled to return.

Mementos

Calendars, t-shirts, candy, mugs, Frisbees, magnets, and other items with your product logo boldly displayed can be great advertising tools. The recipient gets something cool out of the exchange, and your brand is reinforced every time they glance at it. Take care to ensure that the memento does not look cheap, since people assume that shoddy keepsakes translate into a substandard product.

A Program to Remember

Though the chamber group Fringe (www.fringeatlanta.org) performs standard classical literature, their productions are cutting edge. Guests are greeted with a drink to sip while strolling around an art exhibit. Music spun by a DJ combines techno tunes with works to be performed. Concerts begin with a short artsy or cultural film, and documentaries featuring performers link the pieces.

Audience members leave with more than a great memory. The physical program is a souvenir. Beautifully designed, it includes a welcome letter, the evening's program, brief program notes, a thought provoking article about art, and a suggested listening list. A plastic card memento ticket with a code on the backside is attached. The next day, this number can be entered onto the Fringe website, enabling users to download a recording of the performance they had witnessed.

MAINSTREAM MEDIA

Any and all media coverage can be helpful to your cause, either directly or indirectly. Even better—much of this publicity is free. Learn how the industry operates and find ways to use it to your advantage.

Types of Coverage

A majority of American households subscribe to a combination of newspapers, magazines, and newsletters. However, as more people look for their information online, many of these companies are restructuring to adapt. Print media possibilities for publicity include:

- **ARTICLES & STORIES.** A feature about you or your business.
- **SPOTLIGHT SERIES.** A short blurb, often about a community member, highlighting background and activities.
- **REVIEWS.** Assessments of a recording or performance.
- **CALENDARS & EVENT ANNOUNCEMENTS.** Listings of upcoming activities.
- **YOU DO THE WRITING.** If interested in writing, consider submitting editorials/articles or working as a critic.

In today's world, most people have some interaction with radio or television on a daily basis. Broadcast media possibilities for publicity include:

- **NEWS ITEMS.** An interesting upcoming event, activity, fundraiser, or changing circumstance can be covered by news-based shows.
- **FEATURES.** Extended features about individuals, ensembles, projects, and lifestyles are included in many news broadcasts or other programming.
- **INTERVIEWS.** Some talk shows present interviews with artists, including clips of their recordings and questions from listeners.
- **LIVE PERFORMANCE.** Some programs invite artists to perform directly from their studio, and others specialize in live concert broadcasts.
- **CALENDAR LISTINGS.** Many channels plug upcoming events.
- **MUSIC BROADCAST.** Transmitted recordings or videos of your music not only increase sales, but also earn you royalties.
- **YOU DO THE HOSTING.** Become a show host or contributor. Let local stations know about your interests and areas of expertise.

Opportunities

The media world is huge. There are probably many more accessible sources than you realize. Get to know the options and which ones can be useful to your cause.

SOURCE	DESCRIPTION
NEWSPAPERS: Major	It is extremely difficult to get coverage in major newspapers. Competition for space is fierce. If such a paper picks up your story, you can benefit from widespread prestige and notoriety.
Suburban Daily/ Weekly	Much more likely to show an interest, especially during early phases of your career, and they may better reach your target audience.
School	College or high school papers bring your message to young people.
Special Interest	Tabloid sized papers targeting specific groups of readers. Find an appropriate angle that connects with their mission.
MAGAZINES: Trade	Magazines such as 'Jazziz,' 'Opera News,' 'and 'Strings,' written by and geared towards musicians. An article or review circulates information to colleagues with similar interests and backgrounds. As with newspapers, coverage by magazines with wide circulation is coveted and competitive.
Scholarly	Journals open to the academic community for high level articles.
Non-music	Magazines on any number of topics offer creative potential to musicians who can tie their art to its focus.
City Guides/ Entertainment	Published monthly or quarterly, providing an opportunity to reach locals and tourists.

NEWSLETTERS: (Overview)	Existing newsletters cover every interest imaginable. Published monthly, quarterly, or yearly, most are printed on standard 20-pound paper and fairly short (2-8 pages), though organizations with larger budgets use magazine-like formats. Generally a smaller distribution than magazines, so getting attention may be realistically attainable.
School	Elementary through university levels. Provides alumni/faculty reports and relevant stories on current events and education trends.
Community	Sent out to residents to describe local happenings and issues.
Special Interest	Clubs, religious organizations, and other special interest groups may be interested in your story if it relates to their mission.
Music	Numerous music organizations produce newsletters—in fact, you may want to distribute your own.
RADIO & TV: Commercial Stations	Depend on advertisers to pay their bills. The wider the audience, the more they charge for ads. As a result, most are interested only in famous artists or extremely newsworthy stories. Competition for air time is intense, but coverage by one of these channels reaches vast audiences.
Community Supported	Most stations that specialize in classical and jazz programming are nonprofit organizations that depend on donations from businesses and listeners/viewers. Part of their mission is to promote local artists, so excellent publicity potential exists here.
College	Another good source that primarily targets students.
Public Access	Provides the opportunity for community members to broadcast for free. Though the audience is extremely limited, they nonetheless provide complimentary publicity and valuable media experience.

Working with the Media

The media needs compelling and entertaining stories to keep its customers engaged. You want publicity to bring attention to your product. In this light, you and the media have the potential of becoming mutually benefiting partners. When pitching a story, make it easy for your suggestion to be accepted. Have a strong hook, and gear ideas towards the organization's target audience.

Each establishment has its own set of rules for submissions, often clearly laid out on the company website. Follow guidelines religiously, as many stories are rejected solely because of logistical inconsistencies. When is the cut-off date for submissions? Should proposals be presented via e-mail, over the phone, or in a letter? What length is requested, and which information must be included? Triple check for errors in terms of spelling, grammar, and content. Follow through if additional information is requested, and be flexible in terms of scheduling phone interviews.

For print media, submit proposals to multiple writers and editors who deal with music or local news stories (when there is a human interest angle such as a benefit for a sick child, playing in hospitals as music therapy, etc.). This way, there is a greater chance that someone will pursue your story and your materials won't get lost in the shuffle. For broadcast media target the producers and hosts of appropriate programs. Media representatives are extremely busy, constantly under the gun to meet deadlines, so keep correspondences brief.

If someone from the media brings you positive publicity, make sure to send a thank you note. This show of appreciation helps foster healthy relationships and encourages future coverage of your efforts. It's a good idea to save copies of all media mentions so that you may extract quotes, include articles in press kits, and reflect upon your impact.

Multi-Media Coverage

For each market where the touring funk band Mingo Fishtrap (www.mingofishtrap.com) performs, they send hundreds of e-mails to print media, radio, and TV contacts. From this blanketing, they typically receive a few press kit requests. "When you're doing 40 shows, you can't spend a week trying to promote to a single source," explains guitarist Roger Blevins, Jr. "I'd rather get 20 articles in smaller publications than a single write-up in a major one. If your materials are compelling and you put them in front of enough people, someone will bite."

Mingo's press kit consists of 1) their latest CD, 2) a single sheet bio, 3) a specifically tailored news release, 4) a media quote page, 5) business cards, and 6) a concert DVD (their secret weapon). Though this 7-camera production was made relatively inexpensively, it commands more attention than a CD, while showcasing the group's high energy style. "People who preview or review live events want to hear and see the group." In fact, many television stations have provided free publicity, airing brief segments of that video.

On Becoming Newsworthy

Let's begin by discussing what does NOT fall into this category—the fact that your product will be of extraordinary quality. Hopefully everything you submit to the public will be high caliber, but excellence does not an interesting story make. Other un-newsworthy items: standard literature presented in typical ways, musically technical descriptions, an advertisement.

Something is newsworthy when it has an interesting angle. Five minutes of any news program confirms this. Whether the information is good or bad, heartwarming or terrifying, it has some kind of hook and interest. Capturing media attention often requires an extraordinary element. When judging the potential interest level of a story, consider whether it would be compelling enough to capture your own attention. Some newsworthy issues:

- **FIRSTS.** The premier performance by an artist in a prestigious venue, the first use of Chinese instruments with the local orchestra, the inaugural Pizzicato-Only-Convention.
- **SOMETHING NEW.** Commissions, premiers, newly discovered compositions, recently invented instruments.

- **SOMETHING UNUSUAL.** Atypical presentations (interdisciplinary, multi-media, multi-cultural, themed) or venues (museums, bowling alleys, highways).
- **SOMETHING CONTROVERSIAL.** The media loves any and all things controversial.
- **SOMETHING INTERESTING.** Intriguing stories about how the music was composed, where the group recorded, or the life struggles of an artist.
- **SOMETHING MEANINGFUL.** Significant community issues such as a veteran's musical memorial or diversity awareness concert. This category includes negative stories such as music funding cuts threatened by a school board.
- **SOMETHING FAMOUS.** A performance with someone or something "famous."
- **SOMETHING EDUCATIONAL.** Special ways in which musicians educate the public.
- **SOMETHING CHARITABLE.** Benefit events for worthy causes.

In many cases, the wackier the story, the more likely it is to attract media attention. For example, getting a classical music magazine to cover an unknown string quartet performing standard lit is nearly impossible, as many groups compete for precious few slots. However, the same ensemble backpacking across country on trains might have a good shot at attracting attention from travel magazines (that may never have covered musicians in the past). Ironically, after such a kooky story has been released, the music journal just might rethink its position.

Classic Politics

In 2004, CNN, BBC, and NPR ran stories on soprano Elender Wall (www.elenderwall.com) performing art songs by Bryant Kong (www.stuffedpenguin.com). The lyrics were based on quotes from Donald Rumsfeld, then the U.S. Secretary of Defense. Accounts mentioned nothing about the quality of his compositions or the singer's voice. Instead, they focused on this controversial political figure and their transformation of his words into art music. Nonetheless, Bryant's music was seen and heard across the globe on television for the first time.

News releases

News releases are essentially short news stories. They are sent to the media, booking agents, presenters, clients, and others who might be interested in your activities. Though releases are not advertisements, they can help augment sales, exposure, and image.

Media organizations receive far more leads than are printable, so be sure yours merits attention. If an editor pursues your story, she may print the release word for word, edit it down, or have a staff writer conduct supplementary interviews and research.

Upon receiving a release, reporters first assess timeliness. Does this require prompt attention, or can it wait? Always include the indication "FOR IMMEDIATE RELEASE" or "FOR RELEASE ON (INSERT DATE)" towards the top of the page. Additionally, clearly list all pertinent contact information (company name, contact person, address, phone, fax, e-mail, URL) high on the page.

To determine a compelling angle, answer this: If there were just one minute to pitch your story, what would you say? Why should someone pay attention to your news? Now boil that information down to a single, sharp, focused sentence. *Violà*...you have your hook.

After creating a thought provoking title, craft the first paragraph. It must 1) intrigue the reader, and answer 2) who, 3) what, 4) where, 5) when, and 6) why. If these six crucial elements do not appear in the opening sentences, assume your release will be unsuccessful.

CHECKLIST

Omitted details can mean omitted opportunities. Does your news release include:

- ☐ An event description & title?
- ☐ Location & directions?
- ☐ Date & time?
- ☐ Names of people involved?
- ☐ Background information?
- ☐ Ticket prices & where to buy them?
- ☐ A web address with more info?
- ☐ A great & compelling angle?
- ☐ Reasons someone should care?

FOR IMMEDIATE RELEASE
September 15, 2006
Media Contact: Laurie Townsend
(604)822-9161
laurie.townsend@ubc.ca

The Nu:BC Collective Inaugural Concert
BASIC ELEMENTS
Telus Studio Theatre – October 14th
Redefining the Music Concert Experience

Vancouver, B.C. ~ Not to be missed! Vancouver's new cutting-edge performing arts collective, the **Nu:BC Collective**, presents its inaugural season at the Telus Studio Theatre on October 14th. As the newest ensemble-in-residence at the UBC School of Music directed by flutist **Paolo Bortolussi**, Nu:BC brings together the spectacular talents of School of Music faculty and those of Vancouver's outstanding creative artists. This season features repertoire from some of the most exciting and influential contemporary composers from Canada and abroad. Joining forces with choreographers, lighting designers, video artists and others, the Nu:BC Collective seeks to bridge the gap between artistic media to offer an extraordinary and unique concert performance experience. Be there at the beginning and experience the newest voice on Canada's contemporary music scene.

- **BASIC ELEMENTS** features works by Howard Bashaw, Stephen Chatman, Keith Hamel, Chen Yi, and György Kurtág and Christian Calon.

  Featuring celebrated UBC bassoonist **Jesse Read** performing **Keith Hamel's** *Obsessed Again...* for bassoon and interactive electronics paired with sound-generated video; the dynamic duo of **Gwen Thompson** and **Eric Wilson** bringing home their high flying New York premiere of **Stephen Chatman's** duo *From Pent-up Aching Rivers* - with choreography by UBC's **Cathy Burnett**; Chinese-American composer **Chen Yi's** luminous work *Qi* for flute, cello, piano and percussion; new music specialist **Paolo Bortolussi** performing Montrealer **Christian Calon's** haunting *Souffles Primitifs* for bass flute and electronics; a modern classic in **György Kurtág's** *Hommage à Robert Schumann* for clarinet, viola and piano; and closing with UBC alumnus **Howard Bashaw's** virtuosic *12m-4p-15m* for violin, clarinet, cello, and piano.

- Other performers include a selection of premier artists in Vancouver's contemporary arts scene: Corey Hamm, piano; David Harding, viola; Vern Griffiths, percussion; François Houle, clarinet, and Rebecca Whitling, violin.

Basic Elements – Telus Studio Theatre, Sat Oct. 14, 7:30 pm
Tickets: $20 adults/$10 students available through Ticketmaster [*(604) 280-3311 or www.ticketmaster.ca*] or in person at The Chan Centre Ticket Office.

For the remaining paragraphs, provide additional details in descending order of importance. This way, if an editor curtails your story by editing out the last paragraph or two, the key material will still appear. Effective content includes information about contributors, quotes from participants or external sources (i.e. CD reviews and other positive press), and additional supporting details. End by directing readers to your website for further information.

Though the overall length of a news release should never expand beyond 500-700 words, less is better. Use a journalistic writing style with short sentences and paragraphs. Avoid flowery prose and excessive adjectives, adverbs, or hyperbole. Keep it concise and simple,

Most media contacts prefer receiving news releases in the body of an e-mail. Because attachments can be large, sifted out by spam filters, or infested with viruses, they are generally frowned upon. Before attaching a large file, ask permission. Alternatively, supply a link to the "media resources" page on your website, uploading the information there. Another option is employing a company like **Artspromo** (www.artspromo.org), which distributes news releases of touring artists to newspapers, radio, TV, Internet bulletin boards, and blogs.

Attracting Critics

Concert reviews by music critics put out the word and lend credibility to your efforts. Critics are extremely busy and review space is limited, so be smart when approaching them.

- **SCHEDULING.** When possible, avoid planning performances against other major events. In a bigger city, no time is devoid of competition, but nights earlier in the week are typically freer than weekends.
- **INVITATION.** Send a brief, personalized e-mail with a news release. It's usually appropriate to contact critics directly, instead of going through the supervising editor. Provide plenty of warning—2-4 months of lead time is best.

- **USE A CONNECTION.** If you do not know the critic personally, it may be helpful to have a mutual friend or colleague do the inviting.
- **MAKE IT INTERESTING.** Make sure the concert offers something intriguing for the reviewer...as well as other audience members!
- **TICKETS.** Always offer a pair of complementary tickets to reviewers.
- **MEETING.** If possible, meet briefly with the critic to describe the project and its goals.

What's Critical to Critics

Joshua Kosman (www.pacificaisle.blogspot.com), the San Francisco Chronicle's classical music critic, is a busy man. Eighty percent of his workload consists of reviewing performances by A-level organizations with a regular performance season. Competition for him to attend events not on this list is fierce. To even be considered requires 2-4 months lead time, perhaps some follow-throughs, and an out of the ordinary newsworthy concert experience. "If a string quartet plays Brahms, Haydn, and Shostakovich, don't expect me to make it...maybe if there is some kind of hook, like the group is all blind."

If you receive a negative review, try not to get too bent out of shape. See if anything can be learned from the comments, but remember that they are just opinions. Critics, like anyone, bring their own biases and preconceptions along with them. Case in point, see Nicolas Slonimsky's book "Lexicon of Musical Invective: Critical Assaults of Composers since Beethoven's Time." This text reprints horrendous attacks waged by critics against compositions now considered timeless masterpieces.

UNLEASHING YOUR MARKETING GENIUS

A surprising number of musicians who make inventive musical interpretations cower at the notion of a marketing campaign. This is an area where artists can shine! Devising an approach will prove more fun and effective when viewed as a creative endeavor instead of an arduous task. When initiating or refining a marketing campaign, brainstorm every idea imaginable for your product without editing, no matter how absurd it may seem. In this moment, when the mind is free from its usual filters and judgment, you may just find your moment of marketing genius.

Chapter Four

PRINT MATERIALS THAT SCREAM SUCCESS

Chapter 4

PRINT MATERIALS THAT SCREAM SUCCESS

What do you look like on paper? Print materials, along with web presence and recordings, are the public face of your musical product. Prime marketing real estate—often the entry point for new "clients" and a reminder of your existence to previous ones—they make the case for what you do. Stellar documents may place you one step closer to a sale or even tilt the scale in your favor. *No product can realistically thrive without powerful physical marketing materials.*

That said, even the most brilliantly crafted materials in isolation rarely close the deal. A great poster will not bring people to your concert...An amazing resume will not get you hired...A lovely brochure will not populate your studio...at least not by itself. With the occasional exception of dumb luck, success requires an exceptional product and a multi-pronged marketing campaign. Print materials are only one step in the process, albeit an essential one.

Savvy musicians understand that not all documents are created equally. In order for them to work effectively, they must:

- **GET NOTICED.** Marketing messages are everywhere, and as a result, most are overlooked or disregarded. Making documents stand out often requires some unusual aspect: unique message, placement, size, design, etc.
- **REINFORCE BRAND.** Every document should strengthen your brand identity, incorporating name, logo, and slogan, while shaping the core image/message you hope to convey.
- **INTRIGUE.** To advance your agenda, materials must reach the right people while captivating attention and piquing curiosity. Boring is never acceptable!
- **INFORM.** Clearly provide critical details with carefully chosen words.
- **PROVE MEMORABLE.** Repetition, multiple streams of publicity, and a strong or distinct message all contribute to making your message stick.

In their book "Made to Stick: Why Some Ideas Survive and Others Die," authors Chip and Dan Heath discuss in detail six features that make some messages more powerful and memorable than others. The traits, represented by the acronym SUCCESs, are:

1. Simple
2. Unexpected
3. Concrete
4. Credible
5. Emotional
6. Stories

ESSENTIALS

The Writing

Musicians are responsible for written materials on a regular basis: news releases, website content, bios, grant proposals, program notes, business plans. Do not underestimate the power of writing. A well-crafted statement can be persuasive in promoting your message, while consumers assume that poorly written materials parallel inferior workmanship. Even a carefully "wordsmithed" e-mail to someone you don't know can lead to huge opportunities. If unconfident in your writing abilities, consider employing a publicist or working closely with a coach.

The most effective writing captures four critical elements: 1) relevant message, 2) comfortable style, 3) accurate text, 4) fascinating angle. Though strong writing skills alone will take you far, it requires imagination to draft text that is memorable and captivating. Find a distinctive take that immediately draws in readers. A good title and attention grabbing thesis are essential, since it's difficult to recover after a weak opening. Keep content focused and relevant throughout, and always end on a strong note. Just as the final sounds of a composition disproportionately affect a listener's reaction, your conclusion should make a strong impression.

Omissions, incorrect information, and careless mistakes are not only sloppy, but they can bias others against you. Obviously, use spell check, but beware that even computers can miss errors. Before submitting any text, proofread at least three times, hunting for typos, grammatical inaccuracies, or awkward writing. Read text aloud, checking that passages flow naturally. Return for another pass a few days later with a fresh pair of eyes, and after you are satisfied, have colleagues check it. Make no mistake, writing is serious business.

The Look

The good news: It is now easier and cheaper than ever to make print materials sparkle. Computers come loaded with fonts galore, sophisticated templates, and user-friendly graphic editing capabilities. The bad news: Everyone has access to these resources. An average looking presentation is rarely good enough to make an impression. Make all documents visually striking, considering the spectrum from large-scale impact to minute details.

Some businesses pay thousands of dollars to hire graphic designers, but effective artwork can be acquired even on a shoestring budget. Printing companies often offer graphic design as part of a package deal. Friends, students, or local artists may be willing to create something for a small fee. And if you are visually inclined, inexpensive computer programs make relatively high-quality graphics attainable.

View text in various typescripts to see which best represent the impression you hope to convey. Too many fonts make a document appear cluttered and unprofessional; with the exception of special effects, limit this number to two or three. It is, however, often appropriate to establish a visual hierarchy through the use of **bold**, *italics*, SMALL CAPS, ALL CAPS, and various sizes, as long as comparable passages employ the same style. Underlining is typically limited to web and e-mail addresses. Use non-decorative, easy-to-read characters for extended passages, and make text large enough to be easily deciphered from a likely viewing distance.

Always employ clean, clear formatting. Create a layout that is easy to read and navigate, making the most impressive data pop out. Lists, bullets, charts, and graphics can be effective when used appropriately. Consider the density—words per line; spacing between lines; width of margins; lengths of paragraphs.

Well-placed, visually appealing graphics including logos, photographs, drawings, paintings, sketches, cartoons, and computer-generated images bring a level of interest that no amount of text can capture. If you don't have access to an artist, free public domain images are available on the Internet and through specialty software.

Color can add zest and visual interest to documents, highlighting key points while adding variety. Though color copies are more costly than black and white, added impact may justify the expense. Consider the psychological impact of each color scheme.

BUT IT'S JUST PAPER!

Believe it or not, the quality of paper used makes a profound impact. Ordinary 20-pound stock looks flimsy, material from the other side seeps through, and it is ordinary. People may not consciously deduct points because the paper looks cheap, but high quality stock makes documents seem more compelling. Take the weight/thickness, color, and material into account.

PROMOTIONAL VEHICLES

Bios

Bios are sent to presenters, included in press kits, displayed on websites, and printed in programs and brochures. Their job, however, is more than merely presenting appropriate data. Like all marketing materials, the primary goal should be winning the favor of readers. People want to know what you're about. In many cases, they form an opinion without hearing a note of your music. Even when concertgoers read your bio before a performance, the words used can generate excitement or leave them apathetic. Before scripting this statement, brainstorm the following:

- **ACCOMPLISHMENTS.** Awards, residencies, musicians/ensembles with which you have worked, schools attended, major teachers, recording projects, commissions, premiers, organizations, management, publications, major performances and venues, etc.
- **BACKGROUND.** What is fascinating about your personal history? Consider life events, unusual places you have lived, hobbies, interests, and funny stories. Information about overcoming adversity is always interesting (i.e. after breaking your hand, you retrained yourself to play piano).
- **BRAND.** What distinguishes your work or is important to you as an artist? Do you have a specialty? Unusual influences? A legacy you hope to leave?
- **QUOTES.** Powerful testimonials that have been written or spoken about your work by fans, famous people, reference letters, and media sources.

Next, create a hierarchy. What main points do you hope readers will take from your bio? Lead with an attention-grabbing sentence and maintain interest throughout. Place the most compelling information early on—not only should it immediately connect with readers, but some editors shorten bios by eliminating the final paragraphs—and omit unnecessary details. It is better to include fewer points but make a strong impression than to overwhelm with facts.

BIO-FEEDBACK

Feedback on potential lines from a fictional musician's bio:

Guitarist Murray McPickens recently graduated with his doctoral degree from Heaven University. This could appear towards the end of a bio, but never open with your educational pedigree. There has to be something more interesting about you than the fact you studied somewhere, even if it's a really good place.

Murray McPickens is one of the top guitarists of his generation. Exaggerated self-impressed judgments should be avoided. Substantiate!

According to the New York Times, Murray McPickens is "one of the top guitarists of his generation." This is more credible, since the opinion was expressed by someone else.

Murray McPickens has distinguished himself by winning many awards, including the prestigious International Bar Chord Prize in 1974. Don't present yourself as a has-been. If including accomplishments from long ago, be sure to highlight recent activity as well.

Dr. McPickens has performed extensively throughout the United States. Support all claims with specifics. Also, think twice before including titles like "Dr.," since many people assume that overly academic musicians are weak players.

Ever since laying eyes on a guitar at the age of seven, I have been addicted to this instrument. With few exceptions, bios should be written in the third person.

Truly an international musician, Murray McPickens' playing spans from Cuban salsa and American jazz to Spanish flamenco and Italian Baroque. A pretty good opener, especially if you brand is versatility. However, this sentence fails to mention what Murray actually does (plays guitar)—be sure to include your area of expertise early on.

One windy afternoon, Murray McPickens found himself stranded in Mexico City with nothing but a guitar and a toothbrush. Wow, you have my attention...

Far too many musician bios look essentially identical—uninspired laundry lists of accomplishments. There is absolutely no reason a bio must read like an obituary! Why not create a statement that reflects the image you hope to project? Bios may employ various literary styles: character pieces, comedic accounts, performer "trivia" lists, poems, etc.

Some of the most engaging bios have been composed by relatively inexperienced performers with no option but to embrace a creative approach. Always consider the audience, however—some constituents may be turned off by anything that strays too far from the norm.

The BEST Trumpeter Ever!

Born out of frustration that people take their MySpace pages far too seriously, Ken Watters (www.myspace.com/kenwatters) gave his profile a makeover. "Up until that point, my page was boring, just like everyone else's." He replaced the professional studio photo with a bizarre Photoshop® concoction, and rewrote his bio as if he were the cockiest musician in the world. Poking fun at self-impressed primadonnas, it begins, OK... *I am the BEST & MOST IMPORTANT jazz & ALL STYLE trumpeter in HISTORY.* He continues with mountains of politically incorrect over the top hilarity. As a result, the site began generating buzz and attracting heavy traffic.

Ken maintains a more serious, factual account on his personal homepage (www.wattersbrothers.com). "That bio describes what I've done. The MySpace page depicts who I am." He directs contacts to the site that seems most appropriate.

Various length bios may be requested. It is a good idea to maintain several versions. Standard lengths include 100-word, 250-word, and full-page. Conclude with your web address so that interested parties are directed to further information. Update your bio at least once a year.

Publicity Photos

A photograph in itself will probably not get you work (though this has happened!), but it can certainly pique someone's interest or lead to disqualification. Photos function a lot like bios in that they tell a story. What do you want yours to say? When people see your picture, how will they complete the sentence, "That artist seems so _____"?

Photographs are reprinted in newspapers, magazines, concert programs, posters, flyers, CD booklets, and websites. They are required from singers at most auditions, and play a central role in press kits.

Some musicians consider eliminating photography expenses, using a friend instead. Think twice before travelling this route. Expectations run high, and amateurish shots do count against you. Unless you know someone who produces outstanding, magazine quality work, hire an expert. If you're really in a pinch, consider approaching a photography student at your local art school. They always need interesting portfolio subjects, and work is generally done under the supervision of a teacher. Cost is usually minimal or free.

When possible, locate a photographer who has worked previously with musicians. Ask colleagues for referrals, and view work samples to make sure you like their style. Get the pricing up front, and fully comprehend what that amount includes. How many prints does it buy? Can you obtain digital files? Do you have permission to reprint images without additional fees? When strategizing with the photographer, share existing photos from magazines, websites, or other sources that demonstrate the spirit you hope to capture.

GETTING SHOT

On the day of the shoot, it is better to bring along too many items along than not enough. Pack several outfits including performance attire (typically all black), instruments, makeup, hair products, jewelry, accessories such as hats or scarves, and other possible props. Sessions typically include hundreds of shots and require 2-4 hours. Posing for that long can be exhausting! Therefore, conserve energy, drink plenty of water, and trust your photographer.

So what makes a good publicity photo?

1. STRONG IMPRESSION. The image should make a statement, stir an emotion, and reinforce your brand. Many classical musicians portray a classy formal aura, but if your product pushes the envelope in any way, a more artistic expression may be appropriate.

2. APPROPRIATE LOCATION. Possibilities include the photographer's studio, a concert venue, or external sites such as gardens, beaches, train stations, etc.

3. RECENT & CHARACTERISTIC. A decade old photo or one that does not resemble your appearance is like false advertising. It can get you into trouble with presenters or audience members who were "expecting something else."

4. HEADSHOT/ARTISTIC SHOT. Many sources require *headshots,* which frequently expand beyond your face to include the upper torso and a portion of your instrument. Even if you send full body *artistic shots,* some editors may look for ways to crop the photo.

5. SIMPLICITY. Except for special effects, keep the shot simple and clean. Too much clutter diminishes impact. Take strides to prevent unnecessary items from muddling up the shot, such as electrical outlets, cords, unnecessary objects or people, etc.

6. FOCUS. In most cases, have a single focal point rather than multiple elements competing for attention.

7. SPONTANEITY. As challenging as it may be, try to look natural and comfortable. Contrived facial expressions and overly posed shots convey insincerity.

8. CONTRASTS. Contrasting colors, textures, and images sharpen photos. This becomes even more important in black and white. Beware of outfits that are too close to your skin color and other elements that camouflage rather than distinguish.

9. GOOD LIGHTING. Successful shots are not too dark or overexposed.

10. HIGH RESOLUTION. When a photo will be printed from the digital version, use the highest resolution available. At a minimum, it should be one megabyte.

For physical copies, black and white 8 x 10 shots with a glossy finish are the industry standard, though color prints are increasing in popularity. The image may span from edge to edge, or a white border or design can frame the periphery.

Your name, contact information, website, and instrument/voice type should be imprinted somewhere so that people know who they're seeing. This information may appear towards the bottom of the portrait or on the backside. Another possibility is typing onto an adhesive label that is affixed to the back. Do not write on photos! Not only does this look unprofessional, but the impression of your pen can seep through.

Got the Picture?

The following musicians have wonderful photos posted on their websites. Not only are these shots high quality, but each effectively conveys an image of the performer and the music they play:

- Zoe Keating (www.zoekeating.com), cello
- Meg Okura (www.megokura.com), composer, erhu, violin
- Piers Adams/Red Priest (www.piersadams.com), recorder/Baroque ensemble
- Pamela Z (www.pamelaz.com), composer and vocalist
- The Portland Cello Project (www.portlandcelloproject.com), cello ensemble
- America's Dream Chamber Artists (www.adcany.org), chamber music society

Resumes

There must be a thousand resources detailing the considerations of putting together a resume, yet so many musicians still don't get it right. A resume is *not* simply an historical account of what you've done. It is a marketing tool used to gain employment, grants, and other opportunities that are often extremely competitive.

Do not simply throw together a resume. Take the time necessary to craft one that presents you in the brightest possible light. It is not unusual to spend a week or more perfecting this document. The following points can help your resume stand out from the competition.

1. CUSTOMIZE. Custom-tailor each resume. A document sent to a booking agent should highlight different points than one mailed to a teaching job. Include only information that is directly relevant to the position sought.

2. OPENING STATEMENT. Begin with a short, 1-3 sentence declaration emphasizing your strengths, objectives, or philosophy, stressing how they make you the ideal candidate.

3. PROVIDE THE ESSENTIALS. Typical headings: Work Experience; Skills; Performance Highlights; Awards & Grants; Recordings; Publications; Education; Teachers/Coaches; Conductors; Other Accomplishments. Don't be shy about including summer festivals, master classes, internships, volunteer work, and self-initiated projects if helpful to your case. List dates and locations. In particular, people want to know what you are doing now (i.e. 2006-present).

4. SHOW BENEFITS. The best resumes illustrate not only what you've done, but also the special features you bring. If you did something exceptional while on a job, for example, take a few words to articulate the contribution that sets you apart from the pack.

5. ACCENTUATE THE RIGHT STUFF. An excellent way to evaluate a resume is holding it about three feet from your face, seeing what you notice. Make sure the design stresses your strengths. For example, if you have performed in many states, those locations should naturally draw a skimmer's attention, perhaps spaced in a particular way or italicized.

6. PLACE STRONG SUITS EARLY ON. With the exception of academic positions, begin with professional accomplishments rather than education. Stress your professional accomplishments over the fact that you have attended school somewhere.

7. DE-EMPHASIZE WEAKNESSES. If an area of your background is particularly lean, combine headings to avoid bringing attention to this weakness. For example, if you have only made one recording but perform frequently, merge these sections to create the general impression of success in both areas. However, always tell the truth; avoid the temptation to exaggerate. If an "embellished fact" is discovered during a reference check, your reputation and integrity will be compromised.

8. BE CONCISE, BUT THOROUGH. Because resumes are short, typically limited to one page, choose every word carefully. However, it is better to create a comfortable well-spaced two-page document than to cram everything down to one.

9. MAKE IT BEAUTIFUL. Approach your resume like artwork. Aim to make a nicer looking document than the competition, mirroring the high quality of your work.

10. MAKE IT CONSISTENT. Since reviewers typically spend around 30 seconds glancing through this document, keep the formatting clear, consistent, and logical.

11. MAKE IT PERFECT. People notice mistakes, and these can count against you. Proofread, make sure punctuation is unified throughout, etc.

12. SUPPORT WITH COVER LETTER. Always send resumes in conjunction with a cover letter expressing interest in the opportunity and highlighting why you are the ideal candidate. In most cases, a couple short but compelling paragraphs are more than enough.

AN OPPORTUNITY TO REFLECT

Constructing a resume forces you to evaluate contributions. It not only points out areas of success, but also makes shortcomings blatantly apparent (and everyone has these). Though well-written documents disguise weaknesses, being forced to confront holes in your professional life can be positive, helping identify where energy and activity should be focused.

Curriculum Vitae

Far less information is available about *curricula vitae* (CVs) than resumes. As a result, many people are not quite sure how to approach them. In fact, some musicians send what is essentially a resume, but call it a CV. Needless to say, their file is not approached favorably.

If a resume is a career snapshot, then a CV is a detailed bibliography. Requested for grants, faculty searches, and other specialized work, they are longer, more in-depth accounts of your history. Someone fresh out of college might have a CV of only 5-10 pages, while one from a veteran could easily span 30+ pages.

Because of their length, it is even more important that formatting guides the eye to significant triumphs; you still only have 30 seconds to make an impression. Understand that committees will not read your CV from top to bottom—it will surely be skimmed. However, you never know which data will be noted, so pay meticulous attention to details throughout.

Though formatted similarly to a resume, CVs provide more details and additional explanation. Without turning into a novel, the luxury of space allows you to address particulars about what you have done and how you have contributed, especially when this information strengthens your case. For example, if outlining teaching experience, include the number of students, topics covered, your responsibilities, and what made you stand out in that position. With awards, explain the meaning and competitiveness of each honor. Do this, however, with bullet points and extremely concise explanations.

Instead of highlighting only a few main accomplishments, as with a resume, CVs provide a thorough list of experiences spanning several years or even an entire career. Quantity, as well as quality, often counts. In addition to categories commonly found on resumes, CVs often include repertoire or composition lists, professional memberships, community service, languages spoken, or even hobbies (who knows, your beloved pastime might catch someone's eye and advance the file). References and their contact information often appear on the final page.

Other Promotional Tools

Consider a range of issues when designing publicity tools. How do they reinforce your brand? What is the main message you hope to convey? What kind of hook will be incorporated? Do a series of items refer to similar themes? Will there be a funny, informative, or emotional approach? Which fonts and colors are best? What makes your materials distinctive? Always get feedback from multiple colleagues before printing large quantities.

View on-line templates and designs used by other musicians, assessing their efficacy. In fact, keep a written list of the best materials, noting specific aspects you like. These references will prove helpful to your designer when describing the effect you hope to capture. In terms of content, too much information overwhelms, while omitted essentials can frustrate or even lose sales. Weigh the importance of every word. Possible items to include are:

a) Your name/band name/product name/name of participants
b) Title of event
c) Service(s) provided/instrument/voice type
d) Appropriate contact information (phone, e-mail, fax, address)
e) Web address
f) Logo/slogan (if they exist)
g) Art work/photography
h) Date & location of event/ticket information (price, where to purchase)/repertoire
i) Testimonials/review quotes
j) Major awards/recordings/ management/record label/other accomplishments
k) Brief bios/description of product/frequently asked questions

ITEM/CONTENT	NOTES
Business Cards *a, c, d, e, f, (g)*	Effective cards make an impression! Consider intriguing graphics, flashy fonts, glossy finishes, and/or double-sided designs. Always carry cards with you or risk forfeiting opportunities—Phone numbers on napkins are unimpressive and will be lost! Business cards are necessities.
Letterhead *a, c, d, e, f, (g)*	Letterhead is stationary designed specifically to represent you or your service. The same type of information found on business cards should appear, usually covering the top portion of the page in a visually appealing manner.
Posters *for concerts:* *a, b, (c), (e),(f), g, h, (i)* *for businesses:* *a, c, d, e, f, g,(i), (j)*	Consider a range of designs, content, artwork, and uses of color. A series of themed posters can be effective. Make sure writing is large enough to be read from a distance, and do not oversaturate with information. Find unique ways to make posters stand out: size (post-it notes to jumbo banners), shape (non-rectangular), material (glued elements, 3-D formats), location (stairs, ceilings, floors, bathrooms), message (controversial, funny, weird, touching).
Flyers *on front:* *a, b/c, (f), g, (h)* *on back:* *a, b/c, (d), e, (g), (h), (i), (j), (k)*	Flyers serve as mini-posters that can be mailed, hand distributed, or left in strategic visible locations to be picked up by potential clients. Used for single events and ongoing businesses, common formats include postcards and 7 x 10 printouts on various weights and colors of paper. Unlike posters, flyers can include information on the backside. Make sure to leave room for an address and stamp if they will be mailed without an envelope.
Brochures *a, c, d, e, f, g, i, j, k*	Brochures, more informational than flyers, are used to promote ensembles, teaching studios, and other ongoing businesses. Many possible designs are available, including bi-fold, tri-fold, and multiple page booklets.
Miscellaneous	Magnets, bumper stickers, envelopes, return address labels, business checks, folders, greeting cards, invitations, stationary, and a number of other items can be custom designed to represent your product.

Press Kits

Press kits are marketing packages containing information about musical acts. Distributed to concert presenters, managers, agents, record labels, individuals looking to hire musicians, and of course the press, they are used to acquire some kind of opportunity.

When creating a press kit, begin by making an "all-purpose" version that can be used for most occasions. Later, you can tweak the cover letter and contents to fit each recipient. Press kits consist of several loose items placed neatly into a folder. Many folder designs are available, including those with slots for business cards or built in CD holders. Groups often have folders custom designed with imprinted photos, graphics, and typesetting.

All press kit items should incorporate easily readable fonts and type size. Inserts should be limited to a single page each, and may include:

- **COVER (PITCH) LETTER*.** Designed to spark interest, it should include contact info, a statement about why you are sending the press kit, and instructions for proceeding.
- **NEWS RELEASE*.** Provides all of the pertinent information about your newsworthy event.
- **SUMMARY SHEET/ARTIST BIOS*.** A synopsis of the product offered and those involved. This should provide compelling commentary to hook the viewer and distinguish your offerings. It may list recent performances, awards, other accolades, and interesting facts. Bulleted lists or short paragraphs are possible.
- **PHOTO*.** A good headshot or an artistic photo that serves double duty as a headshot. People want to know what you look like.
- **CD/DVD RECORDING.** A full-length recording or demo sampler. Videos are helpful if the performance is visually appealing. No more than 1-2 disks should be included.
- **FAQ SHEET.** Answers to Frequently Asked Questions.
- **FLYERS/CONCERT PROGRAMS.** From past or upcoming engagements.

- **REPERTOIRE LIST.** Cataloguing sample literature by composer, genre, or instrumentation. If several shows are available, provide a description of each.
- **PRESS CLIPPINGS.** A few newspaper or magazine articles/reviews demonstrate that people are paying attention to your work.
- **QUOTE SHEET.** Quotes excerpted from reviews, testimonials, or thank you notes. Obviously higher profile personalities hold more weight. Indicate the source and date of statements.
- **OTHER SERVICES.** If you offer master classes, educational workshops, or additional relevant services, include a sheet providing details.
- **BUSINESS CARD.** Include a couple cards so they can carry and share your information.
- **ACCESSORY.** Something as simple as a refrigerator magnet can make a press kit stand out.
- **ENVELOPE.** Use a distinctive envelope, so even that intrigues.

* *Top priority*

Do not insert all of the aforementioned items into a single press kit! An effective package provides enough information to interest the reviewer without becoming overwhelming. The more material included, the less likely each item will be studied, so make sure attention is focused appropriately. Make the kit easy to navigate, nice to view, and rich with substance.

The cost of duplication, photographs, recordings, and postage make press kits fairly expensive. Even if the price tag is limited to $4-7 per unit, this quickly adds up when compiling multiple packets. And they have a remarkably low rate of success when sent unsolicited. Rather than building a marketing campaign around press kits, network, build relationships, and mail off these packages only after a sincere interest has been expressed.

ON-LINE SUBMISSIONS

Many presenters today prefer to receive press kits through websites like *Online Gigs* (www.onlinegigs.com) or *Sonicbids* (www.sonicbids.com). After charging a fixed fee for each submission, these sites automate the submission process. Both companies cater to self-managed ensembles and fulfill a number of additional functions.

All of the elements above may be uploaded as an electronic press kit to your website. In fact, physical press kits are diminishing in popularity as more organizations post this information on-line. This eliminates expenses on your end and allows interested parties to examine your materials instantaneously. Maintaining both physical and online documentation allows you to compete in a variety of ways.

Press Kit Power

Hoping to get more gigs with orchestras, the saxophone foursome Capitol Quartet (www.capitolquartet.com) mailed out 300 beautifully crafted press kits costing $15 apiece. The effort was a total flop—nothing.

The next year, CQ member Anjan Shah served on a committee to select guest artists for the Baltimore Symphony. Any of the 250+ press kits that didn't grab jurors' attention in five seconds were thrown into the trash. The packets that advanced looked amazing, had impressive content, and immediately clarified essentials. Without a great photo, proposals were doomed. This experience taught Anjan that his group had included too much info, and that their demo CD should have featured only recordings with orchestra instead of chamber performances.

Years later, the group now employs a multi-faceted promotional approach. They send direct e-mails to a different employee each week within targeted orchestras: the Educational Director learns about educational offerings; the Operations Director discovers they have great looking manuscripts (string parts are bowed!); the Marketing Director hears of pre-recorded TV commercials and radio spots. For the marketing encore, they send key people a cover letter and clearly branded CD visor containing a few of their disks. These coordinated efforts have yielded exponentially better results.

A CHANGING WORLD

As the world becomes more digitized, the need for materials that are actually printed on paper is diminishing. This is good news for savvy musicians, who no longer have to spend as much capital on duplication expenses. But the requirement of producing remarkable promotional vehicles continues. Resumes, CVs, bios, photos, press kits, and other publicity tools remain critical to the success of savvy musicians—the only difference being that they are moving to cyberspace.

Chapter Five

POUNDING THE VIRTUAL PAVEMENT

Chapter 5

POUNDING THE VIRTUAL PAVEMENT

The Internet changed all the rules—how we communicate, spend our time, receive our news, socialize, and even find love. It redefined the ways in which we learn about music, advertise music, sell music, buy music, and listen to music. The Information Super Highway has made geography largely irrelevant, allowing anyone anywhere to have access to just about anything.

With such a radical shift in the way society operates, the wellbeing of established businesses continuing to operate on past sales paradigms was inevitably affected. In the music industry, this evolution has been detrimental to major record labels, as described in the next chapter. Large publishing companies are suffering a similar fate for parallel reasons. These firms are simply unable to maintain the extreme market domination they enjoyed in the pre-Cyberspace era.

But the Internet also paved the way for new winners. At the top of that list, you will be happy to hear, are entrepreneurs. Suddenly, *even an individual running a home business can compete against the big guys.* Major superstars and emerging artists are placed on equal footing, since it is no more costly or difficult to access information on one over the other. The World Wide Web allows savvy marketers to reach their target audience inexpensively and effectively.

THE THEORY OF CONSTANT EVOLUTION

The technology and trends of the Internet are changing at breakneck speeds. The hippest fads of today may fade into oblivion tomorrow, overtaken by new crazes. Any book that deals with technology will find itself outdated within a matter of months. Therefore it is imperative for savvy musicians to stay current and adapt to the quickly changing landscape.

MARKETING ON THE INTERNET

The Entrepreneur's Internet

There are many wonderful, non-business oriented reasons for having a presence on the Internet: social networking, exchanging photographs, voicing opinions, sharing knowledge. This chapter, however, focuses on marketing and career advancement strategies. Some talented musicians maintain beautiful websites that fail to clarify what they hope to gain professionally, much less take steps that help them achieve those objectives.

In order to formulate a salient Internet marketing strategy, you must first clarify your goals. What exactly is it you hope to accomplish? Sell CDs? Get commissions? Build a fan base? Accumulate work? All of the above? *Every piece of information released to the Internet should serve some larger purpose*, even if that means simply directing the reader to your website (which in turn serves a function). Any item that does not invite onlookers to take some action is a squandered opportunity.

This in no way implies that only advertisements are beneficial. Helpful, entertaining, or provocative postings are fantastic ways to attract new customers or reconnect with old ones. But once you have their attention, the most difficult step of any marketing campaign, what is the next step? How can you use that momentum to build the relationship?

Of course, the mere mention of your name can help (remember name recognition?). If you're already well-known, even a slight reference may be enough to remind people of your existence, convincing them to check out your website and see what's new. But for musicians starting out, you may only have one opportunity to catch a viewer's attention. Use it wisely before they move onto something else.

Web Presence

In the eyes of many, something that cannot easily be found on the Internet does not exist. By extension, this means that a musician without strong web representation does not have a career. Obviously, the logic is flawed, but perception is everything. So how successful have you been? "Google" your name to find out.

Just think about it. Let's say you are looking to hire a trombonist for a high profile gig, and a friend provides two referrals. A keyword search on the first name turns up only three listings, all of which mention her peripherally. For the second player, 130 unique hits emerge: an artist website, social networking pages, news releases, calendar listings, extensive blogging, etc. True, it may be impossible to assess who is the better performer from this exercise, but contestant #2 certainly has a lot more "fame." Who would you contact?

YOUR PRIMARY WEBSITE

Why You Must Have a Website

A website is the ultimate marketing tool. In addition to providing the cheapest and most wide-reaching form of advertising available, it allows you to convey a carefully crafted message around the clock in a relaxed, non-threatening fashion. It provides reference material for the media, an easy way to communicate with fans, forums for selling merchandise, and the opportunity for others to check out your work. In fact, because websites allow for an essentially unlimited amount of content to be included, it can fulfill just about any function you envision.

Without a website, your product is invisible. Without a good one, your sales potential will be severely crippled.

Logistics

There are many paths to creating a website. Learn to program in HTML and do it yourself. Start with a pre-programmed template—some are quite nice and flexible!—and drop in the content. Ask a friend to do the designing in exchange for a year's worth of bassoon lessons. Employ a high school or university student for a small fee and the promise of a "great resume builder." Drop thousands of dollars into hiring a pro. The road travelled is inconsequential. My concern here is not that you won't be able to get a website up and running, but rather that you craft one that maximizes its potential for professional success.

What Really Matters

The exciting news is that any website may be visited by anyone with Internet access and the inclination. Unlike television, however, which has a limited number of channels, the Internet is infinite. This makes attracting new visitors significantly more difficult, and even if someone decides to peek inside, they are likely to leave quickly unless material presented proves its relevance immediately.

While websites are a relatively new invention, the concept behind making them effective is not: *know your audience and understand what they want.* Offer information, services, or features that resonate and inspire confidence—often quite different than what you find interesting. Begin by determining what really matters:

1. WHAT ARE YOU TRYING TO MARKET? Recordings, private lessons, compositions, a band, engineering skills, concert tickets, loyalty, your playing, a deeper level of music appreciation? *Attention savvy musicians: If you are not actively promoting something, don't expect the site to help your career in any substantive way.*

2. WHAT STEP(S) WOULD YOU LIKE VISITORS TO TAKE? Buy an album, offer a commission, join a mailing list, share contact info, make a donation, hire you?

3. WHAT'S IN IT FOR THE CUSTOMER? A great experience, free information, joining a community, a special deal?

4. WHAT QUESTIONS WILL GUESTS LIKELY HAVE? What, where, when, who, why, how much?

5. WHAT WILL DRAW NEW VIEWERS TO YOUR SITE? Reputation, word of mouth, an invitation, other marketing, a cool feature, outlandish content, freebies, in-depth information? Unfortunately, cool music or a fancy site design can't be the answer, since they won't know that until after visiting.

6. WHAT ELEMENT(S) WILL HOLD THEIR ATTENTION AND BRING THEM BACK? And what will convince them to invite their friends?

ATTRACTING REPEAT VISITS

When considering the emphasis and structure of your website, consider which elements are likely to attract repeat visits. The main reasons people *return* to a music website are:

- **Entertainment.** To re-watch, re-hear, or share something with friends that is fun, interactive, quirky, beautiful, relevant, or a conversation piece.
- **Additional information.** To continue perusing material not viewed or absorbed during the first visit. However, no one cares about a bunch of text that fascinates you; they are only interested in content directly benefiting them. Helpful forums might address making reeds, practicing effectively, Baroque sociology, marketing music, or a database of compositions for a particular instrument/ensemble.
- **Helpful tools**. To use online tools, such as a metronome, manuscript paper generator, ear training exercises, or music games.
- **Order merchandise**. To purchase items such as CDs, scores, or memorabilia.
- **Communication**. To contact someone associated with the website, participate in a chat session, or add comments to a blog.
- **Updates.** To see what is new, such as upcoming performance dates or recent developments. Which brings us to an important point: *update your site regularly.* If not, fans may feel cheated, and presenters whose events are missing will become irritated.
- **Invitation.** Because an e-mail or other marketing reminds them about your great site.

Content

Once you have a clear idea about what really matters, compile the content: text, audio, video, and graphics. It may take weeks or even months to organize and perfect this information. How much should be included? Enough to adequately address the six questions above and not a kilobyte more. The purpose of a business site is not to show off impressive but irrelevant stuff you've done or share photos of your high school reunion (unless marketing directly to fellow classmates). Focus on your message.

All critical information must be clearly addressed. Omitted details such as the geographic area covered, contact information, and pricing structure cause viewers to become frustrated and leave. If pricing is variable, make it clear and easy for guests to request a quote.

A more common problem, however, is overloading. Visitors don't even know where to begin. Have you ever been handed a stuffed 25-page restaurant menu? Sure, they probably have heaps of nifty recipes, but identifying a single selection is stressful.

If your goal is to sell apple pie, just put that on the menu. Less is more. And unlike the eatery, where customers who enter almost always stay, websites have a much lower success rate. Entry is anonymous, and leaving is a cinch. If someone becomes the least bit confused, overwhelmed, or annoyed, they'll leave more quickly than you can say "mp3." Have one central focus for each page, and make it easy for people. Keep it succinct, simple, and clear.

As you conceptualize content, be sure to visit many websites representing musicians and non-musicians. Much of the time they demonstrate what *not* to do, but every once in a while you'll run into a gem. Keep precise notes on what you like and dislike, jotting down exceptional addresses. This list of URL's will be invaluable to your designer. Certainly, visit sites of competitors, understanding that your goal is to create something that exceeds their standard.

Relevant content is crucial. No matter how many visual bells and whistles your site boasts, visitors won't stay long if the information provided is not helpful, intriguing, well-organized, and concise. Include only the most pertinent items.

PAGE/ITEM	TIPS
Audio	No music website should be devoid of audio. However, nothing is more irksome than unwanted music that cannot be silenced—a sonic assault on the hapless surfer who accidentally left their speaker volume up! If your site loads music automatically, make the play and stop buttons VERY easy to locate. Avoid extraordinarily large files.
Bio	In addition to your main bio, include several downloadable versions of various lengths. Word processing formats allow editors to copy and paste without risking typos.
Blogs	Short for "web log," a blog can be anything from a personal diary to a public forum. It may incorporate links, audio files, graphics, or even video. Postings are shown in reverse chronology.
Calendar	Be sure to include pertinent details such as the location, time, repertoire, cost, and method of purchasing tickets for events. Include links to venues or series with websites that provide additional information. Update regularly.
Composition List	For composers interested in disseminating music. Include duration, instrumentation, year composed, premier info, awards, program notes, audio/score samples, and purchase instructions.
Contact Info	Make it easy for people to contact you. Include e-mail, phone, and fax. However, e-mail addresses may be detected by *spambots* that add you to annoying spam lists. Two solutions to this problem are typing out the address (i.e. infoATmysiteDOTcom) or using a special form for e-mails. Think twice before placing your home address on the web.
Description of Services	Clearly outline services offered, how they benefit clients, and what distinguishes your product. Address likely questions.

Home Page	The entryway to your site, many people will decide whether to stay based on their 2 second impression. It should look great, clearly illustrate the site's purpose, and tempt viewers to get engaged. Don't overload with information.
Links	Not only do links drive traffic to websites of colleagues and organizations, but there is a fabulous fringe benefit. When someone does a keyword search for those entities, your site may emerge.
Mailing List	Include a clearly visible place where fans can subscribe to your mailing list. If regularly using bulk messaging, make it easy for uninterested parties to opt-out. While relevant and appreciated communications help your business, unwanted ones do little more than get people grumbling.
Merchandise	For recordings, include purchasing instructions and other pertinent details (tracks, performers, durations, notes, etc.). Scores, ringtones, t-shirts, bumper stickers, and additional merchandise may also be sold. Make shopping easy or risk losing customers–many people flee from sites because the ordering process is confusing or cumbersome.
Miscellaneous	Practice tips, trivia, music jokes, special fonts, details about unusual instruments, or other non-standard pages can expand and diversify the number of hits you receive.
News/ Newsletters	Keep your news section updated, and place something impressive on the top of the page.
Photos/ Graphics	At the least, include one photo, probably a head shot. Small resolution sizes under 50k load quickly and appear adequately online. Images to be downloaded and reprinted in programs or by the press should be at least a megabyte. Credit the photographer.
Podcasts	Podcasts are recorded online "radio" clips that may be downloaded to computers or other media players, presenting an opportunity to interview musicians, talk about the creative process, or air recordings.

Electronic Press Kit	An entire downloadable copy of your press kit saves time and money while adding convenience to potential presenters and the press.
Reviews/ Testimonials	Praise from external sources, such as newspaper/magazine reviews or satisfied customers, lend credibility to your product.
Repertoire List	Helpful for performers who want to demonstrate versatility, promote fixed programs, or allow presenters to choose pieces.
Video	Effective performance or promotional videos add pizzazz and impact. Video opportunities include *vlogging* (video blogging), *vodcasting* (video podcasts), and *webinars* (on-line video seminars).

Presentation

Your goal should be to produce a personal, unique website that is nothing less than visually stunning. This in no way suggests that overly complex, animated graphics overwhelm visitors at every turn! Moving graphics do little more than turn people off—even more so if they waste time loading. Avoid a *splash page* (initial entry screen) that can't easily be bypassed, streams of floating notes that chase the cursor, and other frenetic graphic metamorphoses. If you have to consider whether a particular feature is annoying, the answer is probably yes. Keep it simple.

Create an intuitive, user friendly, easy to navigate sitemap with a clear unified layout. The placement and appearance of navigational tools should remain consistent on every page, never requiring visitors to hit their browser's back button because this menu disappears.

Stick to a limited number of standard fonts. Systems arbitrarily choose substitutes for those not in their font folder, changing the look and spacing significantly. Make sure text is large enough to read on computers set at a number of resolutions, and avoid hard-to-decipher colors. Divide large text blocks into short paragraphs and long passages into separate pages, as reading endless prose on a computer monitor is fatiguing. Edit out anything that's less than your best most crucial material. Remember that websites are read differently from books, relying heavily on the visual. Consider placing more extensive passages in .pdf attachments.

The eventual design of your site will undoubtedly evolve over time and through trial and error. Work closely with the designer throughout this process. Your final product should be outstanding across the board, since visitors will assume a direct correlation between its quality and your professional workmanship.

Checking Functionality

Before the going public, make sure everything works. Proof the content thoroughly and repeatedly, accepting nothing less than a convincing writing style. A website is not ready to be unearthed if parts are still "under construction." Too many eager newbies jump the gun and frustrate viewers with their incomplete presentation.

Be sure all pages and graphics appear correctly. Check links to be certain that all pages, graphics, and audio/video files open quickly. Then perform these tests on a number of other browsers and computers using various operating systems. There are often differences that are not apparent when designing the site.

Seek critical feedback and a variety of opinions from friends and colleagues you trust. Beware of individuals who simply concede that everything is flawless the first time around—there is always potential for improvement, so perhaps this says more about their lack of insight than the perfection of your work. When confident about your new creation, proudly unveil it to the world, but continue to collect reactions. Even a "completed" website should be a work in progress rather than a masterpiece frozen in time, updated regularly to reflect new performances, products, and information.

Attracting Attention

So you followed the advice above, and are now the proud owner of one of the world's great websites. Only one problem...nobody knows about it. If you've done the job well, those who become familiar with the page will return many times. But the first trick is getting them to visit—you must market this marketing tool!

Send an e-mail *blast* to everyone you know celebrating your new domain and inviting them to take a peek. Ask them to kindly forward the link to others if they like what they see.

Include your web address on everything—fliers, business cards, e-mails, brochures, posters, letterhead, CDs, e-zines—and conclude bios with a sentence inviting readers to visit. Mention your site every time you do a media story or radio interview, and proudly plug it during public performances. Heck, affix it to the back of a t-shirt if that gets attention; be creative. For more ideas, visit *The Savvy Musician* (www.savvymusician.com. I couldn't resist).

A growing number of local, national, and international *internet directories* are available on the web, representing just about every kind of musical product: chamber groups, private lessons, music retail, piano tuning, recording studios, etc. Do a keyword search for your area of expertise and sign up for all the free ones. Beware of directories that charge, however. Too often, they are fly-by-night operations that have little traffic and prey on inexperienced users.

The web is a viral place where visitors often stumble upon information, as opposed to seeking that exact person or thing. One of the most certain ways to drive traffic to your domain is having its URL linked to many, many other websites. Secondary sites and links from pages of friends, colleagues, and organizations help achieve this goal. Blog posts also increase visibility—suddenly a lot of people know something about you and are able to click on your link to learn more. You can never be too rich, too good looking, or have too much web presence!

If you've done things wisely, the uniqueness and quality of content alone will be enough to attract some guests. Be sure to have the designer embed appropriate *meta tags* (keywords) so your site pops up when someone does a relevant search engine hunt.

Great Music Sites

Here are some effective music websites and the reasons why:

- The piano duo Anderson and Roe (www.andersonroe.net) features dynamic videos, eye catching flyers, a polling booth, and a blog presenting this duo as hip, pop culture icons.
- Trombonist Tom Gibson (www.trombonelessons.com) hosts a series of video podcasts including lessons, performances, and interviews.
- Pianist Katya Grineva (www.katyagrineva.com) makes it easy for the press, booking agents, and other visitors to learn about her work by means of an electronic press kit, video interview, newspaper articles, and downloadable photos.
- Bassist Jason Heath (www.doublebassblog.org) presents an extensive blog dealing with all things bass related.
- Not only is Tasmin Little's (www.tasminlittle.net) album *Naked Violin* available for free downloading, but she offers spoken introductions to each piece and even suggests strategies for using the music in classroom settings.
- Saxophonist and bandleader Ralph Wilder (www.ralphwilderorchestra.com) directly answers questions that prospective clients might have through a series of videos.

EXPANDING WEB PRESENCE

Unveiling a website is a crucial step for your marketing campaign, but it should not be the last. Building an extensive web presence delivers many benefits:

1. NAME RECOGNITION. More web representation can increase name recognition, place your postings higher on search engines, and make your business appear more successful.

2. MORE CONSTITUENTS. Each site has the potential of reaching new audiences.

3. VARIED MESSAGE TYPES. People access information in different ways: text, audio, video. An assortment of message types helps you connect with a greater pool of individuals.

4. MOTIVATOR. All postings should steer viewers to your site and/or provide a call to action.

Increasing web presence doesn't mean that unique material must be generated for each entry! On the contrary, look for ways to rework or recycle content.

Social Networking Sites

Social networking sites offer incredible benefits. Better yet, most are free (paid for by advertisers) and easy to operate. Hosts are often equipped to handle just about any type of data: text, photos, sound clips, video files. In many cases, providers offer various formatting options, making design infinitely easier than starting from scratch.

Networking sites allow members to list "friends" who are also members. While a large circle of friends may give the impression of success, this is not the only benefit. In the real world you obviously know your connections, but probably not all *their* associations. On these sites, you can easily bounce to pages of your friend's friends, their friends, and so on. Needless to say, it permits you to "meet" people who would never cross your path outside the virtual pavement. It also allows others to find you. Because we tend to have acquaintances who share our interests, these sites allow niche communities to blossom. If your message is strong and relevant enough, it has the potential to spiral into out of control popularity.

Popular networking sites include *MySpace* (www.myspace.com), *Facebook* (www.facebook.com), and *LinkedIn* (www.linkedin.com). Try *Classical Lounge* (www.classicallounge.com) and *Dilettante* (www.dilettantemusic.com) for sites geared specifically towards classical musicians and fans, and *Jazz Musician Space* (www.jazzmusicianspace.com) to visit a "Social Hang for Jazz Musicians."

Early Music Meets New Technology

Gwyn Roberts, co-artistic director of the Philadelphia Baroque Orchestra Tempesta di Mare (www.tempestadimare.org), comments on some ways in which *Facebook* has been helpful to her ensemble. Hours after posting a 2-hour concert broadcast on their "page," she began receiving comments from Latin American admirers who had learned about the group and were interested in purchasing CDs. As it turns out, a "friend" had posted that "event" on a Spanish language Early Music group forum, allowing it to reach hundreds of new "fans."

After a personal emergency forced a contracted ensemble player to back out of a gig at the last minute, Gwyn tried calling some subs, but could not reach anyone. Then she thought to check *Facebook* and see who was online. Shortly after, someone agreed to step in.

Video-Sharing Sites

Video-sharing sites, like networking sites, typically allow members to post free of charge. Consider uploading live performance excerpts, carefully staged productions, or music related talks. The most viewed videos are usually extreme or unusual in some way, whether demonstrating virtuosic brilliance or outrageous wackiness. An intriguing clip has the potential to generate a huge viral buzz. Obviously, make sure that posts represent your work favorably. The most popular video-sharing site today is **YouTube** (www.youtube.com). Check out **The Music Page** (www.themusicpage.com) for exclusive music content.

YouTube Superstar

For years, Greg Pattillo (www.whatisproject.org) had been "beatboxing" (vocal percussion) while playing flute. But it wasn't until videos were uploaded to *YouTube* that his career took off. A posting of his *Inspector Gadget* rendition received almost a million hits within days of appearing on the site's main page. Other videos have appealed to vast and additional audiences.

Greg has since been featured on shows broadcast by Nickelodeon, BBC, Fox, and German radio. Esquire magazine, Flute Talk, and the New York Times have run feature articles on his playing. He now has a flute endorsement, touring trio with management, beatbox/flute instruction manual, and an international profile. "*YouTube* single-handedly launched my career. It has given me the sort of exposure previously limited to big corporate stars, without the drama and big bucks required in those deals."

Organization Sites

Sites representing ensembles, universities, companies, and arts associations often post individual pages on employees or members. Treat these as marketing opportunities.

Blogging

There are many ways to utilize blogs: host your own, appear as a guest writer, have a blogger cover your story, add comments to an existing post. Every entry should link to your primary site. Most bloggers are constantly in search of interesting content, making this an ideal way to communicate your stories and ideas.

Web-Based Media

There are three major branches of media coverage: print, broadcast, and Internet-only. Yet even the first two categories are closely linked to Cyberspace. Most newspapers release many or all articles on-line, and some radio and TV stations upload interesting shows in the form of podcasts. Therefore, even brushes with traditional media outlets can boost your web presence.

The number of Internet-only "newspapers" and "magazines" is quickly proliferating. Being picked up by them requires steps similar to that of other media sources (newsworthy news releases, cover letters, etc.). However, because an essentially unlimited amount of material can be featured, most Internet-only publications are constantly in search of interesting content. These sources will likely take notice if proposals have something enticing to offer readers. You may also want to pursue Internet radio stations to disseminate your music or conduct an interview.

Web Calendars

Many publications and web sites host online calendars. Listing events is typically free. Submit information at least one month in advance.

Internet Registries

Existing Internet registries catalogue just about every musical business imaginable: wedding bands, private teachers, independent record labels, recording studios, composers, etc. Most allow you to provide name, contact information, and a description of services offered. Sign up for all the free registries; think twice before paying to be listed.

Links

See if colleagues, complementary businesses, and other organizations will provide a link to your site. Reciprocal links are always appreciated.

Always E-Present

Though composer Alex Shapiro (www.alexshapiro.org) lives on a small remote island, she is more connected to the world than ever before, thanks to the Internet. Her extensive web presence consistently leads to new opportunities, often from people she hasn't met. For example, a conductor recently offered her a commission after discovering her *MySpace* page.

Alex writes articles for on-line magazines like *NewMusicBox*, and has been featured in interviews, profiles, and CD reviews with several e-journals. In addition to maintaining her own blog, she posts comments on a number of others. Each contribution links to her website, where she consistently notices a spike in hits after something new is posted. As a full-time concert music composer, these networking tools are essential. "If you have something interesting to say, take the initiative to put it out there. This e-presence helps you become a known quantity to peers and other readers, and delivers new fans and clients to your musical doorstep."

INTERNET COMMUNICATION

E-mail

You are undoubtedly familiar, or perhaps even obsessed, with e-mail. It provides a free, convenient, and instantaneous way to communicate while offering a quick cost-effective way to "send" documents such as musical scores and recordings. For now, let's focus the discussion on e-mail as a means of—you guessed it—marketing.

E-mailing provides an easy way to ask members of your network for support, make unsolicited contact with new personalities, and unveil your latest products to old clients. But for a message to have any sort of impact, the content and structure is imperative. Most people's inboxes overflow with offers "to good to be true." Usually they are moved quickly to the *spam* folder. For the greatest chances of delivering a positive, fruitful e-mail experience, make sure messages are compelling, relevant, and to the point.

- **SUBJECT HEADING.** A clear accurate heading not only establishes expectations, but makes it easier to locate the message at a later point.
- **PERSONALIZE.** Personalized messages are taken more seriously than generic ones.
- **GOOD OPENING.** Most people read the first few sentences of an e-mail and then decide whether to continue. Grab their attention quickly.
- **SHORT AND SWEET.** Busy people (i.e. everyone except perhaps grandma) have no appetite for e-mail "novels." Get to the point and make every word count.
- **CALL TO ACTION.** Be clear about what you hope the person will do as a result of your message. What action would you like them to take?
- **LAYOUT.** Most people skim, rather than read, e-mails. To convey maximum information, favor short paragraphs, bullet points, etc.
- **TONE.** One problem with e-mail is that words are presented without inflection. Go out of your way to convey a friendly air.

• **PROOFREAD.** Assume that spelling, grammar, and other errors will be noticed. Mistakes cause others to take you less seriously.

• **ATTACHMENTS.** Do not clog someone's inbox with an exceedingly large attachment without first warning them.

• **SPAM.** Never do it. If you send mass e-mails, always include a way for people to opt out if they desire, so they don't become annoyed by your contact.

YOUR SIGNATURE PERFORMANCE

Submitting a business letter without contact information would be unthinkable, yet many musicians omit this critical feature from e-mails. Every work-related message (and perhaps personal one) should conclude with a *signature*, usually 4-8 lines of text consisting of at least your name, website, position/company, and contact information.

For even better results, use the opportunity to promote your site or product by emphasizing a benefit: "For 23 revolutionary practice tips that *will* transform your music making, visit www.yourwebsite.com." You may even want to stock a variety of signatures, choosing the most relevant one for each communication.

Response

There tend to be three categories of e-mail responders. The first group typically answers messages within 5 minutes, and certainly never takes more 24 hours. Not only does this practice convey a sense of extreme professionalism, but it removes a "chore" from your to-do list. The second group often procrastinates 3-7 days before offering a reply. They eventually follow through, but sluggishly. The last faction simply does not acknowledge messages unless they feel that communication benefits them directly. You have probably been irked by people who subscribe to this philosophy.

Of course you are busy, and responding promptly to every note isn't always possible. But understand that your reputation rests largely on perceived dependability. Many gigs are simply awarded to the person who hits "reply" first, and even when a communication does not offer immediate gain, good service now leads to future reward. Make it your policy to exceed expectations. If you truly are too busy to answer messages, hire an assistant or generate an automatic response explaining the circumstances. That way, at least people won't take your lack of action personally. This just makes good business sense.

Keeping Fans Engaged

Chapter 7 addresses the importance of building a fan/client list and staying current. E-mail provides a host of free and easy ways to remain in plain view, making it more likely these individuals will offer you work, buy your product, or see your show. How much communication is the right amount? Inundation results with diminished interest or even irritation, while a disappearing act may cause them to forget about you altogether. Depending on what you do, *aim for at least one relevant e-interaction each 6-month period,* with no more than two per month excluding personalized contacts.

There are many ways to keep fans engaged. One possibility is simply sending out e-mail invitations to upcoming events. Whet their appetite, clearly state the details, and include a short news release.

An *e-zine* is an e-mail newsletter. If using these, commit to releasing them regularly since it speaks to your reliability. The best newsletters encourage loyalty, create a sense of community, and distinguish your work. Include content that will be anticipated and appreciated by readers. For example, a recording studio e-zine might include recording tips (running a smooth session, editing strategies), perspective on releasing a CD (label vs. do-it-yourself, marketing techniques), articles submitted by recent clients, and a plug or two for the business.

Another interesting option is creating a 2-3 minute *video postcard.* This could containg a photo slide show underscored with your music, live recent clip, or spoken message. Because this concept is still unique and underexploited, it is an attention grabbing way to stay in touch. If the file is too large to include in an e-mail, upload it to a special web page and forward the link.

Internet Connections

The string quartet Ethel (www.ethelcentral.com), known for performing a diverse range of musical genres, uses the Internet to connect with current and potential fans in several ways. Among other functions, networking sites allow new listeners to discover the band. "*MySpace* is like a mall with millions of stores. Window shoppers who come across our webpage often wind up attending a concert at some point," explains violinist Mary Rowell. Presenters, the press, and others interested in digging deeper can find more detailed information on their blog and their website. Finally, *ETHELzine* keeps current enthusiasts engaged. This visually appealing e-mail newsletter, sent to around 5000 subscribers each month, includes photos, upcoming events, and blog entries by group members.

The Internet as a Resource

This chapter focused on Internet techniques that promote professional activities to others. Of course, the World Wide Web is also an incredible research tool, making it easier than ever to discover opportunities such as gigs, competitions, job listings, calls-for-scores, conferences, etc., while learning about recent trends and happenings. For each area of interest, there are Internet-based organizations you should join and websites to visit regularly. For an extensive list of resources for musicians, visit *The Savvy Musician* (www.savvymusician.com).

Chapter Six

THE NEW RECORDING PARADIGM

Chapter 6

THE NEW RECORDING PARADIGM

MAYDAY, MAYDAY!!! Record labels are crashing and burning. CD sales are plummeting, and record stores are on the verge of extinction. The apocalypse for the kingdom of music is imminent. Right???

Well, that depends on where you stand. To executives at major labels, perhaps it is time to consider alternate career options. Similarly, recording artists tied to these companies may need to rethink their strategy forward. But for savvy entrepreneurial musicians with something unique to say, this new set of circumstances may actually be a blessing in disguise.

STATE OF THE INDUSTRY

Things Sure Ain't What They Used to Be...

Increasingly throughout the latter part of the twentieth century, the music industry was dominated by a handful of powerful record labels. These companies were profit-minded business organizations, representing artists they hoped would maximize earnings, often irrespective of musical merit or depth. They used radio stations and TV channels like MTV and VH1 as powerful marketing tools, influencing which "songs" would receive airtime. Music that quickly caught on was forced upon consumers repeatedly, ad nauseum.

In a sense, record companies controlled public taste. They determined what was "hip" and, therefore, what was purchased. Under this system, some recordings sold through the roof, and companies made out like bandits. The phenomenon of the megastar was born, making a relatively small percentage of artists filthy rich.

Record labels took on significant risk, investing heavily in their roster. In addition to the high price tag of recording, duplication, and distribution, they marketed intensively and organized tours in order to sell their products. Of course, with that kind of investment, a majority of albums lost money. Musicians only got paid after all related project expenses had been recouped, and that rarely happened. If one recording by a particular artist managed to turn a profit, but others did not, the surplus would cover the remaining deficit before any compensation was disbursed. The majority of recordings were not lucrative, and musicians who did not prove profitable were quickly dropped from a label's roster.

While popular music styles generated the lion's share of recording revenues, several major labels maintained non-pop wings. Sales were still important, to be sure, and the principles outlined above were mirrored. However, by the end of the century, classical and jazz recordings in the United States each accounted for only a few percent of total music sales—down significantly from the 1960s, when classical albums alone captured over 30% of the market.

More often than not, these recordings lost money, requiring companies to subsidize such "experiments in vanity" with profits from the other side. Eventually, labels began shrinking these arms of their business. Independent, non-pop labels also emerged, usually tackling projects that required smaller investments (i.e. chamber as opposed to orchestral). Many "indie" labels failed to survive, but some managed to eke by and a few did well. Helping to disseminate classical and jazz recordings, public radio stations surfaced in many metropolitan areas.

During most of this time, it was essentially impossible for independent artists to develop a major reputation without the backing of a record label. Recording was expensive, and there was simply no affordable way to advertise and distribute this kind of product without the backing of a label. Independent musicians could certainly work locally, but competing with the "big guys" was impossible. Even signed artists had their hands tied to a certain extent. Their fate was largely up to the amount of support record companies were willing to invest in promoting their careers. Executives with no musical background commonly dictated "artistic" choices with the sole hope of increasing the bottom line.

This summary is quite simplified, but it paints a rough picture of prevailing conditions in the late 20th Century. Which brings us to today...

...So Here's What they Are Now

The music industry has had an extreme makeover, thanks in large part to the Internet and other technological advances. In particular, two major transformations have changed all of the rules.

CHOICE. In years past, the amount of exposure the average Joe had to recorded music was limited. True, he *could* have purchased any record, cassette, or CD in the store, but most people favor that which is familiar. Joe learned what was "cool" primarily through radio and music videos. His favorite stations—a subset of the 18 music options available in his area—reiterated the same tunes repeatedly. Not so ironically, these became his preferences. Of course, classmates and friends also influenced his tastes (after listening to the same channels). The music he bought was predictable, and his collection closely resembled other folks in town, or across the country for that matter.

In the present era, the average Jane has unprecedented access to a huge array of recorded music options: mainstream radio, satellite radio, TV radio, Internet radio, podcasts, YouTube, independent artist websites, and the list goes on. She discusses musical taste not only with classmates at school, but also "friends" from all over the world through MySpace, Facebook, and Twitter pages. Sometimes when surfing the net, she accidentally stumbles upon exciting unfamiliar sounds, broadening her taste. The downloads on her iPod are significantly more eclectic than Joe's collection, and not necessarily a close match with other folks in town.

Today, with so many choices accessible, it seems logical that musical taste will de-centralize and expand. As a result of this shifting paradigm, more mid-level artists will be able to find an audience as the "distribution of (listening) wealth" is re-proportioned. Under these circumstances, even non-mainstream emerging artists have the potential to shine in ways previously unimaginable *if* they can find a way to attract attention and become part of the conversation. While the increasing amount of choices presents new challenges, lack of access is no longer a problem. Great news for savvy musicians!

EXPENSE. In the past, every phase of the recording process was quite costly: recording, design, duplication, packaging, marketing, and distribution. It could easily require $25,000-100,000+ to create and promote an album. Today, recordings can still cost that much, but it is also possible to drastically reduce that amount. Let's consider these issues individually for a hypothetical recording released only through a more recent means of acquisition: *downloads.*

1. **RECORDING.** The expenses associated with the recording process still exist, and this is the priciest aspect of many projects. However, equipment costs have dropped while quality has improved, allowing some kinds of work to go faster (editing, mixing, etc.). These circumstances also make it feasible for musicians to operate home recording studios. Once the initial investment has been made, they can record to their heart's content without worrying about soaring hourly rates.

2. **DESIGN.** For downloads, it is still necessary to design "cover art," which is displayed online. However, affordable and user friendly graphics programs make this step feasible and inexpensive for those willing to self-design.

3. **DUPLICATION.** No physical product must be duplicated. This expense is eliminated.
4. **PACKAGING.** Downloads do not require packaging. This expense is also eliminated.
5. **MARKETING.** Internet advertising is substantially cheaper than traditional mass marketing schemes. It also makes it easier to target customers interested in a particular type of product.
6. **DISTRIBUTION.** Once a company is set up to distribute through a particular on-line vendor or site, it costs little more to offer ten or ten thousand products.

WHAT ABOUT CDs?

CDs are still a significant medium through which music is sold, and this will remain the case for the next few years. However, it is easy to understand why so many people prefer downloads: instantaneous access, cheaper prices, no shipping charges, avoidance of clutter (hundreds of hours stored on a single gadget!), the ability to purchase only tracks desired.

As a result, compact disk sales have fallen drastically, and this downward trend will continue. When producing disks, understand their benefits and market them so that you won't wind up with a mountain of leftovers after their obituary has been written.

- **Habit.** Some people, especially among older communities, are not comfortable with download technology. Others just prefer CDs. Classical and jazz audiences currently buy these disks at a higher rate than fans of many other genres.
- **Sound Quality**. In order to make downloads faster, files are converted to smaller formats with lower sound quality. However, new technology is working to correct this discrepancy as bandwidth for distribution grows.
- **Information.** CDs come with informational booklets. If this is a selling point, make sure your packaging adds value. However, more and more, full details are available on-line, diminishing the importance of this issue.
- **Demo**. The physicality of CD demos reminds reviewers to take a listen.
- **Souvenir/Impulse Buying**. The main advantage of a CD is that you can hold this tangible object. When attending a concert, some people like to acquire a physical keepsake. *You can't autograph a download!* In essence, the strongest argument for CDs has nothing to do with musical content. In the future, another physical form will likely emerge to take its place. For example, check out download cards at *Dropcards* (www.dropcards.com).

Of course, this new price reduction also creates challenges. Today, just about anyone has the means to record, and as a result, a slew of really horrible music is spewed at every turn. And more products mean more competition, at least in terms of having your voice heard.

In most cases, recording still requires a sizable investment. But these figures have lessened, making it feasible for savvy musicians to raise this money without the backing of a major label. Now the "little guy" has a chance of succeeding in ways previously unimaginable. The Internet and other technological innovations allow artists to have more control over their own destiny, thanks to increased choices and decreased expenses. That's why the fall of the recording industry could just be, for the emerging savvy musician, a four-leaf clover.

THE BUSINESS OF RECORDING

Paying Recording Artists

Mechanical royalties are paid when recordings are sold. For each composition, record labels disburse payments to publishers who then typically split this amount with the composer 50/50. A fixed rate for each work that appears on the recording, based on the duration of the "song," is multiplied by the number of units purchased. Mechanical royalties are also paid to recording artists. A certain percentage of the retail price, usually 8-25%, is divided among performers.

Though this formula may appear simple enough, it is actually quite complex. All funds "advanced" by the label must first be recouped before royalties are paid. This includes recording, marketing, touring, and other expenses. Once the initial investment has been recovered, a host of additional factors shrink the royalty amount including issues as ridiculous as "anticipated product damage." The bottom line—most artists generate little if any capital from recordings. With the exception of blockbuster hits and highly visible ensembles, projects typically lose money. However, a good product can attract gigs and other revenue producing opportunities.

Labels representing pop groups often sponsor tours which help boost album sales. Conversely, classical and jazz artists typically record for the opposite reason—to help them get tours!

The music industry is now faced with a new dilemma. In a world where recordings can easily be duplicated and downloaded, often for free, how will artists, composers, songwriters, publishers, and labels get paid? That is the 23 million dollar question, and one that has a lot of experts scratching their heads. "Photocopying" music today is a snap, as every computer is equipped with a CD-R drive. Though it is illegal to duplicate most recordings, effectively policing this practice is impossible.

The bigger issue, however, is downloading. In 1999, the website Napster became the first peer-to-peer music file sharing service. It allowed people to swap and download music recordings without charge, avoiding the need to make a purchase and violating a host of copyright laws. A lawsuit forced Napster to shut down in 2001, but the habits it instilled in consumers fundamentally changed the way music is accessed and distributed.

When recordings are obtained for free, nobody gets compensated. But the public is increasingly resistant to the idea of paying for recorded music, and certainly unenthusiastic about handing over $15-20 for a single album. Companies and artists are scrambling to invent download solutions that are legal, generate cash flow, and attractive to consumers. Some possibilities:

- Many sites, such as **iTunes** (www.itunes.com), allow people to download music by paying a flat fee such as 99¢ per track. Consumers are not forced to shell out big cash to purchase an entire album, choosing only selections of interest. About 75% of each download fee is allocated for royalties, which pays the distributor, label, and musicians.
- Sites like **Rhapsody** (www.rhapsody.com) offer subscription services. For a monthly fee, patrons can listen to any of the music in their archives, unlimited. This is like customer-controlled radio. Music cannot be downloaded, but heard only via the Internet.

Royalties are distributed proportionally based on the number of hits for each track.

- Similarly, **Apple** has considered charging a higher fee for iPods and iPhones in exchange for a service that allows users to buy or rent an unlimited amount of recordings.
- Peter Gabriel's website **We7** (www.we7.com) allows members to either 1) purchase individual tracks, or 2) download them for free. However, for option #2, downloads force patrons to watch advertisements of up to 10 seconds before each listening for the first four weeks. In other words, advertisers buy the music instead of consumers.

The Record Label Conundrum

Getting a record deal today is easier than ever before. No kidding! There are small, independent companies popping up all over the place, and if you have a unique marketable product, signing on is absolutely feasible. What's the catch? In many cases, you have to be willing to pay them.

Gone are the days of labels investing heavily in artists they represent, especially in the jazz and classical worlds. In fact, most of the majors are no longer willing to take on the risk of new talent within these genres. Instead, they favor reissues and new recordings by established celebs, or eliminate this part of their business altogether. Even top symphony orchestras face this reality—not a single American orchestra holds a multi-CD contract.

On the other hand, the number of smaller, independent companies is proliferating, thanks to the diminishing cost of doing business. Most of these labels operate more like service centers than full-blown sponsors. The more they do, the less payment you receive per unit sold. "Signed" artists are frequently required to raise all funds necessary to cover recording expenses. Some labels even charge additional fees. However, they may offer a variety of benefits, including:

- Recording (if you are lucky)
- Their brand name
- Prestige
- Design (booklets, inserts, etc.)
- Packaging
- Duplication
- Logistics (copyright, royalties, etc.)
- Submissions to radio & reviewers
- Distribution
- Promotion (usually limited)

Distribution is a particularly important benefit. A good label will already have an existing fan base and be set up to market to an international audience through their own website, Amazon, Barnes & Noble, Wal-mart, and/or other retailers.

If seeking a label, search for companies that specialize in the kind of music you perform. Get referrals from musicians and do research on-line. Several websites, such as *All Record Labels* (www.allrecordlabels.com) and *Musical America* (www.musicalamerica.com), catalogue hundreds of labels.

Each business has unique submission policies. Some don't accept unsolicited materials, while others consider proposals from just about anyone. Regardless of size or prestige, all labels have one predominant concern: will your product sell? Do not approach a label until you've identified likely consumer groups and formulated a strong marketing strategy.

Be sure you fully understand the terms of the agreement upfront. Do you retain the rights? What expenses will be required on your end, and how is payment allocated? Can the contract be easily terminated? How will they actually promote your product? Beware of over-promising. Seek feedback from artists who have previously worked with the label, and consult an entertainment attorney before signing any agreement.

Getting Labeled

Jazz trumpeter Sean Jones (www.seanjonesmusic.com) has a multiple release contract with *Mack Avenue Records* (www.mackavenue.com). For each recording, the label provides a cash advance, covers recording and marketing expenses, and even sponsors tours. To recoup their investment, they market aggressively through jazz catalogues and trade journals, magazines like *The New Yorker* and airline publications, internet sites, and a host of other places. They also push to get maximum airplay on radio and TV music stations. This kind of deal is quite rare.

More common is the agreement jazz trombonist, singer, and arranger Scott Whitfield (www.scottwhitfield.com) has with his label, *Summit Records* (www.summitrecords.com). With each CD, he is responsible for funding all recording, editing, and mastering expenses, while the label covers graphic design, duplication, and printing. In addition, they make recordings available on their website, Amazon, iTunes, other Internet vendors, and even some retail outlets. For each unit sold, Scott receives a small royalty. The label also allows him to purchase a minimum of 500 disks at a discounted $5 rate, which may be marketed for a profit at gigs. This is how the vast majority of his recordings are sold.

Oboist Nancy Ambrose King (www.kingoboe.com) has released six albums with three companies. As with Scott, she was responsible for recording expenses, while the labels financed post-production expenses. Nancy has generated no revenue through these transactions. "I never intended to make money with recording. Instead, I did them for the experience, to be the first to record certain pieces, and to put my name out there. But my CDs have led to other opportunities that do pay." Even if making a CD causes the artist to lose money (often the case), it can help facilitate other artistic and professional goals.

Go-It-Alone

The entrepreneur in you may be perplexed, wondering if the arrangement above is really such a great deal. If responsible for so many expenses anyway, why not start your own label? The price of CD duplication has dropped considerably: a few thousand dollars can buy 500-2000 disks. Perhaps a friend with artistic inclinations can design packaging materials for a reasonable rate.

With self-releases, higher profits can be earned even if fewer copies are sold. To emphasize with a grossly oversimplified example...Let's say a store sells your CD for $15. About half ($7.50) goes to the label. Your contract stipulates that artists receive 10% of the label's cut, or $.75. But by going-it-alone, you retain the full $7.50. It would take 10 times as many sales to yield the same profit margin! Better yet, selling the disk after gigs or through your own website earns you the full $15. Needless to say, carefully weigh each model:

EXTERNAL LABEL	YOUR OWN LABEL
less control	more control
less time & energy	more time & energy
less risk	more risk
distribution already established	distribution more difficult
some $ investment usually required	more investment $ required
less bookkeeping required	organization/bookkeeping required
more potential sales	much more $ earned per unit sold

One of the most challenging aspects when starting a label is distribution. As the owner of an independent company, you are responsible for making all arrangements and delivering physical copies to retailers, either personally or via mail. It's essentially impossible for new companies to get their products into chain CD stores, bookstores, and some Internet music sites. However, the number of accessible options is quickly proliferating.

Another possibility is hiring a *pass-through*, which allows the use of an established label's distribution pipeline for a fee (typically 10% to the pass-through and another 10% to their distributor). By the time your label has 15-20+ products and an established history of sales, you may be able to hire a distributor directly for a 10% commission.

To summarize, each stage of a recording project—recording, design, duplication, packaging, marketing, and distribution—takes time, energy, and resources. When you take on all the financial risk, you will rightly be entitled to the highest reward when and if your product sells. If other parties share this risk, they will take their cut. Some labels today require you, the artist, to make the big investments while they retain the majority of profits. Think carefully before entering this type of agreement. Going-it-alone requires significantly more work, but the potential difference in payoff can be substantial.

Release Yourself

In the early 1990s, when flutist Laurel Zucker (www.laurelzucker.com) first decided to record, she spoke with several artists signed to labels. Many complained they weren't getting paid well, didn't have artistic control, and were unsatisfied with their firm's marketing. So she began her own company, before it was fashionable. To date, *Cantilena Records* has released an impressive 45 disks and 4 teaching DVDs. "Though my recordings do generate income, I'm not in it for the money. I truly love sharing flute music with the world."

From time to time, Laurel has received small subsidies from flute companies and other businesses, but most projects are completely self-financed. By now, recording sales generate enough revenue to bankroll future ventures. For each release, she sends out copies to various magazine reviewers, mails CDs to every classical radio station in the country, purchases a full page color ad in *Flutist Quarterly,* and makes disks and downloads available through sites like CD Baby, Amazon, Flute World, and her own domain. She also sells disks at concerts.

Off-Line Sales

Even if you have an external label, it is the musicians' responsibility to sell recordings. True, companies may independently push some copies through various channels. But if you are not visible, actively developing a fan base, and marketing vigorously, it is unlikely that many units will sell. Here are a few off-line options:

- **PRE-SALES.** Take orders even before the recording is released (see Chapter 11).
- **MAILING LIST.** Use e-mail or direct mail to notify your network about the new release, providing album details and purchase instructions.
- **CONCERT SALES.** There is no place better than a performance to sell recordings. Don't be timid about plugging them.

• **CD RELEASE PARTY.** Hosting a release party is a great way to create hype while selling copies "hot off the press." Make this celebration an exciting event, with live performances of tracks from the album, food and drinks, and other fun activities.

Chamber Music on Tap

The Bassoon Brothers (www.bassoonbrothers.com) scheduled a CD release party in a brewpub series called "Chamber Music on Tap." This group, which dresses similarly to the Blues Brothers, designed a fun and engaging event filled with surprises: they unveiled the *Top 10 Reasons YOU should play the Bassoon*; a "secret guest soloist" wearing a wig and playing electric violin emerged; the audience joined in to perform *Fanfare for the Common Bassoonist* on kazoos; free CDs were given to audience members who answered musical trivia questions. Recordings were sold at a discount, and members participated in CD signings. This anticipated event received much media coverage, resulting in a packed house and solid sales.

• **CD STORES.** For small independent labels, getting major national chains to carry your music is nearly impossible. However, many stores reserve an area for local artists. See if the branch manager is interested in a *consignment* agreement. This means that a certain amount of CDs are displayed, but you are paid only for copies sold, making it a no risk agreement for them.

• **OTHER VENDORS.** Why not sell recordings on consignment through non-music merchants (independent bookstores, local cafés, tourist info centers, etc.)? Be creative, partnering with stores that *do not* normally stock CDs. This way, your product won't be competing against thousands of others. Perhaps the store is even willing to pipe your music through their speakers.

• **EVENT RECORDINGS.** Live recordings have a special appeal to those who were in attendance, especially if the show features personal touches. Perhaps patrons can pay a fee and have the CD mailed when ready. Another possibility is selling passwords that allow fans to log onto a website and download the show.

Visibility is the Key

Tuba soloist Patrick Sheridan (www.patricksheridan.com) stresses the importance of being visible in order to sell recorded music. "If you don't perform in public regularly, don't count on recordings doing very well." At times, he has played as many as 250 concerts per year, with 5-8% of the audience in smaller venues and 3-6% in larger ones consistently purchasing his albums. Performances and web distribution are the primary sources of sales.

Additionally, Patrick stocks CDs at large music stores and other places where musicians go. He sells recordings through *Walking Frog Records* (www.walkingfrog.com), which sends out its catalogue quarterly to 50,000 people. (Recently they've shifted emphasis from physical to online catalogues, consistent with market trends.) Though that company purchases disks from him for almost nothing, the publicity generated by reaching such a large clientele makes it worthwhile. Other projects, including his pedagogical book *The Breathing Gym* and sponsorship from Jupiter Band Instruments, Inc. also increase name recognition which in turn moves recordings. Finally, his bizarre album designs intrigue, such as the cover for *Bon Bons*, which features a photo of Patrick's head decorated with chocolate sauce and cherries.

Web-Based Distribution

Many artists sell CDs through their own website. By getting people to make the purchase there, you maximize profits. Clearly outline the process for ordering. Be sure to obtain shipping address and payment details. Mail orders promptly.

The easiest type of fee to collect is a check or money order, sent to you before the product is mailed. However, most people prefer the convenience of credit cards, e-checks, or bank transfers. Since overseeing these financial transactions is complicated, consider using a service such as *PayPal* (www.paypal.com). PayPal accounts are easy to setup and require a small commission of around 2%, a good deal for those selling in low volume.

Another possibility is selling through established online retailers who take care of logistics such as shipping and payment. Each vendor has unique policies, payment structures, and customers, so research thoroughly to determine which sites are best suited to your needs. Some merchants only charge commission, while others require an annual or per item fee. Few vendors mandate exclusivity, and most allow you to track sales around the clock.

• **AMAZON ADVANTAGE FOR MUSIC PROGRAM** (www.amazon.com). Amazon is the world's leading Internet retailer. For an annual $30 fee (unlimited products) plus 55% of the CD sales price, Amazon will stock a small amount of disks and contact you when supplies run low. For each album, they provide a webpage displaying cover art, track names, liner notes, music samples, and additional information. A number of independent album "browse lists" can direct unfamiliar listeners to your product.

• **CD BABY** (www.cdbaby.com). CD Baby is the second largest Internet retailer of independently released CDs, next to Amazon. They only carry disks provided directly by musicians, not distributors. Artists earn $6-12 per CD sold.

• **GARAGE BAND** (www.garageband.com). Garage Band charges $35 to register each album. They allow you to select the sales price, and take a $4 commission for each CD sold.

Downloads, discussed earlier, offer benefits to musicians, labels, and vendors. Artists can release individual tracks as soon as they are ready, before an entire album has been completed. The single is back! They eliminate expenses such as duplication, packaging, and shipping, and online stores do not have to worry about maintaining a physical inventory. Even if a particular item does not sell for a while, no expenses are associated with carrying that product. This is the opposite of traditional record stores, where merchandise that fails to sell is returned.

Reviews & Radio

Not only does a good CD review provide free publicity, but it loans credibility to your work. A great resource for finding magazines that review recordings is your local bookstore or music library. Also visit *The Savvy Musician* (www.savvymusician.com) for links to magazines that review. Take note of journals that include emerging artists in your genre. Newspapers within a few hours of your home should be considered as well.

After compiling your media list, compose a single page personalized letter to each contact on nice letterhead. Briefly describe the CD's content, who performs, and what makes it interesting. Also specify where the music can be purchased, since reviewers are only interested in easily accessible products. Most reviewers are inundated with requests, so be patient. It typically takes at least 3 months for a commentator to address a project. If no word comes after 6-8 months, assume that your request has been denied.

For radio play, send your CD to program directors at stations that feature the kind of music recorded. Once again, write a short personalized letter, and include a bio. Many stations are particularly interested in work by local artists or those with upcoming performances in the area. If that describes your situation, let them know you are available for interviews.

If the actions above seem daunting or require more time than you are prepared to give, consider hiring a publicist. Though their services can be expensive, typically $1000+ per month, publicity generated may justify this cost. A good publicist will already have media contacts and work aggressively to promote your music.

GENERATING THE PRODUCT

Demos

Demos—recordings distributed free of charge—are primarily marketing tools. They are submitted to presenters, employers, publishers, record companies, artist managers, contractors, film directors, grant committees, competitions, auditions, and clients, with the hopes of being offered opportunity and building reputation. Similarly, educational institutions and ensembles distribute demos to prospective students or performers they hope to recruit. They can also be gifted as complimentary recordings. CDs are still the standard, though that is changing as more people email sound files and post audio clips.

February 23, 2009

Robert Decisionmaker *(fictional name)*
Program Director, WMPG
Greater Portland Community Radio
96 Falmouth St., Box 9300
Portland, ME 04104-9300

Dear Mr. Decisionmaker,

Enclosed is an advance, radio-ready sample copy of the upcoming CD by **Kinobe & Soul Beat Africa**, to be released on Multicultural Media (www.multiculturalmedia.com) in mid-March. As was mentioned in my e-mail, Kinobe & Soul Beat Africa will be performing at One Longfellow Square on Saturday, March 21. It's a rarity for a Ugandan band to make an extensive tour of the United States (exciting for Portland as well as the musicians!), and the work of the media is invaluable in getting the word out to the communities they visit. I appreciate you taking the time to introduce their music to your listening audience.

A press kit with additional information about the band, including a copy of the materials I e-mailed you previously, is also enclosed. To learn more about the group, visit www.kinobemusic.com.

Please let us know if any of your hosts are interested in interviewing Kinobe. He is available by phone at your convenience, and there are even possible times he could visit the station in person during his Portland area visit. March 8 would ideal for an in-station interview, and March 4-5 or 12-14 are also possibilities, depending on the time and pending certain arrangements.

Thanks again for taking a look, and feel free to contact us if you have any questions. I hope you are able to attend the concert yourself—nothing compares to hearing these incredible musicians and their unique instruments in person!

Sincerely,

Andy Edelen
andy@classactsontour.com
410-374-9059
443-286-5057 (cell)

It often seems that the more someone can do to help your career, the less likely they are to listen to your demo. Certainly there is little sense in mailing unsolicited recordings, but even if you have an invitation, the following points increase your odds of making an impact:

1) Design visually appealing packaging that makes your recording stand out.
2) Mark the artist's name, recording contents, and contact information clearly on the CD label. This way, even if packaging is lost, people will still know what they are hearing and how to get in touch.
3) Place the strongest track first, and make sure "good stuff" occurs right at the top. If juicy playing doesn't begin until the 4 minute mark, consider fading in at that point. When someone's attention is not immediately secured, they will probably listen only long enough to locate the eject button.
4) Place the next best track second, using similar logic, and so on.
5) Busy people "skim" demos; they rarely listen from beginning to end. Therefore, break long movements into separate tracks. Assume that no one will fast forward.
6) In the not so distant past, people accepted that demos would be lower grade than professionally released CDs. This is no longer true. Expectations run high, and mediocre recordings lose gigs.

DEMO-LICIOUS

Some musicians leave business cards with stores around town in hopes of picking up clients. But it is doubtful that someone will make an inquiry just because they like your card. Instead, why not leave demo CDs at businesses (wedding shops, music stores, etc.) that cater to your clientele? On the disk, clearly indicate your product's name, contact info, web address, and a 1-2 sentence description of what you do. True, this technique requires a $1-3 investment per disk, but chances are high that you will reach your target audience.

Commercial Releases

There are numerous motivations beyond generating revenue for releasing a commercial recording: documentation, building reputation, establishing credibility, disseminating great music, motivating your fan base, attracting concert engagements. Many artists never make a penny from their recordings, and others lose capital with every project, pursuing this path solely for the love of the art. However, there are ways for savvy musicians to generate revenue from recordings sold at gigs and through on- and off-line retailers.

What to Record

So you want to record? Great. You have a donor willing to foot the bill and a group of musicians eager to get busy? Perfect. Only one question remains—what to record?

This depends on the recording's intended function. In the case of an audition tape, specific literature may be required. A playing sampler might contain snippets from several performances. Wedding band demos should incorporate a smattering of styles as well as some classics, while aspiring film composers demonstrate a variety of cues showcasing writing strengths and breadth of talent. For performing artists who market primarily to fans at concerts, the choice of literature is relatively insignificant in that energized audience members will likely purchase whatever is available.

If, on the other hand, you hope to create a commercial recording with national or international appeal, the considerations are different. All "standard literature" has been archived numerous times within the astoundingly comprehensive catalogue of recordings that exists. Is there really a need for yet one more version of these masterworks? No matter how authentic or revolutionary your interpretation might be, don't count on selling many copies to non-family members. After all, how many people would opt for an unknown artist over an array of celebrities? Would you? Most labels won't even consider this kind of proposal.

You are more likely to create a splash by recording something unique: new commissions, arrangements, originals, improvisations, underrepresented composers, etc. A brass transcription of a standard string quartet may have more potential than an actual string quartet playing the same piece! Concept albums combining standard works in a special way also have the chance of standing out. However, as people increasingly download individual tracks to create their own mixes, this technique's efficacy is lessening.

A good concert program does not necessarily make the ideal recording, and vice versa. For example, it's common for recordings to feature a compilation of works by a single composer or particular stylistic bias. This lack of variety might (*might*) make for a boring show. As with a live performance, recordings should be unified, logical, and attractive. Consider the aesthetics, ordering, flow, variety, and overall arch of the album.

A Pianist's Dirty Little Secret

Pianist Andrew Russo (www.russocentral.com) propelled his career by specializing in contemporary American music. His performance of George Crumb's *A Little Suite for Christmas* in the Van Cliburn International Piano Competition distinguished him as the first musician to perform inside the piano for this event. Largely as a result of publicity generated, he formed a relationship with Black Box Records, for which he has recorded six single-composer disks by Americans such as John Corigliano, John Adams, and Aaron Kernis.

His affiliation with another label, Endeavour Classics (www.allegro-music.com/end), resulted in a different model: compilations. The album *Dirty Little Secret* contains fourteen jazz-inspired compositions, most of which are between 3-5 minutes in duration, mirroring the structure used for pop albums. Similarly, *Mix Tape* features a collection of works based on popular, rock, or hip-hop tunes, recast in the style of concert music composers. Some works are for solo piano, while others incorporate electronics.

Packaging & Duplication

After a mastered CD has been completed, you may be itching to release the project, but there is still more work to be done. The final stages often hold up progress for weeks or months. With this in mind, make arrangements for these tasks early on.

When mastering a CD, make sure the engineer embeds an *International Standard Recording Code* (ISRC) to each track, obtainable for free. This digital number is like a license plate, making it possible to identify recordings automatically for royalty payments. For more information, visit *Recording Industry Association of America* (www.riaa.com).

If you plan to sell CDs through any kind of merchant, you will need a bar code on the back cover. This universal code, placed on most retail products, allows electronic readers to recognize the item. Barcodes can be bought from the *Uniform Code Council* (www.gs1us.org) for a whopping $750! If you just fainted, take a deep breath, because there is a cheaper way. Record labels cover this cost, and CD duplication/distribution outfits such as *CD Baby* (www.cdbaby.net) offer packages that include barcodes for little or no charge.

When releasing a compact disk, a label and all physical inserts must be designed. There are three parts to this process: 1) writing the text; 2) compiling the artwork/photography; and 3) creating the graphic design. The content and presentation should be high quality, appropriate, and intriguing—people do judge CDs by their covers! Before working with a designer, raid your own collection to find examples that capture the spirit you like. The following content is typical:

BOOKLET	TRAY CARD (BACK COVER)	CD LABEL
CD Title Artist/Ensemble Name Titles (comps & mvmts) Composers (w/ dates) Performers & Instruments Bios Program Notes Texts (for vocal music) Acknowledgements Label Name Copyright Notices	CD Title Artist/Ensemble Name Titles, Tracks, Timings Label Name CD Copyright Information Contact Info Short Quote/Description Bar Code	CD Title Artist/Ensemble Name Titles & Track Numbers Label Name CD Copyright Information **SPINE LABEL** CD Title Artist/Ensemble Name Label Name Catalogue Number

There are numerous companies that duplicate disks, print labels and inserts, place CDs in casing, and shrink wrap. These firms are easy to find on the Internet and through music technology magazines. Fees vary, based on the kind of packaging, number of items purchased, and company. Do comparison shopping, but also get referrals from fellow musicians. You certainly don't want to be stuck with a mountain of defective disks!

Office supply stores sell inexpensive, easy-to-design, printable CD labels suitable for demos. It is also possible to engrave some recordable CDs directly from special printers. If you must write on a CD, be sure to use permanent markers, as ball point pens damage the disk and destroy audio data.

Copyright & Licensing

Recordings are *intellectual property.* This means that someone cannot use an existing recording for a film score, TV show, video game, web site, etc. without first paying for the right to use it. Theoretically, a musical creation is automatically protected under copyright law the moment it is represented in tangible form, whether notated or recorded. However, if someone "steals" your music, it may be difficult to prove that you are the legal owner.

To be safe, submit an SR form (Sound Recording) for recordings and PA form (Performing Arts) for original compositions to the *United States Copyright Office* (www.copyright.gov). The $45 fee due with each application is discounted by $10 when submitted through the website. This domain also answers a host of copyright related queries.

When placing non-original pieces on a commercial recording, you may need to obtain the rights. Compositions fall into the following three categories:

1. PREMIER RECORDING. If this is the first time a composition protected by copyright law is recorded, obtain written permission from the publisher, composer, or estate that owns it. A signed contract should outline the stipulations of the agreement. Obviously, you're off the hook if performing original music.

2. PREVIOUSLY RECORDED, UNDER COPYRIGHT. If a work has been previously recorded but is still under copyright, you do not need special permission. Instead, obtain a *compulsory mechanical license* through the *Harry Fox Agency* (www.harryfox.com). For each recorded work, you are required to pay a small fee (approximately 8-9¢ for a 3½ minute selection) multiplied by the number of recordings made. The expense is minimal, and mechanical licenses are not difficult to obtain. However, they are crucial. Without one, you can get sued.

3. PUBLIC DOMAIN. For works no longer protected by copyright, there are no restrictions or payments required. This includes all music composed before 1923. Since then, the length of copyright has been expanded drastically. For example, works written after 1977 are protected for the life of the composer plus 70 years. If unsure whether a piece is PD, search *Public Domain Info* (www.pdinfo.com). *Please note: It is possible to copyright a new arrangement of a PD work.*

Peering into the Future

Nobody knows exactly how the enormous changes to the recording industry will turn out. Musicians will undoubtedly continue to record, but how they'll get paid is the elephant in the room. The solution is not yet clear, but I remain cautiously optimistic. The industry will find a way to keep itself lucrative. What alternative does it have?

Chapter Seven

EXTRAORDINARY PEOPLE SKILLS

Chapter 7

EXTRAORDINARY PEOPLE SKILLS

The music business is first and foremost about people. Not music. Not business. Not money. Not talent. *People.* Interpersonal skills can make or break someone in any environment, and they usually do.

Professional satisfaction often has more to do with collegiality between co-workers than the content of tasks completed; chamber ensembles succeed or fail largely depending on how members interact; more opportunities are offered to friends and respected colleagues than unknown "wildcards." Making and maintaining harmonious interactions is essential in this industry that revolves around human relationships. Savvy musicians understand that *honing people skills is every bit as important as refining musical craft.*

SAVVY RULES OF ENGAGEMENT

By adhering to the suggestions below, you increase the odds of turning acquaintances into friends and friends into advocates.

RULE #1: BE NICE—TO EVERYONE

It really doesn't matter how strong your musical skills are if you're a jerk. Some musicians are charming to people they think will help their career, and rude or dismissive to just about everyone else. Not only does this create bad karma, but it winds up closing many doors in ways not always obvious. People can see through transparent insincere motives. Be good to everyone, whether interacting with the president of Sony, hired stagehands, young children, or a complete stranger. The payoff will be considerable, on multiple levels.

RULE #2: BE POSITIVE

Smiles and laughter are free, powerful, and contagious. Optimists are much more likely than complainers to win the favor of others. Of course, everyone has bad days, and sharing difficult moments with close friends is necessary at times. But when existence gets stressful, take a step back to gain perspective. Remind yourself how lucky you are to be pursuing something you love. Cheerful behavior has an additional benefit: you will be happier and healthier.

A SAVVY SECRET?

When conducting interviews for this book, one striking feature was how positive most of these individuals were. Despite serious challenges, they overwhelmingly maintain a sense of humor and optimism. Quite a few even declared that there has never been a better time to be a musician than today.

RULE #3: BE RELIABLE

Dependability is just as important as likeability. Arrive early, prepared, and sober, finish projects before the deadline, and follow through responsibly. Many musicians have blown great opportunities simply because it took them too long to return a phone call.

RULE #4: BE LOYAL

Reciprocity is essential in the music industry. Demonstrating benevolence to those who have helped you will unleash rich rewards.

RULE #5: INVOLVE THE COMMUNITY

Consider the many ways in which your music can create community while enhancing the quality of life for those that experience it. Embrace projects that inspire others to get involved. People become more excited about your successes when they play a role in getting you there. Projects take on a vitality of their own when enthusiastic proponents partake.

Caretaker of Culture

Cellist and Artistic Director of *El Paso Pro-Musica* Zuill Bailey (www.zuillbailey.com) fondly recalls the many ways in which musicians have profoundly touched his life. He hopes to make the same kind of positive impact on others. "Music is not about me, me, me. That kind of ego-driven approach is extremely empty and lonely. On the contrary, our art should be a celebration." Viewing himself as a "caretaker of culture," Zuill asks himself how every activity undertaken will make a difference to individuals and communities that surround him, whether performing, teaching, proposing a new project, practicing 12 hours per day, or engaging in a conversation about music.

RULE #6: ALLOW OTHERS TO FEEL IMPORTANT

A primary motivator for every human being is proving our existence has meaning, to the world and ourselves. In order to feel important, we seek family, friends, fame, fortune, and fanfare. Without resorting to superficial flattery, sincerely endeavor to make others feel valued and of great consequence. Let them know that their actions are noticed, appreciated, and valuable.

RULE #7: ASK QUESTIONS & LISTEN ACTIVELY

The act of asking questions shows you are sincerely interested. People who refrain from such inquiries usually don't care, or at least give that impression. Similarly, nothing is more flattering than the feeling of being listened to attentively, without distraction. Look the person in the eye, and think twice before answering a cell phone during the conversation. Focus complete attention on your conversation partner.

RULE #8: CLEARLY ARTICULATE EXPECTATIONS UP FRONT

Don't beat around the bush. Let people know the amount and type of commitment expected early on, whether working with an artistic collaborator, contracting an employee, or dealing with a client. It is better to have someone walk away from an agreement than to con them into accepting and later regret it. Changing rules partway through is frustrating and harms relationships.

RULE #9: ARGUE SMART

Most musicians are passionate people with passionate viewpoints, but the savvy ones pick their battles. And while high level debates about the nuances of a phrase may be important, be clear that opinions expressed are purely musical, not personal. Never lose your temper—you are much more likely to get your way under conditions of goodwill. Chewing someone out usually sets back your cause, and regrettable statements can easily slip out during these passionate moments. It is better to be friends than to be right.

RULE #10: NEVER SPEAK BADLY ABOUT ANYONE

Not only does this practice spread negativity, it *always* come back to haunt you, especially in a community as small as the music world.

RULE #11: THINK LONG-TERM

Make choices that allow relationships to thrive over time. Capitalize on ways to increase the longevity and vibrancy of each connection. Be wary of burning bridges behind you.

RULE #12: THANK PEOPLE

Proudly give credit where it is due. Everyone, even those who contribute in small ways, enjoys feeling appreciated. Thanking someone too much is better than not enough.

A SPECIAL TOUCH

To really make an impression, send a thank you note the old fashioned way. While e-mails may be appreciated, they do not require much effort, and will quickly be forgotten. A card, on the other hand, demonstrates that you are willing to go the extra mile to express appreciation.

NETWORKING

Why Your Network is Important

Practice, practice, practice→excellence→dream gigs appear. This is a formula young musicians often assume, but 98% of the time it works differently. More likely: practice, practice, practice→schmooze→solidify contacts→someone who likes you and believes you are qualified sends work your way. Sure, some offers are based simply on performance merit, but these are the exceptions. More often, people hire their friends. The bigger and stronger your network, the more opportunities will find you.

Every person you meet has the potential to benefit your cause in some way, though it may not be immediately apparent how. Please do not interpret this in a sinister way, implying that you should simply manipulate others. Relationships are two-way streets—you have something valuable to share with those who meet you as well. Here are a few ways in which members of your network can help you achieve professional and artistic aspirations:

- **EMPLOYMENT.** Hiring you for anything, from a single service to extended work.
- **PATRONAGE.** Attending an event, purchasing merchandise, or becoming a client.
- **FINANCIAL SUPPORT.** Contributing capital.
- **GIFTING SERVICES AND TIME.** Volunteering to help with some aspect of a project.
- **LOANS.** Letting you borrow gear, props, clothing, or other items for an event.
- **INTRODUCTION.** Introducing you to new contacts who join your network.
- **RECOMMENDATION.** Referring your name.
- **ENDORSEMENT.** Supplying testimonials about your work.
- **INFORMATION.** Teaching you something or revealing an opportunity.

Networking is a skill unto itself, requiring more than simply meeting people. In order to transform contacts into advocates, several factors must fall into place. Individuals will only pro-actively help if they like you. They need to understand which skills/talents you possess and the types of opportunities sought. And you must stay current; individuals are most likely to help those with whom they've recently interacted.

Defining Your Network

When it comes to networking, some musicians become so obsessed with the "rich and famous" that they forget about the "little people." Sure, it would be great if Lorin Maazel personally invited you to solo with the New York Phil. But chances of that happening are slim to nil, even if you did manage to exchange a few sentences with him in the bathroom of the Hilton six short months ago. Most musical superstars are spread too thin and solicited too often to give much thought to Joe Newcomer, regardless of talent or vision. If you have a celebrity connection, by all means pursue it, but there are many other potentially lucrative contacts.

Much of the time, it is the "ordinary folk"—familiar faces, non-musicians, and those in a comparable or lesser stage of their career—who are willing to invest significant energy and resources into your professional development. The people you already know may be infinitely more helpful than you realize. Take a moment to brainstorm the members of your current network. This list probably spans easily into the hundreds.

The first layer of your network is family and friends. Do not take these individuals for granted. They will prove to be your support structure and biggest advocates time and time again.

The next level includes all the people with whom you currently interact: fellow musicians, work colleagues, teachers, students, advisors, neighbors, clients, and other acquaintances. As you list these individuals, consider the background and resources each offers.

The Social Director

Trumpeter Chris Volpe seems to be known and liked by all involved with the Minneapolis music scene. Nicknamed "The Social Director," he often orchestrates communal interactions (i.e. dining or drinks) after gigs and rehearsals, whether with a few colleagues or a large group. "Relationships enriched through casual socializing often prove more beneficial and long-standing than those fostered solely during business contexts. True, this process takes time, but it can be a lot of fun and is crucial for strengthening your network."

Chris has noticed that many people go out of their way to schmooze with conductors and celebrity soloists, while ignoring local or young musicians. Yet these very community members are the people who often become strong allies and connections. Chris makes a point to treat everyone well, regardless of position or fame. When gigging with someone new, he prioritizes befriending that person. "I know how hard it is to be the new kid on the block."

Next, recall individuals who played these roles at earlier points of your life. Even if you've lost touch, it may be simple to re-activate their membership into your fraternity of support. Track down long-lost buddies. Most people are thrilled to hear from a "voice from the past." In fact, the act of reacquainting may result with a stronger bond than was originally held.

Another group is just steps away from your active network: fans and clients. Many musicians do not make sincere efforts to form relationships with these constituents, but this is surely a squandered opportunity. Who knows what potential they hold? Already impressed with your talents, they may be delighted to become better acquainted, or even serve as enthusiastic foot soldiers for your cause.

Growing Your Network

There is a world of people out there. The trick is finding ways to bring them into your "inner circle," or at least establishing some kind of personal contact. The simplest way to do this is by expanding existing connections by one generation. In other words, try approaching a friend-of-a-friend, neighbor-of-a-client, or a parent-of-a-student. Having the mutual associate introduce you makes this process even easier and more organic.

Many activities can further expand your network, placing you shoulder to shoulder with fresh personalities. Quality time with fewer individuals usually yields better results than unmemorable fraternizing with the masses.

- **MUSIC SCHOOL.** Aside from improving your craft, one of the top benefits of music school is networking potential: teachers, students, guest artists.
- **LESSONS WITH A "CELEBRITY."** Studying with a big name allows you to make a valuable connection. The problem is that switching from "student" to "colleague" status in the mentor's mind is sometimes difficult.

• **FESTIVALS.** Music festivals present fabulous settings for bonding with like-minded individuals. National and international events provide access to others who can expand your network geographically.

• **CONFERENCES.** Attendees share common interests, and out-of-town visitors likely have a fairly flexible schedule—the perfect environment for quality mingling.

ADVANTAGES OF THE "WRONG" CONVENTION

A composition conference is a great place for composers to mix with other specialists. However, it may be difficult to generate commissions from this setting, since most participants compete for the same types of gigs. More lucrative might be a woodwind convention, for example, interacting with performers eager to recruit composers to champion their instrument.

• **CONCERTS.** Performances are great places to mix with musicians and music lovers.

• **GIGS.** Gigs permit associations with musicians, non-music employees, and guests.

• **BOARDS.** Joining the Board of Directors of an arts organization allows you to work closely with other arts advocates.

• **HOBBIES/INTERESTS.** Meet people who share your non-music interests, including activities that involve your children.

Jazz Praise

Pianist Jim Martinez (www.jimmartinez.com) earns a good portion of his living performing "Jazz Praise" services at churches throughout the United States. Events typically blend traditional hymns with jazz contexts (i.e. *Amazing Grace* meets Dave Brubeck's *Take Five.*)

Extraordinarily outgoing and friendly, Jim attributes a large part of his success to networking skills. He prioritizes becoming a trusted part of each community visited: mingling with worshippers, eating with the congregation, staying in member's homes. People who like him, share his values, and enjoy his music often work pro-actively on Jim's behalf.

• **PARTIES.** Celebrations, receptions, reunions, and other organized merrymaking activities give you access to attendees in a relaxed setting.

SCHMOOZE FACTOR

"Schmoozing," or informal conversing, is an art form requiring diligent practice, but it pays off when mastered. In social situations, set goals early on about how many exchanges you hope to instigate, and don't let yourself chicken out!

- **Relax.** Ironically, the most intimidating place to initiate conversation can be a room packed to capacity. Keep in mind, however, that most people are just as "mingle-phobic" as you, and they will be delighted to chat if invited.
- **Break the ice.** Many people can be "unlocked" with a single question or opener.
- **Body language.** Handshakes should be firm but reasonable—soggy or bone-crushing hand clasps do not create a good first impression! Make eye contact and utilize body language that shows you are engaged.
- **Drop the agenda.** People can tell if your primary motivation is self-serving. Just be likeable. The more you bond, the more likely you will help each other in the future.
- **Be positive.** Negativity is a turn-off. Folks you just met don't want to hear about your nightmare gig or the depression that accompanies male pattern baldness (unless it's a funny story).
- **Stick to appropriate topics.** Avoid controversial subjects such as politics or risqué matters unless you're sure they are appropriate.
- **Carry business cards.** Many people blow long-term networking opportunities because they forget to carry and exchange business cards.
- **Stay in touch.** Within 48 hours, send an e-mail affirming how much you enjoyed the meeting. We all encounter many wonderful people. At a minimum, it requires a second contact for someone to become a true connection.

- **VOLUNTEERING.** Volunteering for a worthwhile cause, perhaps arts related, benefits both you and the organization. In addition to meeting people and doing something nice, there may be extra perks such as free admission to events or behind-the-scenes training.

- **GUEST ARTISTS.** When out-of-town musicians visit your community, offer to serve as a host, chauffeur, or meal companion. This presents you with a unique brand of VIP access. Touring can be lonely; your willingness to help out will not be quickly forgotten.

- **NETWORKING MEETINGS.** A trend of growing popularity. Professionals are invited to present business ideas and receive feedback, often during a monthly breakfast. A local Chamber of Commerce may organize these gatherings, or you can initiate one yourself.

• **INTERNET.** Blogs, chatrooms, and social networking sites provide a host of opportunities to "meet" others.

The Connector

Operatic mezzo-soprano Ja-Naé Duane (www.ja-nae.com) hosted a 72-hour e-mail based networking event called *The Connector*. For a $19 registration fee, the 60+ musician participants were sent morning, afternoon, and "happy hour" questions, in addition to nighttime "homework." One task was to list 10 things they wanted or needed (sponsorship, collaborators, recording studio time, business cards, a haircut) and 20 assets they had to offer. Responses were submitted to the entire group, and then individuals could correspond directly with parties of interest. The result: participants bartered services, got gigs, and found new collaborators.

Contact Lists

Knowing a thousand people won't help if you cannot get a hold of them. Keep track of everyone. In addition to contact information (phone, fax, address, e-mail, website, company), it is a good idea to jot down personal information (birthday, anniversary, names of spouse and children) or even stories and memories. If your network grows as large as it should, it will become impossible to remember all these details. When you decide to reestablish contact five years down the road, wouldn't it be nice to say, "How is your daughter Julie? She must be 8 by now!" or "Do you remember the time that juggler's ball flew into your tuba bell?"

Contact books are often organized alphabetically by last name, but it is helpful to cross-reference by geography or discipline. Several databases should be maintained, including:

1. INDUSTRY LIST. Performers, composers, educators, and other contacts from the field (contractors, producers, presenters, engineers, etc.). Keep notes on areas of expertise and the types of projects preferred. Make this list as complete as possible for times when you hope to generate new opportunity ideas.

2. MEDIA LIST. Contacts from print, broadcast, and Internet media. For each individual, include organization name, special interests/biases, and policies/deadlines for receiving news releases. When promoting a new project, use your media list to quickly track down connections that have been helpful in the past.

3. FAN/CLIENT LIST. Use this list to communicate news, upcoming events, and your latest services. You may want to create an e-mail listserve for this purpose, but use it wisely and always give an opt-out option.

A Delicious Treat

Jazz singer Kayla Taylor (www.kaylataylorjazz.com) maintains a fan list that, at last count, contained over 1600 names. A sign-up sheet is placed on the merchandizing table during shows, and enthusiasts can subscribe through her website. Beautiful e-mail newsletters, constructed through *Constant Contact* (www.constantcontact.com), are distributed every 7-10 days. Because Kayla finds it difficult to promote activities by writing in the first person, she assumes the penname "Lucy Lalala."

The media list for her group, which performs locally (as opposed to nationally), is limited to around 10 contacts. Understanding that they are inundated with requests, she is careful not to overwhelm with submissions. To capture their attention, a unique approach accompanies each mailing: colored envelopes, a coloring book and crayons, chocolate bars with custom designed wrappers reading *Kayla Taylor Jazz—A Delicious Treat for Everyone*, etc. "That may sound silly, but it works. People notice, and nobody has turned us down."

Staying Current

In the music industry, the saying "out of sight, out of mind" is particularly applicable. When someone seeks a cellist, for example, odds are they will direct it to the last qualified player with whom they connected. For this reason, it is essential to stay at the top of your connections' mental Rolodex™.

As a rule, make contact with each valued member of your network at least once a year. Remind people you are still alive and appreciate their acquaintance. Of the many ways to stay in touch, e-mails or text messages may be easiest, but in-person visits, cards, letters, and phone chats make a stronger impact. Sometimes it is nice to check in with no agenda other than, "Hello, I've been thinking about you." Avoid coming across as a pest or stalker, but it is also inadvisable to approach only when you want something after having faded into oblivion for eons.

GETTING RESULTS

Every once and a while, a phone or e-mail message may appear completely unprompted. On the other end is a member of your network, or even complete stranger, eager to offer you some kind of opportunity. Most of the time, however, it works differently. Making things happen requires self-initiation, a relevant cause, perseverance, and the ability to interest others in your vision.

But making the "ask" can be difficult. Many musicians feel embarrassed or guilty about the notion of requesting assistance, though there is no reason to feel that way. We all need support in this world. You may be amazed how much just asking for referrals, donations, advice, or work can accomplish. And you may have little choice. At times, soliciting assistance may be the only way to advance your career or bring dreams to fruition.

Emphasizing Benefits

For the past 4 decades, jazz trumpeter Mike Vax (www.mikevax.net) has begun each Fall with an empty slate. During September and October, he focuses energy on booking clinics and concerts throughout the upcoming year. This used to require sending out hundreds of letters and press kits, but now most correspondence is done through e-mail. He follows up determinedly with subsequent e-mails and phone calls.

Mike stresses the many benefits his services offer. For example, when marketing to high school band directors he explains, "I will emphasize the same things you say every day. But when students hear it from an outsider, it will have added power." Mike specializes in talks on practicing and work ethic, both which motivate students and ultimately raise the program's level. His high energy visit will surely be inspirational for all, and by marketing the concert well, tickets sales can pay for his fee and even raise additional capital.

"Cold Calling"

One of the most dreaded phrases in the English language must surely be *cold calling*. It means phoning someone you have never met and asking them to help you reach a particular goal. Though the probability of rejection is high, this is one practice that savvy musicians cannot avoid, at least occasionally. Perhaps you just moved to a new city and need to find work, or are trying to convince new presenters to book your show. While cold calling is never easy, there are steps that raise the success rate.

A good start is making the contact a little less arctic. In other words, find some personal connection with the recipient. Become the internal candidate. If you share a mutual acquaintance, drop the name. Better yet, have that person call first, say some niceties, and ask permission for you to get in touch. Another possibility is finding some congruency between your backgrounds (attended the same university, share a specific interest, etc.). These associations shift your contact from the pesky-telemarketer to actual-human-being category.

Before making contact, do some preliminary research. Make sure you address the appropriate individual and learn about their background and priorities. Information about most people involved with the music industry is readily available on the Internet. Then take time to structure your "sales pitch," during which you must:

1. Introduce yourself
2. Develop rapport
3. Describe product benefits
4. Generate interest
5. Receive an invitation to schedule a meeting, re-contact at a later point, or submit materials for consideration

You typically have 1-2 minutes to accomplish all five goals, underscoring the necessity of developing a script that is attention grabbing, specifically tailored, effectively delivered, and succinct. When phoning, use notes to help stay focused, but avoid word-for-word reading. Without rambling, answer all questions, and maintain a friendly tone.

Take notes on the conversation, from pertinent business details to personal information (if they mention family, wouldn't it be nice to bring that up next time?). Before hanging up, try to obtain permission to keep the relationship alive in some way. Always end with a thank you.

Cold, But Creative

After completing studies in the UK on a Fulbright Scholarship, composer Christopher Tin (www.christophertin.com) moved to Los Angeles to try his hand at film scoring. But months went by and the phone stayed silent. So he devised a plan.

Christopher asked the Fulbright Commission to write a letter on his behalf, mentioning his recent award and explaining that they were trying to set him up with a mentor. He then wrote personalized letters to the top 27 film composers in Southern California. In each, he introduced himself, described his background and admiration for their music, and asked if they would be willing to chat for 15 minutes. He included a beautifully designed, self-addressed stamped postcard with the text "Sure Chris, I'd be delighted to speak with you! You can reach me at _____. The best time to contact me is _____. Sincerely, (their name)." The idea was to make responding as easy as possible, while doing something creative that captured their attention.

Nine responses came—a whopping 33% success rate! In fact, some composers were so impressed, they phoned him directly. And one of these contacts eventually offered Christopher his first professional writing opportunity.

Working Your Network

The act of cold calling will certainly give you a new perspective on the importance of networking! Whatever you hope to accomplish, it is much more difficult to obtain positive results from a stranger than a known associate.

After identifying the members of your network who most readily have access to resources you seek, make contact. For large requests, arrange an informal meeting if possible. Think things through ahead of time, and arrive prepared with at least one supporting document (resume, project summary, budget, press kit, etc.) that provides something concrete to digest.

Present a pitch that is distinct, well-designed, and connected to the person's interests. Cover the points addressed in the previous section. Be clear and direct about appeals; don't beat around the bush. And never take people's time for granted. If meeting is not possible, phone conversations are preferable to the impersonal nature of e-mails.

Follow Through

Unless asking for a small favor, it usually takes time and multiple interactions to get results. If there is any indication of interest, try to establish the next step by the end of your initial exchange. For example, if they suggest you reestablish contact, ask for a good time. Record it in your datebook and follow through. If a press kit or other documentation is requested, mail these items out ASAP so your contact is still fresh. Always include a brief personalized cover letter referencing your recent dialogue and expressing appreciation for their interest.

After the first follow through, communication often becomes quiet. People are busy. Despite the best of intentions, your proposal may slide down their priority list. A follow-up phone call about 1-4 weeks after the material has been received is appropriate. Of course, you can't just ask "so, do I get the gig?" Therefore, make sure everything arrived safely and present some new information such as an invitation to an upcoming event or an offer to send supplementary materials. During this call, also try to extract additional information, such as when the decision will be made or what steps can help move the process forward.

PERSISTENCE vs. PESKINESS

Maybe you sent off promotional materials or left a voice-mail. As each day passes, it becomes less likely a reply will come. Did the person simply get too busy to respond, or is their silence an indication of disinterest? Should you follow through yet again? When do you cross the line from being responsibly persistent to an irritating pest?

Most musicians give up way too easily, throwing in the towel after one or two communication attempts. However, *it often takes at least five interactions before an agreement is made*. Unless non-interest is explicitly stated, follow-ups are absolutely appropriate. Allow time for a reasonable turnaround, but waiting too long may cause your proposal to escape consciousness. Perseverance pays off!

Do not expect anyone to get back to you. Everybody is busy and everything takes time. Despite the best of intentions, your project will probably drop down their priority list. Consider using alternative communication methods to grab attention (i.e. a phone call or fax following an e-mail) and always remain pleasant. If no sign of life is made after 5-7 reasonably spaced efforts, move on.

If you have been irritated by people failing to respond, practice what you preach. Make a commitment to answer messages promptly.

Make it easy for people to help you. If hoping for a newspaper feature, send contacts a well written article they can use verbatim if desired, and make downloadable photographs available on your website. When contacting presenters, include a plan explaining how *you* will promote the event. Demonstrate that your proposal is not only a smart move, but also a stress-free one.

If someone turns you down, ask for permission to stay in touch. Even though things didn't work out this time, the relationship is not necessarily dead. In fact, since you already have an established association, the odds of achieving results in the future are higher.

Increasing the Odds

From a young age, percussionist Lisa Pegher (www.lisapegher.com) dreamed of soloing with orchestras. In order to bolster her reputation, she and composer David Stock (www.davidstockmusic.com) applied for a commissioning grant from *Meet the Composer* to fund a percussion concerto. To increase their odds, they sent letters to one hundred smaller-budget orchestras throughout America, inviting them to join a "consortium." Participants would be listed as co-commissioners and entitled to offer one of the first performances. They eventually secured seven commitments, and were awarded the grant.

From this experience, Lisa notes two lessons. First, only ensembles with whom they had a previous, personal connection got on board. Their network proved crucial. Second, it required many follow up contacts to persuade groups to commit. In fact, sometimes this process felt a bit like pestering. But in the end, everyone involved benefited—soloist, composer, orchestras, and of course, audiences.

BEING A GOOD COMMUNITY MEMBER

The music industry is a competitive place. However, things get bad when we fight against each other. As artists, we have a much better chance of thriving when working together. We are more powerful when joining forces, collaborating, and supporting one another.

NO WONDER!

After rehearsal one day, a group of musicians was bemoaning the fact that yet another orchestra had declared bankruptcy. As they lamented, someone asked how often each person actually attended orchestra concerts. Thinking years back, not a single member could recall the last time they appeared at such an event without a comp ticket. If artists do not find music meaningful enough to give it a place in our lives, how can we expect others to cherish it?

Attend concerts of colleagues, not only for personal fulfillment and "research," but also to encourage their efforts and support the local scene. When someone else succeeds, view this as a triumph for all music, not a threat to your self-worth and preservation. Be good to those who have helped you, and seek ways to create alliances with artists. As a result, everyone benefits: you, others involved, and the community.

Chapter Eight

PERSONAL FINANCE FOR MUSICIANS

Chapter 8

PERSONAL FINANCE FOR MUSICIANS

When choosing music as a career path, your top priority probably wasn't becoming an instant millionaire. If earning a six-figure salary had been the predominant concern, you probably would have selected a vocation in the legal, business, or medical sectors. But instead you followed a passion—for this you should be commended. And though you are willing to make sacrifices "in the name of great art" (everyone knows that musicians have a deeper commitment to artistic integrity than personal prosperity...), does becoming a musician really mean that economic stability must be forfeited, instead buying into a life prone to poverty?

NO!!! It is absolutely possible to achieve financial well-being as a savvy musician. And in order to accomplish this, you needn't become a rock 'n roll icon, concertmaster of the New York Phil, or famous Hollywood film scorer. But success will not occur automatically. It requires hard work, financial literacy, and clear planning.

ART vs. MONEY

Prioritizing economic issues and performing with integrity need not be mutually exclusive! There is no reason to feel ashamed for thinking about money or making a satisfactory living, and it is possible to do these things without selling you artistic soul to the devil. Ignoring such matters, instead using music for occasional episodes of escapism in order to forget about the collection agency pursuing you, is not a good solution. We must balance artistic passions with financial realities.

Musicians who follow the kinds of suggestions outlined in this book often earn a solid, middle class income, forcing them to face the same types of economic issues that challenge other middle-class earners. Therein lays the problem. Most of our population does not understand the money game, and as a result, they struggle with finances. You see, building wealth requires more than simply raking in piles of cash. In fact, *many financial gurus argue that one can "retire rich" on almost any income level.* But your entire financial profile must be considered—earning, spending, and saving.

This chapter is by no means a comprehensive financial guide. It does, however, have three primary goals:

1. To convince you that financial literacy is essential
2. To explain some basic financial premises
3. To encourage you to prioritize financial issues and pursue further research

For additional information, there are numerous money books available, covering everything from basic economic know-how to detailed investment strategies. Many colleges offer personal finance classes. You may also want to consider employing a financial advisor. Their insight can be invaluable, and some are willing to set up "free" appointments. But be forewarned—any professional will try to sign you on as a client, which may or may not be optimal for your situation. Make sure you understand how they make money and what potential conflicts of interest may affect your well-being.

YOUR FINANCIAL PLAN

The best time to take charge of your financial life is today. The earlier this occurs, the better off you will be in the long run. Even students without a steady income have a great deal of money entering and exiting their existence: student loans, scholarships, food and housing costs, part-time job income, gig payments, entertainment expenses, etc. The choices you make now have a tremendous impact on your future.

1. DEFINE YOUR DREAMS & PRIORITIES. What are your short-, medium-, and long-term financial goals? What kind of lifestyle do you desire? Do you hope to have a family? Buy a house? Invest in your career? When would you like to retire? Where would you like to live? What will it take to fulfill your dreams?

2. ANALYZE YOUR CURRENT PROFILE. Is your present income level satisfactory? What debt do you have? How much is saved? What is your net worth (everything you own minus everything you owe)?

3. CREATE & IMPLEMENT A PLAN. Make staying disciplined and on track as easy as possible. Simplify and automate whenever the opportunity exists. Your bank or employer can automatically deduct investment money each month, and automated payments for regular expenses such as mortgages and phone bills translate into less work for you. Computer programs such as Quicken® (www.quicken.intuit.com) provide a painless and straightforward way to track income and expenditures. Using software also simplifies things considerably at tax time.

EARNING

There are a number of ways musicians earn money:

MONEY MAKING PURSUITS	COMMENTS
Music Jobs	Full or part time work for an employer in the music industry
Self-Employed Services	Income earned from musical services such as playing, teaching, recording, etc.
Merchandising	Earned income from the sale of merchandise
Competitive Awards	Financial awards from grants, competitions, and fellowships
Royalties	Royalties are paid to composers, authors, and recording artists when their products are sold or performed publicly
Non-Music Income	Any kind of income generated by work or assets outside of the music industry, including investment income

While some musicians generate 100% of their revenue from a single source, most draw from a combination of income streams. In fact, this is one advantage of becoming a musician—there are usually ways to create additional earning opportunities. Remember, any skill you possess has the potential to become profitable with a little creativity and the right marketing.

Music Jobs

From a financial point of view, salaried or hourly positions in the music industry have the advantage of regular predictable paychecks. In addition, many employers contribute to health insurance and retirement funds. Downsides include fixed schedules, inflexible working conditions, and a salary that is non-negotiable. Some self-employed musicians maintain a "day job" in order to take advantage of the benefits. Conversely, many employed artists enhance their income by freelancing.

Self-Employment

The advantage of self-employment is that you get to be your own boss, determining schedule, agenda, wages, work environment, and which projects to pursue. When the enterprise prospers, you are the beneficiary of all the glory since you alone are responsible for its success. The sky is the limit in terms of earning potential.

If the going gets rough, however, no employer will clean up the mess. Most self-employed individuals see income fluctuate from month to month, sometimes dramatically, making financial stability challenging. Health insurance is more expensive for the self-employed, and it takes discipline to save for retirement without a company helping out.

Most self-employed musicians work as freelancers. They pick up gigs wherever possible, resulting in a varied schedule. Freelance opportunities expand far beyond the performance realm, including commissions, arrangements, master classes, copy work, writing about music, engineering sessions, consulting, and more.

Some musicians run their own business. In this case, start-up costs do not have to be exorbitant. Perhaps it's possible to operate out of your home, negating the need to rent an office. It's imperative to keep clear records of all payments received and business-related expenses for tax purposes, as well as your own accounting and financial planning. The next two chapters focus on self-employment options.

Hometown Business

Cellist Deborah Davis (www.madcapmusiccamps.org) started a chamber music summer camp for local string players aged 10-17. Not only did this venture fill a void in the community, but it created a source of income for Deborah and her faculty. Students were charged tuition to attend the weeklong event, 3-hours per day. That amount was enough to cover renting the venue (a church), faculty salaries, promotional/operational expenses, and turn a profit.

Over the past decade, MADCAP Music Camp has expanded to include jazz, clarinet, guitar, and voice programs. Each session pays for itself. Equally important, it gets participants excited about chamber music.

Merchandising

The sale of recordings, print music, band T-shirts, and other mementos can generate income. In the case of recordings and print music, a higher profit margin per unit sold is claimed by those operating their own record label or publishing company.

Hip Merchandizing

Early in his career, jazz trombonist Michael Davis (www.hip-bonemusic.com) recorded three CDs with record labels that put approximately zero effort into promotion. Hoping to do better, he began his own company, called *Hip-Bone Music*. Beginning with just a few print music publications, his catalogue has grown to include almost 200 products: arrangements, method books, recordings, baseball caps, mugs, and shot glasses (a hot ticket item, though not recommended for high school events!).

Touring with the Rolling Stones taught him the importance of a strong brand identity and logo. Though Michael's merchandising has taken years to become profitable on its own, his products have consistently helped promote other earning streams.

Competitive Awards

Competitive awards include grants, fellowships, and competitions. As the name implies, these can be difficult to obtain, so they are not reliable sources of income. Nonetheless, many musicians have become adept at winning competitive awards as the result of outstanding artistic achievement and well-crafted proposals. These prestigious prizes can also unlock additional opportunities.

Royalties

Royalties are paid to composers, authors, and recording artists when their products are sold, performed publicly, or broadcast. The great thing about royalties is that checks keep rolling in long after the work has been created.

Non-Music Income

Many serious musicians make money through avenues that have nothing to do with music. Possibilities include part- and full-time jobs, self-employment, and investment income.

Building Wealth

Violinist Charles Stegeman maintains an international music career. He is the concertmaster of several prestigious part-time orchestras, an active chamber musician, a college professor, and the artistic director of a music festival. Yet Charles also has a source of income far outside the music world: real estate. At one point, he owned and managed 48 units in three states. "Real-estate, when properly run, is a great retirement wealth building option."

Fees

Some musicians with great poise on the stage begin to quiver with awkwardness when asked how much they charge. There is no reason to feel guilty or nervous when discussing compensation. Think of all the years you have practiced and the education you have under your belt. You are a professional; present this number with confidence.

How much is a product actually worth? The truth: the price your client is prepared to pay and you are willing to accept. *The best business transactions are ones where both parties feel they get a good deal.* Asking too much can scare off potential patrons, while requesting too little leaves you underpaid and sets a precedent that devalues the work of others.

There are several strategies for setting a price tag. In all cases, you should be aware of fees charged by competitors for similar labor, as well as expenses that will arise as a result of your work (supplies, sub-contractors, transportation, room, board, etc.). In the early phases of your career, one possibility is asking slightly less than the competition, providing an edge and compensating for your lack of work history. Perhaps you can maintain this lower amount until attracting a significant customer base, at which point the price starts to adjust upwards.

But there are alternatives to undercharging. Many consumers begin by searching for the lowest price, but are ultimately willing to pay more for something with higher perceived value. It is often advantageous to charge a slightly higher rate, but offer "more for the money." Many people are suspicious of "cheap" products, believing they will also be inferior in quality. In fact, some clients automatically gravitate to the highest fee, assuming that this bloated price tag signifies supreme quality. Whichever tack you take, be sure to give yourself a raise periodically to keep up with inflation.

For some products, you may want to consider an acceptable range. Begin by suggesting a higher number, but if the client indicates your asking price is out of their budget, be flexible. Show that you are sincerely interested in their business, and try to negotiate a rate that keeps everyone happy. Even if the pay is slightly less than you had hoped, a satisfied client may generate additional work in the future. Always be aware of your bottom line, though, and know when it is time to walk away.

BUSINESS ETIQUETTE

- There is no such thing as a "take-back" in the business world. Once you have quoted a price, you may not subsequently change your mind and ask for more, even if you realize the original rate was too low.
- Be upfront about the entire amount—people don't like discovering "hidden fees."
- Use clearly written contracts to avoid uncertainty about charges or details.

Contracts

It seems that every professional musician has one story about a time they were cheated out of payment. It always ends the same way: "There was no contract, so I had to let it go." Most clients are honest and follow through with obligations, but without a contract there is no legal clout when someone refuses to compensate you. A written agreement provides proof in the unfortunate case that you must go to court (usually small claims).

Whether hired to perform, compose, teach, or fulfill other tasks, contracts are essential unless you receive the entire payment in advance.

Clarifying details for both the employer and employee, they minimize the chances of an unexpected surprise. Contracts typically include:

1. **CONTACT INFORMATION.** The name, phone, address, and e-mail of employee and employer.
2. **GIG DETAILS.** Date, time, deadline, location, etc.
3. **FEE.** How much is charged, when compensation is due, and what forms of payment are acceptable (personal check, credit card, cash, etc.).
4. **DEPOSIT.** Is one required, for how much, and when is it due? A 30-50% non-refundable deposit is reasonable, allowing you to get paid something even if the gig is cancelled.
5. **SPECIAL NEEDS/REQUIREMENTS.** Should the piano be tuned? When do musicians arrive? Is a tuxedo required? Who is responsible for room, board, and transportation?
6. **MERCHANDISE.** Can CDs and other paraphernalia be sold on the premises?
7. **CANCELLATION POLICY.** Clearly detail the cancellation policy. How far in advance must you be notified? What is the penalty?

Contracts only become legally binding after being signed by representatives from both parties. If responsible for drafting the agreement, send two copies to the client. Have them sign, date, and return both along with the deposit (if necessary). Only at this point should you autograph both copies and mail one back. It is important that you provide the final signature in case details are added or altered.

If required to sign someone else's contract, make sure to read the fine print, and consult an attorney about unclear passages. There are numerous instances of musicians losing big money because of a clause that seemed "insignificant at the time."

SPENDING

Where is your Money Going?

When people struggle financially, they often convince themselves that the problem is salary. All of life's tribulations would be solved by simply bringing home an extra ten grand (or whatever) per year. But earnings only tell one part of the story. Countless individuals with obscenely high salaries also find themselves broke and in debt. *Much of the time, it is spending habits that prohibit people from achieving financial dreams.*

Many "struggling" musicians waste considerable cash. Take a hard look at your spending routine, and determine ways to cut costs. Even small expenses add up quickly, perhaps more than you realize. It's not what you earn, but what you keep that determines financial success.

Where is your money going? Most people have no idea how to accurately answer this question. A helpful and often surprising exercise is to track of every penny spent during a three month period. Do not allow any cost to go unnoticed. Be specific, noting the reason for each payment, and distinguish between non-controllable expenses (mortgage/rent, utilities, insurance, car expenses, basic food) and controllable ones (eating out, entertainment, gadgets, gifts, vacations). You will probably be shocked to learn your actual spending habits.

YOU ARE WHAT YOU SHOP?

I recently saw a billboard with a disturbing marketing slogan: "You are what you shop." What a pathetic and potentially devastating piece of propaganda! Hopefully life's meaning is more than the kind of watch or suitcase we purchase.

THE REAL DEAL WITH YOUR MONEY

It can be extremely beneficial to keep track of every penny earned, spent, and saved over a 3 month period. Be specific when recording each item so you can accurately analyze the results and determine where adjustments should be made.

INCOME SOURCES (after taxes)
- ❑ Job wages
- ❑ Gigs
- ❑ Contracting
- ❑ Merchandizing
- ❑ Royalties
- ❑ Competitions
- ❑ Scholarships
- ❑ Grants
- ❑ Donors
- ❑ Other music income
- ❑ Non-music income
- ❑ Investment income

HOME EXPENSES
- ❑ Mortgage/rent
- ❑ Homeowners/renter insurance
- ❑ Property taxes
- ❑ Home repair/ maintenance

UTILITIES
- ❑ Electric
- ❑ Water & sewer
- ❑ Natural gas or oil
- ❑ Phone (land, cell)
- ❑ Internet
- ❑ Cable

FAMILY
- ❑ Child related purchases
- ❑ Daycare/babysitting
- ❑ Child support/alimony
- ❑ Other

TRANSPORTATION
- ❑ Car payments
- ❑ Auto insurance
- ❑ Auto repairs
- ❑ Gas
- ❑ Driving expenses (tolls, parking)
- ❑ Other (bus, subway, taxi, etc.)

HEALTH
- ❑ Medical/vision/dental insurance
- ❑ Disability/life insurance
- ❑ Fitness (gym, yoga, etc.)
- ❑ Other (co-pay, prescriptions, etc.)

FOOD
- ❑ Groceries
- ❑ Eating out
- ❑ Other (coffees, drinks, etc.)

DEBT PAYMENTS
- ❑ Credit cards
- ❑ Student loans
- ❑ Other

CAREER EXPENSES
- ❑ Music projects
- ❑ Equipment
- ❑ Instrument maintenance
- ❑ Instrument insurance
- ❑ Scores/recordings
- ❑ Lessons/continuing education
- ❑ Membership dues
- ❑ Other

ENTERTAINMENT
- ❑ Concert tickets
- ❑ Movies
- ❑ Other arts events
- ❑ Hobbies
- ❑ Books
- ❑ Magazines
- ❑ Travel
- ❑ Other

MISCELLANEOUS EXPENSES
- ❑ Toiletries
- ❑ Grooming (haircuts, etc.)
- ❑ Clothing
- ❑ Computer/gadgets
- ❑ Furniture
- ❑ Pets
- ❑ Gifts
- ❑ Donations
- ❑ Other

INVESTMENTS
- ❑ "Rainy day" fund/savings
- ❑ Retirement funds
- ❑ Stocks/bonds/mutual funds
- ❑ College funds
- ❑ Project funds
- ❑ Other

How important are the things you buy? Is another pair of designer shoes really essential? Be careful not to confuse "needs" and "wants." Yet people often acquire things they do not even truly want! Have you ever made a purchase—exercise equipment, jewelry, clothing, computer software—only for it to lie around untouched? Often, these squandered but costly acquisitions occur as the result of impulse buying.

Being financially responsible does not mean you should never spend a cent beyond the bare necessities of basic food, clothing, and shelter. Penny-pinchers who refuse to treat themselves from time to time may miss out on gratifying and inspirational experiences.

However, with every purchase, ask if the expense will genuinely enhance your existence. If you make $20 per hour after taxes and something costs $200, is the purchase worth 10 hours of life energy? If so, the decision to fork over hard earned cash may be worthwhile. Otherwise, save the money. In fact, buying less may even make you happier, directing the search for fulfillment inward, rather than becoming enslaved to consumerism.

A Word of Caution About Debt

America—land of the free, baseball, apple pie, Copland...and debt. Mortgages, student loans, and credit card bills have infiltrated the fabric of our society. Our national motto: "Buy now, pay later." Our philosophy: "You deserve..." Though borrowing allows us to make purchases that may not be possible any other way, interest is charged in addition to principal, sometimes at alarming rates. Though payments are spread out instead of stinging all at once, it essentially raises the price tag. Do you really "deserve" to pay all that extra money?

All debts accrue interest, but rates vary dramatically. Student loans and mortgages usually charge between 3-10%, whereas credit card rates can be staggering, from 10-30+%. A $10,000 loan with an interest rate of 20% paid over 36 monthly installments winds up costing $13,378. This means that over 30% is added to the sticker price. The same loan divided over 5 years skyrockets to a whopping $15,896. Doesn't this seem like a bad deal?

True, there are times where taking on debt is the wisest thing even from a financial standpoint. Beginning a business may require start-up costs that are momentarily out of reach. Musical equipment (often tax deductable) or educational studies may eventually pay for themselves several times over. But before accepting any type of loan, consider the sum total, including interest. Is the purchase really worth that cost?

If you already have significant debt, it is strongly advised that you seek a way out ASAP. Until this balance is under control, your financial future will be held hostage. Many books and experts can help you formulate a plan, but act now. And please proceed with caution before making the next purchase!

Taxes

One expense you won't be able to avoid is taxes. More than one-third of every dollar earned throughout your lifetime will happily be claimed by Uncle Sam.

Most musicians have complicated income streams and, therefore, complicated tax patterns. When balancing employment with freelancing, determining the proper allocation between "employee business expenses" and "self-employment expenses" can be tricky.

Employed individuals should receive a W2 from their employer(s) listing pertinent tax information. If there is no self-employed income to report, filing taxes is usually straightforward, and a 1040EZ (short form) report can be completed.

Things become more involved with self-employed income and deductions to report. Contractors or organizations that have compensated you more than $600 over the year must mail you and the government 1099-MISC forms, which state the amount of payment and show that taxes were not withheld. (If your business has employees or you hired independent contractors, keep excellent records so you will not be charged taxes on their salary.) Smaller amounts, and fees charged to independent clients, must be reported by you. In order to take the maximum number of deductions, complete a 1040 (long form), including a Schedule C for each business.

There are many ways to organize your self-employed business: sole proprietorship, corporation, Limited Liability Company (LLC), or partnership. Each structure has unique tax implications. Most musicians began by running a *sole proprietorship*, or non-incorporated business run by a single person. This is the easiest and cheapest kind of enterprise to operate—essentially just go about your business. But it is worthwhile to consult with an accountant about which format is most advantageous for you.

Resist the temptation to underreport earnings. This decision can come back to haunt you in costly penalties if audited by the IRS, and self-employed individuals are particularly at risk. The good news is that business expenses can drastically reduce the amount self-employed musicians owe in taxes. In order to be legally deductible, each expense must be "ordinary and necessary" for your line of business, at least as far as the IRS is concerned. Maintain clear records proving the costs claimed, and only write off legitimate business, as opposed to personal, expenses. "Proof" can be in the form of clear record keeping, receipts, credit card statements, or check stubs.

DEDUCTION	DETAILS
Business Gifts	Up to $25 for each gift given to a client or business associate.
Computer Expenses	Business computer software and hardware, fees for website design and maintenance, business e-mail accounts.
Driving Expenses	Take a standard rate per mile for business trips, or report gas and repairs. Parking fees and tolls are also deductible. "Adequate, contemporaneous, written records" detailing distances traveled and the purpose of each trip are required if audited, so keep a notebook.
Equipment/Gear	Purchase, rental, and maintenance of instruments, amps, carrying cases, music stands, supplies (reeds, strings, percussion mallets, etc.), other gear.

Home Office	If a portion of your house is used only for business, a percentage of your rental payments, mortgage interest, property taxes, utilities, and repairs can be deducted. Caution: there are strict rules for taking IRS deductions on home offices, so research the laws.
Meals	Up to 50% of the cost for business meals.
Fees	Union, organization membership, copyright, conference registration, and other business fees.
Music Education	Lessons, festivals, classes, and workshops. Tuition for degree programs isn't deductible unless you already have an established career.
Office Supplies	Paper, envelopes, stamps, copies, staplers, printer toner.
Performance Related Expenses	Self-sustained costs such as concert attire, hall rental, program duplication, and reception expenses.
Professional Fees	Agent, manager, accountant, attorney, employees, accompanist.
Promotional Materials	Business cards, photos, press kits, flyers, posters, recording expenses, CD duplication, advertising fees.
"Research" Materials	Scores and sheet music, music books, venue directories, trade journals, "how to" manuals, recordings, instructional videos, concert tickets.
Telephone	If the line is also use for personal use, only the percentage used for business purposes can be written off.
Travel Expenses	Airfare, lodging, meals. Keep receipts for airfare and lodging, but a standard daily per diem for meals may be taken.

If expenses are greater than profits, sole-proprietors may actually claim a loss. In order to be considered a business, however, you must show a profit at least three out of every five years. If not, your music is only considered a hobby, and the benefit of deductions is lost.

Tax code is confusing and often illogical. Computer software like TurboTax® has made tax time more user-friendly, but if you are nervous about filing on your own or worried about missing deductions, hire an accountant. A good CPA can save you significant money.

Self-employed individuals are often required to make quarterly estimated tax payments. Returns must be filed by April 15 unless an extension is requested. However, even with an extension, estimated taxes must be paid by that time to avoid penalties.

Health Insurance

Medical insurance is expensive, and will likely remain that way until a radically alternative health care system is implemented. As a result, many self-employed musicians take a chance and forego this expense. While the desire to save is understandable, this is not an area where skimping is recommended.

Consider this: more than half of all personal bankruptcies result from unpaid medical bills. Unless you live in a sterilized bubble, gambling that you will not have an accident or face a serious medical problem is simply too risky. A single incident can set you back tens or even hundreds of thousands of dollars.

If you or your spouse has a job that offers a health care plan, the easiest and cheapest solution is to take advantage of it. In fact, some musicians maintain jobs primarily for this reason.

A number of musical associations offer health care plans at group rates to members, such as *Chamber Music America* (www.chamber-music.org), the *American Federation of Musicians* (www.afm.org), and the *Music Teacher's National Association* (www.mtna.org). When running a company with at least two employees, you can create a group health plan. Universities offer health care to current or recent students. And "starving artists" may be able to qualify for public assistance, especially for their kids.

SELECTING A HEALTH CARE PLAN

Here are some important issues to consider when selecting a health care plan:

- **Co-pay.** How much will you be charged when visiting your Primary Care Provider (PCP)? A specialist?
- **Deductibles/limits.** What is the deductible when visiting the emergency room? Admitted to the hospital? Treated for outpatient surgery? Is there a limit to the amount paid per incident?
- **Prescriptions.** What is the co-pay for prescription drugs? Which medications are included?
- **Geographic coverage.** Are you covered for emergencies across the country, or only within your region? Which hospitals are connected to your plan?
- **Cost.** Unfortunately, there is no such thing as cheap health care. When dishing out that kind of cash, research to select the most practical plan. If you are in good health and do not expect to see the doctor much, consider higher co-pays and deductibles. But if you have children, make sure they are amply covered.
- **Types of insurance.** In addition to general health care, other types of medical insurance to consider include dental, vision, disability, and long-term care.

The good news is that, thanks to recent improvements in the law, 100% of health insurance payments are now tax deductible to self-employed individuals.

No matter how outstanding your insurance plan may be, the best scenario from both a financial and personal standpoint is to stay healthy! As musicians, our obsessive focus on work sometimes distracts us from basic human needs such as exercising, eating well, and taking care of ourselves. Without health, few things mentioned in this book are possible, so choose a wholesome lifestyle.

A Healthy Choice

The members of So Percussion (www.sopercussion.com) decided to make their nonprofit quartet a full-time "job," therefore operating as "employees." Instead of being paid by the gig, they are compensated with regular and dependable paychecks every other week. In order to set appropriate salaries, a detailed budget estimating income and expenses is projected each year. They err on the side of caution; in the case of a surplus, participants get a bonus.

So Percussion, Inc. pays into a small business healthcare plan, offering general, dental, and vision insurance, as well as workman's comp. (Months before offering this option, uninsured member Jason Treuting racked up hundreds of dollars in bills after slicing his finger on a Snapple bottle!) They are currently considering the addition of a retirement plan.

SAVING

Investing Basics

Wolfgang, Claire-Annette, Johann, and Amanda-Lynn all put money in the stock market for retirement. Wolfgang started investing $5 a day when he was just 20. Claire-Annette waited until the age of 30, but religiously put away $10 per day from that time on. Johann waited even longer, until he was 40, but then came up with the daily amount of $20. Finally, Amanda-Lynn didn't save a dime until age 50. In order to make up for time lost, she forced herself to shell out a monstrous $50 per day. Assuming they all earned an annual return of 10%, compounded annually, let's compare how they did by the age of 60.

	WOLFGANG $5 per day $150 per month		CLAIRE-ANNETTE $10 per day $300 per month		JOHANN $20 per day $600 per month		AMANDA-LYNN $50 per day $1500 per month	
AGE	**Amount Invested**	**Ending Balance**	**Amount Invested**	**Ending Balance**	**Amount Invested**	**Ending Balance**	**Amount Invested**	**Ending Balance**
20	1,800	1,896						
21	3,600	3,982						
22	5,400	6,276						
25	9,000	11,576						
30	18,000	30,219	3,600	3,792				
35	27,000	60,243	18,000	23,152				
40	36,000	108,598	36,000	60,437	7,200	7,584		
45	45,000	186,474	54,000	120,486	36,000	46,303		
50	54,000	311,894	72,000	217,196	72,000	120,875	18,000	18,967
55	63,000	513,884	90,000	372,948	108,000	240,974	90,000	115,758
60	72,000	**839,191**	108,000	**623,788**	144,000	**434,392**	180,000	**302,186**

Wolfgang is the big winner here. He invested the least amount total, yet because this capital was invested over such a long period of time, he had in excess of $800,000 by age 60. Amanda-Lynn, on the other hand, contributed the most, shelling out 250% more than Wolfgang. Yet her retirement savings was far less than half of his, since her funds only grew during a 10-year window.

These numbers are included to illustrate a few points. First, it demonstrates one of the greatest principles of economics: *compound interest*. The amount of an investment increases as money earns interest. In the future, growth is applied to your total holdings, including previously earned interest. As a result, invested capital grows exponentially. The bottom line: start early, allowing money to benefit from the snowball effect of compound interest.

Which brings us to the second point—*it does not require great fortunes to make investing worthwhile, especially if you are young*. Small, regular savings add up quickly (just as small expenses do). Many musicians who "don't have enough money to begin thinking about investing" spend more than $5 a day on non-essential superfluous expenses such as coffee, cigarettes, or eating out. Most people can find ways to save a few bucks per day. Hopefully the chart on the previous page provides the inspiration you need!

HOW QUICKLY WILL FUNDS GROW?

The cardinal rule is that there is no free lunch—the greater potential return, the larger the risk. Safe investments, like Certificates of Deposit (CDs) and bonds, have guaranteed pre-determined rates of return. However, their yield is low. Stocks, mutual funds, and real estate have the potential to earn higher percentages, but are precarious. They can also lose money.

The chart above assumed that money grew at a steady annual rate of 10%. Of course, there is no guarantee that investments will consistently multiply at that pace. However, if the possibility of losing money through the stock market makes you nervous, consider this: from 1926-1999, the average annual return was 11%. From 1990-1999, it averaged 18%. On the other hand, 2008 was a dismal year for investors. At its lowest point, the market dipped almost 45% from its zenith a year earlier. But chances are that it will eventually recover. While past performance is no guarantee of the future, the stock market has a long proven history of growth even with the reality of short-term recessions.

Since there is no crystal ball, it is important to evaluate your tolerance for risk, diversify your portfolio, and invest wisely. Stock investing is not an adrenaline rush or spectator sport, but a means to achieving a less stressful, financially independent future. Do not obsess about daily fluctuations of the market; investing for the long haul is a far better strategy than micro-managing day to day. The younger you are, the more risk you can afford to take (but don't be a fool!). As you approach major expenses such as retirement, conventional wisdom suggests shifting into more conservative funds with less potential of a large swing in either direction.

It can be difficult to put aside money when juggling a music career, student loans, living expenses, and other financial challenges. Many musicians in their 20s and 30s do not even begin to think about retirement investing, either because they lack finance education or believe there is not enough money to make saving worthwhile.

Either way, they usually come to regret this oversight. Are you sure you can afford to wait until you are 30, 40, or 50? Many financial experts recommend that, regardless of how much you earn, 10-20% be directed towards saving. If you cannot afford that amount, start smaller. The important thing is to contribute regularly and plan for your future.

What To Do With Savings

While every individual has a unique set of financial circumstances and goals, there are some basic guidelines on which most experts agree when it comes to saving:

1. PAY DOWN CREDIT CARD DEBT. If you already have debt, get this under control as soon as possible. Begin by paying off the card with the highest rate, then shift focus to the next highest percentage, until debts have disappeared.

2. BUILD "RAINY DAY" FUND. Experts recommend building a *liquid* (money that can be withdrawn without penalty) emergency fund with somewhere between 3-8 months of living expenses. This account serves as a safety net when unexpected expenses arise, a job is lost, or earned income is less than projected.

3. INVEST. After credit card debt is eliminated and a rainy day fund is in place, begin investing. There are many types of retirement funds worthy of consideration: Roth IRA, SEP-IRA, traditional IRA, 401(k). In addition, you may have shorter-term savings goals. Be sure to educate yourself before making any major investment decisions. And remember, the earlier you start investing, the better off you'll be.

Financially Sound

Harpist Jan Jennings (www.harpbiz.com) began her career as a banker. Though now working solely as a musician, this early job taught her many invaluable lessons about personal finance. "What if I couldn't play harp anymore? I need to make choices that allow me to live a good life under any circumstances."

- **Earning.** Jan's primary income source is performance, but she generates additional revenue through other harp-related paths: teaching, writing for harp magazines, selling CDs and instructional books, renting and retailing instruments. She is careful not to undercharge for services.
- **Spending.** Her spending philosophy–buy only that which is necessary. She drives a 17 year old car, mows her own lawn, personally does home repairs, and owns a cell phone purchased for $1 (without text messaging, Internet, or photography capabilities!). "You don't finance luxuries," Jan insists. If a large purchase is important enough, she saves up and pays in cash.
- **Saving/investing.** Jan's goal is to put aside an impressive 50% of everything she earns! Savings are placed in checking accounts, money markets, the stock market, and a SEP-IRA (Simplified Employee Pension Individual Retirement Account). She also views her 18 harps as investments, since they can be sold at a later point for profit.

Investing in Your Career

One important question faced by musicians is how much personal capital to invest in their own career. Should we self-finance recordings and promotional materials? Buy that $100,000 violin? Pay to enter competitions? Shell out cash for a web designer?

The reality is that most musicians regularly invest in their career. All businesses have operating expenses, and the life of a musician is no exception. Because all investments are accompanied with an element of risk, do your homework and make sound decisions. From a purely financial point of view, a good asset is one that eventually produces a positive rate of return.

If self-financing a project, you may want to direct a percentage of your income into a "career fund," just as other currency is filtered into retirement savings. A separate account ensures that you are not tempted to spend this money on indulgences, while providing a clear picture of how much is available. Remember that career investments create tax deductions.

Be careful not to get seduced by unaffordable projects that suffocate your financial future. People get into trouble when spending more than they have. True, some high-price investments eventually pay off many times their original value, but proceed with caution. Things do not always work out according to plan. In most cases, if you can't afford it, you shouldn't buy it. If a purchase seems crucial to the success of your future, find a way to save up by earning more or spending less. Also look for creative ways to curb expenses.

The legendary jazz composer and valve trombonist Bob Brookmeyer once remarked that music is a "very expensive hobby." It sure can be! But remember that while money is important, it isn't everything. Some purchases are bad financial investments, but by bringing fulfillment, their value is much more than dollars spent. Money is important, but it is not the only aspect of life. Weigh the pros and cons of each scenario, considering financing, career development, artistry, and personal happiness. Each aspect directly affects the others.

A Costly (But Wise) Investment

Drummer Sherrie Maricle has led the all female Diva Jazz Orchestra (www.divajazz.com) for 15 years. Over this period, they have self-released 6 albums. Despite corporate sponsorships, fan donations, and sales, Sherrie has lost personal capital on every disk. "But the investment is definitely worthwhile." Each recording raises public awareness for the group, attracting media attention, generating a buzz, and leading to gigs. New arrangements are necessary to keep the band engaged and evolving. And recording projects inspire members, encouraging them to reach for the highest possible level of excellence.

THERE'S NO PLACE LIKE HOME (IS THERE?)

Where you reside is significant on many levels. It determines neighborhood conditions, commute times, weather, proximity to family, number and type of opportunities available, and a host of other variables. In terms of financial profile, this factor contributes not only to your cost of living, but also potential earning capacity.

How important is it to live in Manhattan (or other big city)? This question is complicated. New York is one of the artistic capitals of the world.

The number of creative musicians there is staggering, so finding inspiration is never far away. Lined with halls, clubs, and other performance venues, there is a great deal of work for musicians, along with a community that values creative art making. Opportunities for networking are abundant. In some ways, this city represents every artist's dreams.

On the flip side, New York provides significant challenges. Precisely because it is such a coveted place to live, expect to pay more for just about everything. Forget about becoming a homeowner—according to the real estate appraisal firm Miller Samuel Inc., the average price for a Manhattan apartment in early 2008 was $1.7 million! Some jobs compensate by paying slightly higher wages, but this variance rarely comes close to equalizing the cost of living differential. In fact, payment for some kinds of musical work is less in terms of actual dollars than elsewhere. The end result: Manhattan may be bursting with artistic potential, but getting ahead financially can be difficult for those who call it their home.

There are many other types of places to live: small cities, college towns, suburbs, rural communities. Each locale has unique appeals and drawbacks, and no solution is perfect for everyone. A smaller community may have a dearth of musical work and be lonely artistically, but savvy musicians might find it easier to create opportunities with less competition around. You may even be revered like a super hero. And who knows—with a manageable cost of living, perhaps you will have enough spare change to rendezvous to New York!

Rural Masterpiece

Pianist James Dick grew up on a farm, so after finishing music school, he had little desire to move to a big city. During the summers, he began a small music camp for pianists based in Round Top, Texas (current population: 77), renting space in homes and local businesses. A few years later, he bought 6 acres of foreclosed property consisting of little more than weeds and a rundown school building.

Over a 30 year period, James transformed this area into *Festival Hill* (www.festivalhill.org). Now 210 acres and an international festival-institute for young musicians from all over the world, it boasts a 1000-seat theater, chapel, dorms, garden areas, and other buildings. The center hosts over 60 concerts per year as well as conventions and retreats. James balances a fascinating life, overseeing a multitude of activities at Festival Hill (musical, logistical, facilities, etc.) when not touring.

If one man can build a major musical center in a sparsely populated area over an hour from the closest city, a viable musical existence can surely be created in any environment.

Chapter Nine

NICE WORK IF YOU CAN GET IT, PART 1

Chapter 9

NICE WORK IF YOU CAN GET IT, PART 1

"So, what do you do?" is often the first question a new acquaintance asks after being introduced. Though we know you're a musician, let's get specific.

The music industry offers a vast array of employment opportunities in areas such as performance, composition, education, technology, arts administration, business, retail, repair, therapy, and library science. Savvy musicians typically balance an assortment of activities, often combining several of these categories. Though many mix "jobs" (where an individual is hired by an employer on a long-term basis) with freelancing, the next two chapters focus on self-employed efforts, since several resources focusing on music jobs are in circulation. For a list of possible positions, see Appendix A.

FREELANCE PERFORMANCE

Basics

Freelance work makes up the vast majority of opportunities available to performers. Though it takes time to develop a reputation, build relationships, and establish regular employment, pro-active players often secure significant work within a few years. While some specialties and geographic areas are traditionally more profitable than others, entrepreneurial artists on even the most unusual instrument can create employment possibilities in just about any region.

Work for freelance performers, even those who are well-connected, is irregular and unpredictable. Sometimes, the phone rings off the hook, while others periods are painfully quiet. Certain times of the year tend to be more lucrative than others. For example, the holiday festivities of November and December and popular wedding months of April through June are often busier than January and the hot summer season.

The Freelancer's Life

As a college student, Justin Hines (www.justinhinesmusic.com) had his eyes on the prize: win an orchestral percussion job. Well, let's just say his career turned out a bit differently.

As a professional, Justin is the quintessential freelancer. He plays 1) drum set in jazz combos, 2) bongos in Latin bands, 3) hand percussion in Middle Eastern ensembles, 4) classical percussion in chamber groups, 5) an array of instruments in Broadway pit orchestras, and 6) just about everything in recording sessions. 7) The comedy/pop/cabaret band *Justin Hines and the Headphones* features his songwriting and playing. Oh, and 8) he does in fact take pick up work with a number of orchestras.

In addition to concertizing, a large portion of Justin's income is generated through educational activities. He 9) serves as a public school teaching artist presenting interactive one-man-shows, 10) offers individual instruction through a private school, 11) teaches classes on Latin percussion and 12) composition, 13) coaches young professionals how to construct educational events, and 14) writes curriculum for arts-in-education residencies. One of his most lucrative positions is 15) concert host for the Chamber Music Society of Lincoln Center (www.chambermusicsociety.org). This huge variety of activities keeps Justin energized while allowing him to constantly evolve in exciting new directions.

Because of these erratic conditions, *freelancers must be particularly disciplined about saving money when times are good.* If your workload slows down during particular periods, use those occasions to pursue other income streams, revisit the business plan, update your website, network, and create new marketing tools.

Opportunities

GIG TYPE	NOTES
Formal Concerts	Concert series are sponsored by an array of institutions, each with a unique mission. Some specialize in a type of experience, while others embrace a cross-section. It is often necessary to start small and local, gradually building a following that will appeal to more prestigious national presenters.
Club Dates	Compensation for bar, restaurant, and hotel gigs is often modest, but the deal may be sweetened with semi-regular employment or free food and drinks.
Private Engagements	One-time engagements such as private parties have the potential to pay handsomely, and higher rates can be charged for desirable times such as holidays (i.e. New Year's Eve gigs are typically double or triple scale).
Corporate Gigs	If you can get the work, corporate parties and other functions pay well.
Sideman Work/ Subbing	Orchestras, opera companies, choirs, and other organizations often hire regular members and subs on a per service basis. Amateur and student ensembles also employ "ringers" to beef up their sound. Pay scale is dependent on the budget of the hiring ensemble.
Studio Recording	Recording for television, film, commercials, or "record dates" can pay well, while generating residuals for years to come. However, the amount of work available has dried up significantly since the 1970s, as more companies save money by relying on electronic instruments.

Sacred Music	Many churches, synagogues, and other places of worship employ musicians. Work ranges from weekly service playing to pick up choir gigs and one time guest appearances. Wealthier congregations can pay handsomely.
Musical Directorships	Conductors/musical directors are hired to lead educational, community, and professional groups. Conductors are typically the highest paid musician, though they may be required to do the most work.
Miscellaneous	Cruise ships, amusement parks, circuses, and casinos often hire musicians. Featured acts can command respectable paychecks. Compensation for longer-term employment is usually less impressive, though consistent.
Educational	An entire section below is devoted to educational work for performers.

HOUSE CONCERTS

House concerts are easy to organize, potentially lucrative, fabulously fun, and often overlooked. Here's how it works: find someone to host a performance in their home. They invite friends and colleagues to this novel event, who each pay a small amount. You show up, play for an hour, and then mingle for the rest of the evening. A great time is had by all. Of course numerous variations exist such as organizing a potluck meal, hosting in a barn or backyard, getting paid by the host, or asking for donations instead of a fee.

House concerts offer many appealing features. Financially, they can be profitable. For example, 50 guests might give $20 apiece, and without a middleman to pay, musicians take home the entire $1000. That number shoots up further if selling CDs, which people are more likely to purchase in this intimate environment than they would in, say, a bar or concert hall.

Since house concerts are generally by invitation only, people may attend who would never consider your concert in other settings. Networking opportunities are provided, as guests will surely want to meet you after the performance. These gigs usually lead to at least one other house concert offer, but bigger opportunities may arise as well. Finally, they can be organized virtually anywhere. It is possible to set up a tour of house concerts or earn extra cash while on the road by adding a few to a pre-existing trip.

Contractors & Booking Agents

Music contractors hire performers to fill out ensembles. They usually work for a fixed predetermined fee paid by the employer. Booking agents hustle and secure gigs, typically for a 10-20% commission of the overall amount. Most booking agents also contract their musicians.

When seeking freelance work, find ways to network with the hot shot contractors in town. Request an appointment to chat, perhaps over coffee. Most agents are interested in learning about talented musicians, even if they don't have immediate work to offer. They may ask for a resume, demo, or in-person audition.

Contractors in need of a musician often call several people. The first one to resond gets the offer, so it's essential to be prompt. Do they tend to hire their "pals?" You bet! Do what's necessary to get on the "A-list." Think twice before turning down an offer, and express gratitude to those who are loyal. Since problems with hired musicians reflect poorly on the contractor, contractors aim to find high quality, dependable, likable players. Represent them well. One mistake can cost you countless work while tarnishing your reputation.

Many performers supplement their income by acting as a contractor or booking agent. Doing so also results in additional opportunities, as connections go both ways. In fact, one contractor claims he often calls five people, knowing full well that the first four *can't* do it. This way, he gets "credit" for offering each of them a gig.

Making the "A-List"

Violinist Nicole Garcia (www.pinkmagik.com) has contracted for every type of gig imaginable: live performances (chamber ensembles through full orchestra), recording sessions (film scores, video games, commercials), and high profile events as diverse as Michael Jordan's PGA party in the Bahamas, Kanye West's world tour, and a Raymond Weil watch launch in Las Vegas (for which she hired ten female violinists to play in high heels while standing on a sheet of Plexiglas suspended over a swimming pool!).

Nicole only employs musicians who are strong players, but technical skills alone do not guarantee a place on her roster. Her A-list consists of punctual, professional, agreeable players who have proven their loyalty over the years. A great attitude is essential. "It's all about the vibe." When contracting someone new, she starts them on a small gig to see how they fare.

Getting Gigs

Someone looking to hire musicians stumbles upon your website. After calling for details, they immediately book the group. You play the engagement and all involved live happily ever after.

Is it possible to get a gig like this? Absolutely. In fact, you might even get three or four. But if acquiring significant freelance work interests you, the aforementioned "strategy" needs an overhaul. Consider some of its many potential shortcomings: 1) your site might not be found; 2) the viewer might not contact you; 3) you might not get the booking, losing out to a competitor.

Sure, once in a while you may get lucky every, but do not expect much success with this loophole-ridden plan. If serious about booking gigs, become pro-active. Focusing on marketing techniques discussed in Chapters 2-7, contemplate strategies for the following:

STEP 1: GETTING THE CALL. The hardest stage may be getting prospective clients to make initial contact. Whether word-of-mouth, an outstanding website, or stellar promotional materials give you an edge, *become the obvious choice!*

STEP 2: GETTING THE OFFER. Luck of the draw combined with great public relations may earn you a gig, but it often requires *distinguishing your product*!

Affirmative Action

Violinist Kate O'Brien (www.obrienstrings.com) has been booking private parties for over 20 years, and has one secret: "I always say yes." If a client requests a special piece, she finds a way to make it happen. When no arrangement exists, she transcribes it personally. Any requested style—classical, jazz, bluegrass, Latin, Polish, gypsy, rock, Klezmer, Italian—is performed with a smile. "My job is to make customers happy. Sure, there are pieces I enjoy more than others, but by pouring my heart and soul into everything, I have a great time as well."

GIG ESSENTIALS

When booking a gig, clarify all the essentials. To avoid confusion, clearly articulate this information in a typed contract, to be signed by both parties.

- **Literature**. What styles of music are desired? Any special requests?
- **Time.** What are the starting and ending times? When should musicians arrive, set up, and sound check? When do they break (10-15 minutes per hour is common)?
- **Directions.** Where is the gig? How do you get there? Where should you park?
- **Space.** Is there an elevator? Where should musicians set up? How large is that area? Are there electrical outlets nearby?
- **Equipment.** Is there a piano and will it be tuned? Chairs and music stands? Are clothespins (for windy outdoor performances) or stand lights necessary? Do instruments need amplification? Is there an in-house mic? Should you bring a sound system?
- **Attire.** What should musicians wear? Tuxedo? Dark suit? "Business casual?"
- **Food**. Are performers allowed to eat catered food? Will a separate meal be provided?
- **Contact info**. With whom should you communicate before the gig? During the gig?
- **Payment**. What is the fee for musicians (remember to include the 10-20% booking fee)? Is there an extra charge for transportation or heavy equipment? Who will cover parking expenses? How much is due for the deposit, and how will you collect the remainder?

Getting More Gigs

Too many musicians make the mistake of treating each gig as an isolated engagement. They do what is necessary to secure the work, but then fail to take steps that increase likeliness of generating additional prospects. It is always more difficult and costly to identify new consumers than to have old ones lead you to future work.

Obviously, take advantage of marketing opportunities. Don't be bashful about announcing the group or incorporating visual aids such as displays on music stands or bass drum heads. Distribute business cards freely, print upcoming events in programs, and make fliers available, when appropriate. However, even these steps won't necessarily lead to work.

There is a secret, however, that will drastically increase those odds: *get out of the background.* This is especially important, ironically, when you have been hired to play "background music." If your efforts simply add to the lovely ambiance but fail to make a lasting impression, do you really think guests will remember you the next time they need musicians? It's possible, but you're taking a big chance.

GOLDEN TIP #1: CREATE PERSONAL RELATIONSHIPS. Obviously, wear a smile and be friendly, but there is much more you can do. *Elevate your role.* Use breaks to mingle with guests and non-music employees. Too many performers squander this networking goldmine by yakking on their cell phone or doing some other kind of disappearing act. Don't just hand out business cards, but ask for the recipient's information and add them to your mailing list. Make sure guests enjoy not only the sounds produced, but you as a person. Believe it or not, many people are fascinated to hear about the foreign and exotic lives of musicians.

GOLDEN TIP #2: GIVE THEM A STORY. Offer at least one thing that attendees will remember in 5 years: a special dance, personalized song, party game, hilarious intro, or other interaction. Whatever it is, provide some memory that makes a bigger impression than the nice-but-quickly-forgotten food, flowers, and forks. *Be an entertainer, not just a musician.*

You may be wondering if this approach is appropriate, and there are times when it absolutely is not (i.e. funeral). However, consider why people hire musicians in the first place. Most organizers do not seek "music to be heard but not noticed." They truly hope to add something of value to the mix. If you offer a heightened experience beyond their dreams, 99.9% of clients will love you for it.

Is This Legal?

Mark Katz was hired as a background pianist for a lawyer's association meeting. People seemed to enjoy the music, but nobody actually approached him. During a break, he asked the organizer for permission to play and sing a short piece in a more featured way. She was thrilled by the idea. With everyone's focused attention for these 3 minutes, Mark performed the comic song *My Attorney Bernie* by Dave Frishberg. The audience loved it, and would not leave him alone for the remainder of the evening. Suddenly, his status was elevated to that of celebrity.

GOLDEN TIP #3: CONTINUE THE RELATIONSHIP. Once the gig is done, there are several things you can do to continue the relationship and spawn additional work:

- **ASK FOR REFERENCES.** After the dust has settled, ask for 2-3 references of friends who might have a need for your services in the future. Don't be shy. Someone who already loves your work will be delighted to help.
- **GREETING CARDS.** At the least, send one card expressing how enjoyable the event was. But can you imagine the impact of an anniversary card one year after a wedding gig?
- **GIFTS.** One effective present after a celebratory event is a coffee mug reading "Congratulations from (insert band name)!" Not only will the gesture be touching, but recipients will remember your group each time they sip latte.
- **DISCOUNTS.** Consider offering incentives to clients who rehire the group or provide a certain number of referrals. How about a free lesson? Maybe you can get a new student.
- **ANNUAL GIGS.** If the event is a recurring one, such as a corporate holiday party, feel free to contact the organizer months in advance to lock in the date.

Manager vs. Self-Managed

Many performers fantasize about obtaining management, believing this would be the simple solution to their professional life. Yet those with representation often blame their firm for holding them back. Which is it? In truth, both external and self-management have pros and cons.

In an ideal world, artist managers are part coach, part advocate, and part business executive. Unlike booking agents, who work on a gig to gig basis, managers are concerned with the long-term career development of artists they represent. They book concerts, negotiate payment, set up contracts, and arrange logistics for local, national, or international events. Who wouldn't want this?

In reality, things are more complicated. To start with, it is difficult to obtain management. And it's really hard to get *good* management. More than a few artists make grumbling about their company a daily ritual, charging, "They cost too much and don't get us enough work." Which brings up the next point: management is expensive. Withholdings may be considerably more than individual musicians make, and in some cases, compensation is required when no work is secured. Finally, even the world's best manager will not magically bring you to stardom. *Ultimately, musicians are always responsible for their own success.* Without a marketable product, strong promotional materials, and a pro-active agenda, representation will prove futile.

Most artists with an extensive touring schedule eventually employ management. This route is often ideal for those with a growing or established reputation and significant performance schedule. Some opportunities are open only to those with representation, and managers can spare you a tremendous amount of time and energy in exchange for their substantial fees.

Managing to Succeed

The female vocal quartet Anonymous 4 (www.anonymous4.com), which specializes in medieval repertoire, began as a self-managed group. Without an extensive reputation, they had little choice. But when their first recording reached the classical Billboard chart's top 5 (quite unexpected for a recording of medieval chant and polyphony!), they were approached by several firms.

On their own, the ensemble had booked engagements with local and early music presenters, but struggled to branch into new circles. Their management secured gigs with chamber music, church, and university series across the country and globe, bringing their work to more diverse audiences. (In fact, one piece of fan mail read, "I used to be a Deadhead. Now I'm a 4head!") Another advantage they discovered: it's easier to have someone negotiate on your behalf than doing it yourself.

"Having management doesn't lessen our behind-the-scenes workload," claims Marsha Genensky, "but it does change the type of effort required. With more cooks in the kitchen, there are additional efforts to coordinate. But management allows us to work on a higher level."

Many performers, however, choose to self-manage. This allows them earn a higher profit margin. In some cases, savvy musicians can even take advantage of opportunities that are below the radar of management firms. For example, suppose a date pays $1000. Securing it may require a lot of work for a manager who keeps just 15% ($150). They may not even consider it. But by getting the gig on your own, you keep the whole figure. Self-management also allows artists to maintain greater control of their career, accepting only dates they want. Of course, in many cases the question is a moot point, since representation may be impossible to obtain.

How Management Works

Most often, managers sign on musicians after:

1. They see a remarkable performance and approach the artist.
2. Someone on their roster recommends another outstanding act.
3. Another manager or industry professional refers the artist directly.
4. An artist's reputation grows, and the manager becomes interested.
5. An artist wins a competition, and management is part of the deal.
6. They learn about an artist through cold calling and an outstanding press kit. This is the exception, rather than the rule, though.
7. Another possibility is hiring someone in your network with good administrative and people skills to act as a manager, or at least help out with certain aspects.

> Websites such as *Musical America* (www.musicalamerica.com) list contact information on hundreds of artist managers.

Every manager operates differently. Some work for firms that handle numerous artists, while others take on just one or two clients. There are companies that specialize in a specific type of act, while others maintain a balanced assortment. A less experienced manager with fewer contacts might be willing to devote more time to your cause than someone juggling an extensive roster. On the other hand, they may be unequipped to get you much work. Regardless of structure, it is essential that your manager has a substantial network, clear understanding of your vision, and exceptional people skills.

When an artist manager takes on a client, 1-3 year exclusive contracts are typically signed. Normally, they charge a 20% commission on gross (total) earnings, including even engagements the artist initially orchestrates. They also bill for expenses incurred on behalf of your project such as promotional supplies, postage, etc. Less established managers often require a *retainer*, or upfront fee, and they are entitled to this money even if no gigs are secured.

Because it takes time for promotional efforts to work, this kind of arrangement entails risk. Without results, it's hard to know whether to be patient or if money is simply wasted. Certainly look elsewhere if your management fails to deliver satisfactorily over several years.

Big Promises, No Gigs

For years, trumpeter Rodney Mack (www.rodneymack.com) pursued management companies. Needless to say, he was delighted when an artist manager approached after a performance with the diverse all-star group *Rodney Mack Philadelphia Big Brass*. After several discussions and big promises, he signed a 3-year contract. "Finally someone else will help fight to get us bookings, freeing up time to focus on the music," he hoped.

Their agreement stated that management would receive 20% of all bookings, including those obtained by members, in addition to a retainer fee. Yet after a year and a half and $12,000 in fees, the firm hadn't secured a single gig. When Rodney finally asked why no progress had been made, his manager explained "nobody wants you."

To test that discouraging theory, he spent three days on the phone, obtaining $20,000 worth of bookings. This experience convinced him to terminate the contract and self-manage. "A musical ensemble is like your baby—be careful who you allow to take care of that child."

13 Steps to Booking Concerts

Presenters are dependent on finding exciting acts that will sell to the public, and your product may have the potential to do just that. But please understand if they don't jump for joy at the mere mention of your proposal. The more desirable their series or venue, the more they are approached by those in hopes of being booked. Be prepared for a large percentage of rejections; this is how the business works. However, if your product, marketing, creativity, and persistence are strong enough, doors will eventually open. Booking concerts requires a number of steps:

1. DEVELOP INTRIGUING PRODUCT. (Chapters 2, 12, & 13) Put together a high quality, unique package that will appeal to audience members and, therefore, presenters.

Art. . . With a Function

When speaking with presenters, artist agent Margie Farmer (www.classactsontour.com) wishes she could focus on the talented virtuosity and amazing musical skills she represents. However, that is assumed, and not necessarily the way conversations turn out. Instead, presenters focus on how the proposed show would attract an audience. Does the group or genre represented have a substantial fan base? What kind of hook will sell the event? A specific need must often be fulfilled for each previously designated slot: a particular instrument, world music, something for Black history month, a Christmas show, etc.

Margie works with her artists to develop several programs that fulfill different functions. Though careful never to force musicians to exploit areas for which they have no gift or interest, she finds that with a bit of shaping, an authentic and intriguing offering is usually possible.

2. DETERMINE AUDIENCE. (Chapter 2) Clearly identify the target audience(s) for your show. All publicity materials should reflect that decision.

3. COMPILE PROMOTIONAL MATERIALS. (Chapters 4 & 5) Make sure that content and presentation is superb, a press kit is ready to be shipped, and your website positions your show optimally.

4. RESEARCH OPTIONS. Compose a list of venues or series appropriate for your presentation. Generate ideas from colleagues, Internet searches, the Yellow Pages, newspaper listings, trade journals, and newsletters. Look at other musician's bios and websites, taking note of places they have performed. Local/state arts councils and union offices also maintain presenter lists. When brainstorming, include conventional and atypical options, remembering that more desirable opportunities are also more competitive. Keep thorough notes. Have they hosted similar events? Is the seating capacity appropriate? Do they have a piano, lighting, or other required elements?

5. SCRIPT SALES PITCH. (Chapter 7) Your pitch must hook presenters who want to quickly assess four things: 1) what you do; 2) why it's attractive; 3) when you're available; 4) how much you cost.

6. MAKE CONTACT. (Chapter 7) This is your chance to shine…you have two minutes.

7. FOLLOW THROUGH. (Chapter 7) If any interest is demonstrated, deliver materials ASAP, and be persistent. Hopefully, these efforts will lead to an offer.

8. AGREE ON A PRICE. (Chapter 8) The amount that can be negotiated depends on the type of series, the organization's budget, and your ensemble's reputation. Major presenters may pay $10,000-20,000+ for "celebrity" groups, but these opportunities are out of reach for emerging artists (unless your product is incredibly compelling). More typically, reasonably funded series offer $1500-6000 for ensembles or $1000-2500 for soloists. Smaller community organizations pay only $150-1200. Keep in mind that fees must cover transportation, lodging, meals, performers, taxes, and other expenses that arise. See if the presenter will sweeten the deal by covering hotel stays, meals, or other extras.

9. SIGN CONTRACT. (Chapter 8) Major presenters prepare their own contracts—consult an attorney if anything seems unclear. When working with smaller organizations, you may be responsible for drafting one. Be sure to complete a technical rider.

TECHNICAL RIDERS

A technical rider is a document provided by performers outlining specific needs that should be provided by the presenter. Requirements may include: stage dimensions, electricity, amplification (microphones, speakers, monitors), lighting, instruments, chairs, stands, risers, computer, projector, screen, crew, dressing rooms, and food. A diagram should illustrate the stage setup. Obviously you don't want to unnecessarily burden the presenter, so only request that which is absolutely necessary.

10. STAY IN TOUCH. As the performance date approaches, send requested information such as bios, photos, and program notes in a timely manner. About a week before the show, call to confirm and make sure everything is on track. Always be friendly and accommodating, regardless

This basic performance contract and technical rider were provided by Burning River Brass (www.burningriverbrass.com)

PERFORMANCE CONTRACT

This contract is hereby made this 2nd day of May, 2009, between CONTACT, (called the "Contractor"), GROUP, (called the "Performers"), and PRESENTER (City, State), (called the "Client").

1. Name and address of the place of engagement:

2. Date(s) and starting time(s) for service(s):

3. GROUP will be represented by # musicians.

4. The performers will present a concert consisting of two "halves" separated by an intermission (to be no less than 15 minutes in length).

5. Fee: a. $.00 Concert fee
b. $.00 Total contract fee to be paid in full by check or cash on or before the performance date.
Checks are to be made payable to GROUP.

6. This agreement shall bind all parties, and the Client shall be obligated to pay the full Contract price even if (due to no fault of the Contract or Performers) the engagement is not held as agreed. However, if the Client notifies the Contractor in writing of a wish to terminate this agreement at least 14 days prior to the engagement, then the Client shall pay to the Contractor as liquidated damages, one half the agreed upon Total Contract Price as set forth in Section 5.

7. It is understood and agreed that no performance of this engagement shall be recorded, video-taped, reproduced or transmitted from the place of performance in any manner or by any means whatsoever, by any person or party without the express consent of the Contractor.

8. It is further understood that if for some unforeseen reason one or more of the Performers is unable to participate in the engagement, and adequate professional substitute will be provided under the original terms of this Contract.

9. Warm-up, restroom, and changing facilities within close proximity to the performance location, as well as the equipment listed on the attached rider must be provided.

10. GROUP will be allowed to sell CDs at the venue without charge or commission.

____
Contractor

____
Client

EQUIPMENT RIDER

Sponsors please provide:

- Three (3) pedal timpani with gauges, sizes 26", 29", 31" (please call with questions)
- One (1) concert bass drum (approximately 16" x 36") with stand
- Orchestra bells (MAY be required, depending upon program)
- Twenty (20) black music stands (Manhasset-type)
- Thirteen (13) stand lights (if necessary in venue)
- Five (5) chairs
- Microphone for speaking (if necessary in venue)
- Concert shell (if available)

Optional: Refreshments (e.g. water,juice, cold sandwiches, fruit) would also be greatly appreciated.

of complications that arise. Inquire if there is any way your group can be of assistance: radio interviews, donor fundraiser appearances, etc.

11. MARKET. (Chapter 4) In some cases, you will be responsible for much or all of the marketing. For other scenarios, the presenter oversees promotion. Either way, do everything in your power to help populate the event.

12. HAVE A GREAT SHOW. (Chapter 9) On performance day, arrive early, be good to the crew, and deliver a performance that keeps them talking!

13. KEEP IN TOUCH. (Chapter 9) The name of the game is long-term relationship building. Send a thank you note after the gig and ask for referrals. Maintain communication, keeping the presenter posted with career developments.

How to Concertize for a Living

The husband and wife team Double Play (www.doubleplayfluteandtuba.com) is a flute and tuba duo that performs 150-200 events per year in venues ranging from concert halls and retirement communities to churches and schools. Early on, they worked with management that promised them the world, but had little idea how to promote this unusual ensemble. Ever since, they have self-managed, avoiding the need to pay commissions while maintaining complete marketing control. "We don't get hired because people want flute and tuba music (though they're often intrigued by the combination). It's because they find our personalities engaging and the programming ideas entertaining."

The duo devotes time almost daily towards promoting shows, typically scheduled 6-12 months in advance. They begin by seeking high paying presenters, and then schedule peripheral performances to fill out the tour. Locating potential venues usually entails studying a map, Internet searches, and asking members of their network for referrals. DP also has a fairly steady client base in their home state.

After thorough research, friendly and customized contact is made. They direct presenters to their website, mail off press kits, and follow through consistently. With persistence and a fun product, DP has made their act into a fulltime career for 19 years.

Some Thoughts on Touring

Emerging musicians often dream about becoming international sensations: travel the world, perform to appreciative houses, and be revered as a celebrity. As glamorous as this life might sound, it's not for everyone.

Extensive touring can take its toll. It is difficult to maintain healthy personal relationships when on the road for extended periods, especially if children are involved. Life as a touring artist can be exhausting, lonely, and require extreme stamina. Unless you have a top tier reputation, the money is not always great, especially for the amount of preparation time required. As you sculpt and re-sculpt your career profile, consider how much touring is the right amount for you.

When booking a tour, take the amount of time between shows, travel distances, and lodging/transportation arrangements into account. Typically, this process begins by locking in major events and then seeking smaller engagements that are conveniently placed and timed. Consider supplemental engagements such as educational performances, master classes, house concerts, church recitals, and bookstore gigs.

On the Road Again

The Dixie Power Trio (www.dixiepowertrio.com), a rock and roll playing Dixieland/Zydeco quartet, began as a local act. Within years, they were on the road 4-5 months annually.

According to bandleader and multi-instrumentalist (cornet, accordion, harmonica, and frottoir) Zachary Smith, touring has several benefits. Locally, his group does whatever it takes to keep working, often playing events where music functions as little more than "wallpaper." On the road, they perform nightly for appreciative crowds. Touring allows them to explore the country, cultivate new markets, and the musicians are often treated like royalty. Groups with national profiles also tend to get paid more than local acts, while developing a wider base of fans and the potential to sell more CDs and merchandise.

But with touring comes severe drawbacks. Extensive travel with the same people can be nerve wracking. "The worst fights usually happen on the road—A band is like a marriage." When DPT started touring, Zachary was single. After getting married and having children, this lifestyle became more challenging. "I'd get home and realize I had missed pivotal moments in my child's development." Touring is also expensive. The band's trucks put on 50,000 miles each year, requiring a significant investment for gas and maintenance.

DPT still tours today, but much more moderately than before.

Ensemble Models

There is a continuum of ensemble organizational models. On one end of the spectrum a single leader controls all artistic/business decisions, while others are hired as sidemen. The leader has more responsibilities and power within the group, and gets paid extra for those efforts.

The opposite method entails a democratic co-op. In other words, all members serve as business partners. Responsibilities for each associate should be clearly delegated, preferably in writing rather than attempting the improbable goal of equivalent participation in every aspect. When major decisions must be made, voting takes place, and majority rules. The more participating members, the more difficult this model becomes to execute.

Musical Democracy

The Ying Quartet (www.ying4.com), made up of siblings, is run as an equal partnership. All compensation is divided evenly among the members, and unanimous support for major decisions is required. Each player, however, maintains unique responsibilities. For example, Timothy (Violin I) oversees their ongoing commissioning project; Janet (Violin II) deals with financial (accountant, banking, paying bills) and social (responding to invitations, writing thank you notes) matters; Phillip (viola) works directly with the manager and overseas travel arrangements; David (cello) handles media engagements and CD sales.

Other structures include dual ownerships and outsourcing work to non-members. Regardless of setup, responsibilities and expectations for everyone involved should be unambiguous. Below are a few additional considerations:

- **HOW DO PLAYERS INTERACT?** No matter how much talent is in the room, groups that consistently break into volcanic eruptions are bad ideas. Unless the money is really good, work with people you like.
- **HOW MUCH COMMITMENT IS REQUIRED?** Many players are not willing to invest much time into a group without a guaranteed short-term financial reward.
- **HOW MUCH TOURING IS REQUIRED?** Perhaps the most difficult model is a touring ensemble that works semi-regularly—not enough to quit the day job, but too much to make any kind of consistent scheduling possible.
- **HOW CLOSE DO MEMBERS LIVE?** Obviously, it is easier and cheaper to arrange rehearsals, meetings, and logistics when everyone lives in close proximity. However, decentralized groups also have advantages, such as assigning members to pursue opportunities in their respective areas.

A Hot Business Model: ICE

The unique structure of the International Contemporary Ensemble (www.iceorg.org) has allowed it to expand continuously. ICE is part band, part collective, part booking agent, part presenter. Through this multiple-role format, they are able to offer a vast variety of shows (from full ensemble productions to solo recitals). There are currently 60 annual ICE events; the goal is to reach 100.

Most ensembles focus efforts either on establishing a prominent local presence or developing a national/international profile through touring. ICE does both. They maintain two primary bases of operation, in Chicago and New York, and will soon create a third satellite on the West Coast. In each area, they have developed an enthusiastic following for a regular lineup of events. But they also have an international component, touring shows in Europe, Latin America, and the United States.

ICE operates as a nonprofit, with a five part organizational structure:

1) **Artist Roundtable.** 30 performer and composer members who make the art.
2) **Executive Board of Directors.** Oversees fundraising, finances, organizational structure, artistic growth, and community development.
3) **Advisory Board.** Counsels artistic programming, fundraising, and marketing.
4) **Staff**. Current part-time positions: executive director, program director, fundraiser, graphic designer, webmaster, and an administrative assistant for each location.
5) **Roundtable Committee.** 5-7 musician members who contract guest soloists, conductors, and collaborators.

Musician's Unions

The mission of a musician's union is to support and lobby for its members. Though unions do not provide work, they ensure that affiliates are paid satisfactorily and presented with favorable working conditions when union employment occurs. They also negotiate contracts, determine pay scales, establish and oversee royalty payments, provide information about opportunities and contacts, and offer pension plans and discounted insurance policies. Many professional orchestras, choirs, opera companies, and musicals hire only union musicians.

The largest musician's union in North America is the *American Federation of Musicians* (www.afm.org), but there are others for singers, recording artists, and those involved with theatrical productions. In order to join, an initiation fee and annual dues are charged. Members are allowed to take non-union work as well.

PERFORMERS AS EDUCATORS

Basics

Beyond the obvious philanthropic benefits, there are several reasons for savvy performers to embrace educational pursuits. Not only is there potential work in most regions—groups often pad concert tours with educational events, or even use them as a primary income source—but effective programs increase your fan base while cultivating fresh music lovers. The work can be gratifying, and you will be hard pressed to find more appreciative audiences.

Opportunities

EVENT	DESCRIPTION
Educational Concerts	Geared towards younger children, these events are typically 45 minutes to an hour long and presented to crowds of a few hundred. A series of presentations allows musicians to build upon previous themes.
Educational Workshops	Interactive workshops for smaller groups focused around educational objectives such as learning, discovery, and personal growth. In-school, after-school, summer, and family programs are possible.
Residencies	Residencies in schools, universities, retirement centers, libraries, towns, and other locations allow musicians to combine a number of educational activities. Possibilities include short partnerships, multiple appearances sprinkled throughout a season, and longer term relationships.
Guest Performer	Playing a concerto, soloing with a jazz band, starring in an opera, or serving as another kind of guest artist with educational groups.
Guest Presenter	Master classes, lessons, or presentations about your own work at schools, universities, or summer festivals.

Ensemble Work	Leading or assisting an educational organization: running sectionals, coaching, overseeing one aspect of a school program, etc.
Summer Camp/ Festival	Summer camps and music festivals offer a number of educational roles for performers, from teaching to community engagement.
Competition Adjudicator	Judges evaluate and coach student ensembles. Typically, competitive events are 1-3 days long.

When packaged appropriately, almost any audience is responsive to educational events: young children, K-12 students, college music or non-music majors, parents, concert audiences, young professionals, senior citizens. Some models bring new faces to concert halls, while others deliver directly to communities on their own turf.

Some organizations have an established tradition of importing teaching artists, while others need convincing. Get to know the needs of communities you approach. Offering several programs or the option of custom designing events makes services more desirable.

Once Upon a Concert

As a flute player in regional orchestras, Bridget McDaniel became disillusioned with the kinds of educational programs being offered to children. She felt these events often failed to engage young audiences in meaningful ways, while being watered down musically. Hoping to do better, she founded Tales & Scales (www.talesandscales.org). As the group enters its 22nd season, it's safe to say her experiment was a success.

Tales & Scales performers are charged with bringing stories to life through a technique Bridget calls *musictelling*. Rather than simply narrating and playing, musicians cross train to fully "become" the story—acting, dancing, and transforming their odd combination of instruments (currently flute, clarinet, trombone, and percussion) into props. Each work is a commissioned collaboration involving a composer, writer, theatrical director, and choreographer. Musical numbers, spanning from lyrical new commissions to raucous avant-garde improvisations, are memorized to allow maximum mobility and interaction.

It is amazing to see how this ensemble can mesmerize even a group of 4-year olds. And let's face it, this demographic is more truthful than any other—if bored, it will become painfully obvious as they zone out or begin chattering.

Lining Up Educational Work

Acquiring educational employment is akin to other freelance work, requiring a strong network, good people skills, attention-grabbing promo materials, and entrepreneurial foresight. Create a brochure and website including a description of offerings, testimonials, and FAQs.

Learn who has the authority to approve programs. In schools, this often means the principal or Parent Teacher Association's (PTA) director, though sometimes a music teacher or other individual handles bookings. For local organizations, it can be helpful to meet with the contact person, presenting a compelling description of how your services fulfill their needs.

In some regions, there are booking agents who specialize in educational programs, orchestrating events in exchange for a commission. There are also private organizations that pair schools with artists: many city, county, and state arts councils; *Young Audiences* (www.youngaudiences.org); and *VSA Arts* (www.vsarts.org), which focuses on bringing the arts to those with disabilities.

Getting into School

Pianist and actor Dennis Kobray (www.meetthemusicians.us) makes a full time living playing educational assemblies. During shows, he transforms himself into one of nine composers, from Bach to Scott Joplin. Wearing costumes, he performs and speaks from their perspective. There are three primary ways he lines up work:

1. **Word of mouth.** Teachers, parents, principals, etc. tell others about his engaging programs.
2. **Mailings.** After purchasing elementary school mailing lists from 5- 6 surrounding state Boards of Education, he sends 5000 pamphlets per year, addressed to the PTA/Cultural Arts Director.
3. **Showcases.** Some areas host "showcases" for local PTA members, featuring short samplers of educational performers from musicians and dancers to scientists and inspirational speakers.

Dennis typically performs two shows per school—one for K-2 students (35-40 minutes) and another for 3rd to 5th graders (45-50 minutes)—and schedules two schools per date. He also presents to middle and senior high schools, music teacher conferences, libraries, and retirement homes. After a morning performance is confirmed, he offers a discount to neighborhood schools for the afternoon slot.

Designing Workshops

When planning an educational workshop, begin by determining a compelling theme. Find an intriguing "hook" that allows for exploratory journeying. Programs can be built around a composition, musical element, genre, historical period, holiday/season, or social issue such as leadership, collaboration, multiculturalism, the environment, or self-esteem. Another strategy is connecting with the curriculum in place. By reinforcing what is already taught, your program serves as an aid—rather than a distraction—towards achieving overriding learning objectives.

TIPS FOR TALKS

Some musicians are so accustomed to dealing with experts that they have a difficult time communicating with young students and other "normal people." Consider the following:

- **Make presentations user-friendly.** Leave out technical jargon and specialized language. This is not a conference presentation!
- **Build self-confidence.** Some people are extremely shy about their lack of musical knowhow. Build self-esteem with comments like "that's a great question," and always validate responses even if they're not 100% correct.
- **Don't read.** Whether working from an outline or literal script, practice so that delivery seems organized but spontaneous. Verbatim reading appears insincere and stilted.
- **Keep things moving.** Kids, and adults to a certain degree, have short attention spans. Especially with small children, it is essential to shift activities regularly.
- **Beware of know-it-alls.** There is often at least one person who likes to show off their knowledge. Without being rude, find a polite positive way to redirect attention, creating a comfortable environment where others can participate freely.

Workshops are typically 30 minutes (K-3), 45 minutes (grades 4-6), or one hour (older students). Always consider the attention span of your audience in terms of overall length and pacing. When scripting an event, balance the following elements:

1. MUSIC. Select literature that is audience appropriate and relevant to your theme. Shorter works, individual movements, or even excerpts are possible.

2. ACTIVITIES. Design contrasting but complimentary exercises that accomplish educational objectives. Linking activities to pieces performed make both more meaningful.

3. NARRATIVE. Determine the event's structure. Detail points to be covered, who will say what, and the role of each musician participant. Devise a focused presentation that leaves room for spontaneity and flexibility.

You may want to distribute handouts containing key concepts, vocabulary words, pictures (instruments, composers, etc.), puzzles, recommended listening, or other relevant information. In some cases, it's even appropriate to assign written or listening homework. Even if you won't see the group again, why not suggest steps for continuing their music education?

After a successful event, participants often buzz with excitement for days or weeks. Not only are they inspired, but their musical literacy and appreciation has expanded.

Class Notes

Violinist Sharon Roffman's (www.classnotesinfo.org) nonprofit *ClassNotes* offers week-long educational residencies to schools presented by professional musicians. Each curriculum is custom designed based on material studied in classes. This approach gives students a point of entry, since they already possess some level of familiarity with topics addressed. It also receives more support from faculty, and when teachers are engaged, students follow suit. Planning begins months in advance with a collaborative meeting between musicians and instructors.

One project involved a 3rd grade class preparing for standardized tests. An exercise entitled "Picture Prompt" required students to compose an essay based on a drawing. Sharon began by reading her own writing sample. After discussing its form and content, she inquired how various elements could be represented through music, making the class think they were composing what had in fact been written previously. "What tempo is appropriate for a running man?" "Which instrument is representative of Mr. Jones' deep voice?" Students voiced their opinions, and a string quartet responded with fitting passages. The end result musically emphasized the arc of the story, a point teachers had been trying to drive home.

For high schools settings, ClassNotes has presented to courses as diverse as physics, pre-calculus, literature, Japanese, English as a Second Language (ESL), and of course, music. At times, ClassNotes offers a recital to the local community at week's end, featuring music studied during the residency alongside reflections by the students.

Engaging Activities

Educational events should be engaging, interactive, and experiential. While some programs involve extra-musical elements such as storytelling, costumed characters, movement, or video, the most effective programs extend beyond performers onstage. They invite direct and active audience participation, whether the crowd is 2000 strong or countable on a single hand. Make programs so gripping and fun that, in many cases, viewers do not even realize they're learning. Below is a list of interactive activities, exercises, and games.

AUDIENCE MUSIC MAKING

- **TEACH THE AUDIENCE.** Instead of just demonstrating, have the audience sing actual melodies, clap actual rhythms, or conduct actual excerpts.
- **CALL & RESPONSE.** More than an exercise in retention, this exercise can be used as a vehicle for teaching literature and musical concepts.
- **PERFORM-ALONG.** Play percussion, Orff, homemade, or other instruments along with the "band," developing ear training and building confidence.
- **SING-ALONG.** Consider incorporating words with educational value.
- **IMPROVISATION.** Provide specific parameters that shape learning. One possibility is conducting the audience in free vocal improvisation, suggesting dynamics, register, articulation, texture, and contour. The most challenging aspect of improvising is often psychological, so be sure to create a fun comfortable environment.
- **COMPOSITION.** Small "teams" may compose with the help of a group leader, or a collective effort can be made.

AUDIENCE INPUT

- **Q & A.** Questions can be generated by either performers or audience members.
- **REFLECTION.** After a performance, have listeners comment on their impressions.
- **FOCUSED LISTENING.** One possibility is re-playing a passage several times, encouraging a new perspective with each run-through. Have listeners comment on how each angle impacts their experience.
- **DISCUSSION GROUPS.** Address issues such as what makes the music great, composer intentions, etc.
- **COACHING.** Invite volunteers to "coach" the ensemble. Following a flat and uninspired rendition, ask what could be done interpretively to make it more majestic, melancholic, agitated, etc. Be open to any and all suggestions: changing octaves, adding inflection, altering dynamics, adjusting tempo, re-orchestrating.

HANDS ON

- **PETTING ZOO.** Instrument "petting zoos" allow children and adults to touch, hear, and play musical instruments.
- **INSTRUMENT BUILDING.** Constructing homemade instruments from everyday items is fun and provides a great souvenir.
- **GAMES.** A huge variety of games are possible. Here's one idea: teams guess musical terms (ostinato, pentatonic, minimalism, hemiola, etc.) based on short improvisations.
- **MIMING.** Play "air bass" along with a walking line, mimic trumpets during a fanfare, etc.
- **MOVEMENT.** Improvise or choreograph gestures reflective of the music. For example, march in time, mirror articulation, imitate the character, or move with the bass.
- **WRITING.** Jot down thoughts about a piece or experience; create a *program* (story) to reflect the music; write your favorite musical

memory. Another exercise is composing a poem that reflects the music's character (excited, gloomy) or structure (AABA, rondo).

- **ART.** Draw/paint impressions of the music or portraits of players.

Music Gaming

Bassist Mary Javian (www.philorch.org) has experimented with many interactive games as a teaching artist and Coordinator of the School Partnership Program at the Philadelphia Orchestra. One exercise has students distribute various rhythms throughout their body. Perhaps they stomp quarter notes, play eighth notes on their shoulder, and tap sixteenths on their knee.

Another activity involves handing out cards representing specific notes. As a scale or pattern unfolds, participants stand when their note sounds. Students then reorder the pitches by creating a new formation. The resultant "motive" is used as a point of departure for improvising teaching artists.

A drawing game invites students to represent melodic gestures on paper. If the melody ascends, an upward line is drawn, etc. Participants are also asked to consider the music's character, choosing appropriate colors and angularity/smoothness that correspond to the mood expressed. The activity's process may also be reversed, starting with a visual representation, and then discussing how to interpret it melodically.

Chapter Ten

NICE WORK IF YOU CAN GET IT, PART 2

Chapter 10

NICE WORK IF YOU CAN GET IT, PART 2

COMPOSING & ARRANGING

Basics

Composers and arrangers are natural contenders for an entrepreneurial existence. After all, finding creative solutions to musical problems is a core requirement, and many become obsessed with discovering their own "voice." Hopefully these imaginative impulses translate naturally into self-promotional inclinations, because for them, entrepreneurship is not an option—it is the only way. *The most successful are never shy about marketing their wares,* constantly in search of new opportunities.

Income sources include commissions, publisher royalties for print music, performance royalties for public presentations, music licensing, grants, and competitive awards. Most composers/arrangers also orchestrate, perform, conduct, teach, offer workshops, serve as musical directors, do copy work, and/or pursue other activities.

Composers are faced with a unique dilemma. Their product is abstract: mere marks on a piece of paper that *suggest* musical choices. With the exception of electronic works, they are dependent on performers to realize their vision. Yet many find themselves in relative isolation. The act of writing can be lonely. Unlike performers, who interact regularly with others when rehearsing and gigging, composers have to manufacture such encounters.

There are many steps composers can take to expand visibility. Devote time each week to marketing efforts. Submit works to established sources, such as competitions and calls-for-scores, but also approach musicians who don't typically work with new music. Proudly promote creations to colleagues, and seek performers who will champion your music over time. Composers who also perform or lead an ensemble specializing in original music have obvious advantages. In other words, stay active.

Riding the Wave

Stacy Garrop (www.garrop.com) describes her composition career as a wave—the ups are exciting and busy, while the downs are necessary to get caught up. Her strategy for success combines aggressively promoting music, following every lead, and nurturing past successes to create new ones. "After all," she notes, "if you don't disseminate your music, nobody else will."

Fresh out of school, Stacy attended a music festival, two artist center programs, and two artist colonies, providing the opportunity to mingle with established musicians. She entered every competition for which she was eligible; one work won five awards in a single year! This achievement ultimately convinced the Theodore Presser Company to publish her music.

Stacy initiates a promotional campaign 1-2 times per year, usually mid-season, when programming decisions are typically made for the following year. Once, she sent personalized e-mails with a brief introduction, composition description, and bio to 70 choirs that regularly feature new music. She received several responses, including one ensemble that performed her piece and subsequently commissioned three others.

Opportunities

Composing a Profession

Below are some examples of ways in which composers/arrangers earn income.

- Kevin Puts (www.kevinputs.com) earns the majority of his living by writing concert music commissions for orchestras, chamber ensembles, and opera companies.
- Dean Sorenson's (www.deansorensonmusic.com) jazz writing includes a method book for young jazz ensembles, vocal charts that were toured by the Glenn Miller Orchestra, community wind ensemble commissions, and arrangements for recording projects.
- Miriam Cutler (www.miriamcutler.com) established herself as a composer for documentaries after discovering that this film genre allows her to write creative music while working on projects that share her values.
- David Kurtz (www.dkurtz.me) scores for daytime television shows including *The Young and the Restless* and *The Bold and the Beautiful*. "One great thing about writing for these soap operas is that they have provided a steady source of income for decades."
- Though Gerard Marino (www.gerardkmarino.com) originally envisioned a career as a film composer, he stumbled upon a niche writing video game music. Many of his game compositions have received performances by orchestras throughout the world.
- Vocalists Kerry Marsh and Julia Dollison (www.inhousecustomjingles.com), a husband and wife team, run a business where they compose, perform, and produce custom jingles for businesses advertising on TV, radio, and the Internet.
- Stephen Lias (www.stephenlias.com) has created incidental music for more than thirty professional theatrical productions. Many of these pieces have been rearranged for different ensembles and contexts, generating additional performances and income.
- Nancy and Randall Faber (www.pianoteaching.com) have authored more than 200 publications for beginning and intermediate piano students.
- Tony Alonso (www.tonyalonsomusic.com) composes liturgical works that fill gaps in the literature. Most pieces are set for untrained voices, accompanied by instrumentalists who work within a particular community.
- Trumpeter Chuck Seipp (www.cjseippmusic.com) began creating brass arrangements of classical favorites and wedding music for his own gigs, but the demand for these settings resulted in an unexpected business.

FUNCTION	NOTES
Concert Music	Compositions or arrangements intended for live performance (or recording), written for soloists, chamber groups, and large ensembles.
Song Writing	Music and lyrics for songs.
Educational Music	Method books or compositions/arrangements/transcriptions for educational ensembles. This accounts for the largest portion of the print music market.
Sacred Music	Service music geared towards churches, synagogues, and other religious institutions.
Theater Music	Operas; operettas; musicals; ballets; incidental music for the theater.
Media Music	Music for films; documentaries; industrials; television shows; commercials; radio; books on tape.
Miscellaneous	Ring tones; video games; website music; Internet greeting cards; copy work.

Commissions

One of the primary ways composers earn income is through commissions. Individuals or organizations sponsor compositions in order to 1) create new literature (for instruments or ensembles with limited repertoire), 2) establish a unique identity (difficult to do when playing repertoire that has been presented extensively by others), 3) fulfill a particular function (educational, film score, attract clients, etc.), 4) experience the thrill of being personally responsible for new art, or 5) leave a legacy. Commissions can be funded in a number of ways:

- **ARTIST/ENSEMBLE.** A single artist or ensemble may finance a new piece from their operational budget.
- **ENSEMBLE GRANTS.** Ensembles, in conjunction with a composer, can apply for grants from programs like *Chamber Music America* (www.chamber-music.org).

- **COMPOSER GRANTS.** Composers can apply directly for grants from organizations like the *Fromm Foundation* (www.music.fas.harvard.edu/fromm.html).
- **COMPETITIONS.** The *Sackler Prize* (www.sacklercompositionprize.uconn.edu) and other competitions result in a commission for the winner.
- **SINGLE DONOR.** A single donor, literally anyone, can commission a new work. *Meet the Composer* (www.meetthecomposer.org) has a program that pairs composers with sponsors.
- **MULTIPLE DONORS.** The *Seattle Chamber Music Society's Commissioning Club* (www.seattlechambermusic.org/commissioningclub.html) is an example of a fund supported by multiple donors.
- **CONSORTIUM.** A collective of artists or ensembles can co-sponsor a piece. The composer is rewarded with a reasonable fee and several guaranteed performances. Commissioning entities share the burden of expense while proudly taking credit for its creation.

The Music Commission

Kenneth Radnofsky's World-Wide Concurrent Premieres and Commissioning Fund, Inc. (www.kenradnofsky.com) organized a consortium of 73 saxophonists to commission John Harbison to write *San Antonio*. It received 43 premier performances on a single day and 100 presentations within the year. For a small fee, each participant received an autographed numbered score and "exclusive" performance rights for one year.

Joan Tower's *Made in America* was commissioned by 65 small- to mid-budget American orchestras, including at least one from each state.

Marta Ptaszynska's *Lumen* was made possible, in part, by a Public Commissioning Initiative. Audience members funded individual measures for a $25+ fee. Donors each received the portion of the score they subsidized, and were acknowledged in programs.

Factors contributing to a commissioning fee include the duration, size of ensemble, reputation of composer, and budget of commissioning party. A separate charge may be requested for copy costs, though many composers do this work themselves.

Some commissions come with strings attached. The initiating ensemble may request to give the premiere performance, make the first recording, or even maintain exclusive performance rights for a given period. Stipulations should be clearly outlined in the contract.

Those responsible for facilitating the commission should be credited in all publications, recordings, and programs involving the work. *Meet the Composer* (www.meetthecomposer.org) publishes additional commissioning guidelines.

> When an artist or ensemble decides to subsidize a new work, whom do they approach? The most common answer: a friend or acquaintance. Of course, hopefully they like that composer's music, but only a small percentage of commissions are awarded to strangers. In fact, more than one composer has been solicited by a colleague completely unfamiliar with their work!

Working with a Publisher

In the past, musicians hoping to disseminate compositions or arrangements were dependent on publishers. In addition to their engraving function, these companies were essentially the only resource available for reaching a significant client base.

Today the situation is different. Most composers use computer notation, providing the potential for beautiful professional looking manuscripts. Publishing companies often simply reproduce or slightly alter submitted computer scores.

So the dilemma of whether to sign on with a publisher closely parallels the scenario with record labels or artist management. These companies provide helpful services, but you receive only a small portion of each print music sale or rental, and performance royalties must be split with the publisher. In fact, many publishing houses are struggling for reasons similar to record labels.

Bragging rights and a sense of prestige are earned when a publishing company decides to champion your music. Publishers typically provide services such as editing, packaging, duplication, collecting payment, overseeing copyright, obtaining permissions, and licensing. Some (rare) companies even work with composers on career development.

Major publishers with an established reputation and distribution network make direct marketing to likely clients feasible. In particular, large ensemble directors at the pre-college and college level are often accustomed to shopping primarily with established publishers. Attracting their attention to an independent source may be difficult. For those selling music in large quantities, a publisher is often ideal, since handling that amount of orders may require more time and energy than you are willing to devote.

Publisher Pros and Cons

Don Freund (php.indiana.edu/~dfreund) notes several benefits of working with a publisher. His best selling compositions generate supplemental income each year without requiring much work on his part, allowing him more time to focus on writing. Some organizations are more comfortable ordering from established companies than individual composers. Additionally, as a university professor, this representation looked impressive when he applied for tenure.

But alliances have been far from utopian. "Many composers are under the impression that publishers are there to help them. This is not the case—they are in business to make money. Publishers only invest in composers when they think it will help them achieve that goal." Most of Don's performances result from his own promotional efforts, not the publisher's.

There have also been frustrations. One publisher failed to post audio clips of his music on their website. Another insisted on distributing all his pieces as rentals. Though this practice is common for orchestral works, it is not for chamber music, and ensembles began complaining about the extra fees. Don eventually bought back the rights to his chamber music, and now self-publishes these works.

Self-Publishing

Self-publishing requires more work, but the difference in revenue can quickly add up. You set the price for print music, and are entitled to keep everything minus expenses incurred for duplication, shipping, and marketing. More money can be earned even if charging less or selling fewer units. Better yet, you maintain complete ownership of your compositions, allowing all performance royalties to be directed into your bank account. You may also be a better advocate for your music than a publisher representing a profusion of products. Because of these advantages, some veteran composers pay considerably to buy back rights to older music.

If self-publishing, keep excellent records and pursue all leads. To determine appropriate fees, research prices from other companies for music of comparable duration and instrumentation. Ship orders promptly along with professional looking invoices. Though e-mailing documents eliminates the expense and hassle of shipping, remember that files can easily be forwarded to others without your knowledge or permission.

TOOLS FOR THE SELF-PUBLISHER

The following tools are beneficial for the self-publisher:

- Website. The site should provide details about available works and ordering instructions. It is helpful to post audio clips or even score excerpts.
- Other promotional materials. The usual array, described in chapter 4.
- Nice quality paper. Stock an assortment of high quality paper in the sizes, materials, and thicknesses you require for printing scores and parts.
- High quality laser printer. Ideally, it should be able to print on paper up to 11 x 17, and have the capability of making double-sided copies. Some self-publishers contract printing jobs to companies like Subito Music (www.subitomusic.com).
- Fax machine. Many organizations prefer ordering by fax.
- Binding unit. Copy centers often charge outrageous prices for binding. Purchasing a coil binding unit (priced as low as $100, available at office supply stores) and binding combs (10-15¢ each when bought in bulk) can provide significant savings.
- Long-neck stapler. This great $20 investment allows you to staple in the middle of a folded piece of paper when making parts. Alternatively, you may want to invest in a more expensive rapid stapler, which automatically staples in the correct place.
- Mailing envelopes. Buy in bulk. Consider padded enveloped to ensure that music does not get bent or wrinkled during shipping. You may also need packing tape.

Music for some ensembles, especially orchestras and large chamber groups, is typically rented instead of sold. Groups pay to borrow the score and parts for a given period of time, returning them after the performance. Rentals ensure that the publisher (you, in this case) and composer (also you) receive additional payment each time the work is performed.

The Blessing of Rejection

After Jennifer Higdon (www.jenniferhigdon.com) received rejection letters from all the major publishers, she remembered something Phillip Glass had said in a master class: "If you want to make money as a composer, maintain the rights to your music." So she decided to self-publish. In the early days, this was easy enough, since orders were sporadic. But as her career took off, the workload became overwhelming, making it difficult to find composing time. Of course, that also meant she was earning good money. Jennifer's publishing company now has a part-time employee who fills requests, typically 2-5 per day.

Acquiring Performances

Conductors, performers, and educators are constantly in search of music. True, some only consider works by composers long dead, but many are enthusiastic about recent creations. Just because a fantastic work exists, however, doesn't mean performances will magically accrue. Most musicians consider programming a contemporary work only after they:

1. **SEE IT** — concert, video
2. **HEAR IT** — recording
3. **FIND IT** — catalogue, website
4. **REQUEST IT** — call-for-scores
5. **COMMISSION IT** — previous history
6. **KNOW YOU** — network
7. **KNOW OF YOU** — word of mouth
8. **RECEIVE A SOLICITATION** — promotion

Never send off unsolicited materials. This is almost always a waste of time and energy. Instead, begin by making contact. If a sincere interest is expressed, mail or e-mail a short cover letter referencing that interaction along with a score and recording. Always be clear about your expectations. Are you asking the performer to participate in a pre-arranged opportunity, or proposing that they purchase the score, learn the piece *and* find a way to program it?

GETTING PLAYED

Not all music has the potential for comparable attention, even if the composer, quality, and marketing efforts are equivalent. For maximum performances, consider the following:

- **Function**. Certain categories of music, such as educational and religious, have a wider client base than others.
- **Accessibility**. Most performers seek music that will resonate with their audience.
- **Score clarity**. Nobody wants to struggle through sloppy notation and careless mistakes!
- **Orchestration**. Non-standard combinations may result in beautiful and unusual colors, but finding groups to program these works is often challenging. On the other hand, traditional settings (piano, violin, string quartet, orchestra) are forced to compete against endless amounts of music. Writing for solo instruments or existing ensembles with less literature available (English horn, harp, saxophone quartet, percussion ensemble, band) optimizes performance potential.
- **Difficulty**. Extremely challenging works may see few performances, since most players are not advanced enough and professional ensembles often shy away from extensive rehearsing. Alas...time is money.
- **Duration**. Shorter pieces often have a stronger appeal than longer ones. Many groups favor contemporary works under 10 minutes.
- **Uniqueness**. A well-written but "normal" composition may attract limited attention, whereas a quirky, fun, or out-of-the-ordinary experiment can quickly garnish notoriety.

Over 1000 Performances Annually!

There are 1000-2000 performances of Frank Ticheli's (www.frankticheli.com) compositions annually. Several factors contribute to this success. First, his music is immediately accessible. "As a student, I wrote what I thought I had to, music that was much more hardball. It wasn't until after graduation that I discovered my true voice." This change of aesthetic was not a deliberate attempt to appease audiences, but rather an admission of his own musical values and instincts. "Be true to yourself—never compose just to prove something to others."

Frank discovered a niche: appealing and sophisticated works for band and wind ensemble. Middle and high school band directors are constantly seeking interesting literature, and many college conductors are adventurous proponents of contemporary music. His reputation spread rapidly within these communities. This notoriety led to guest conducting offers which, in turn, increased exposure and income. Currently, he is expanding into a new area—choral music.

Another career booster was the enthusiasm of a few key individuals. A handful of conductors, who had been mentors or fellow classmates, championed Frank's music early on. "Even a single advocate of your compositions can become a tremendous asset."

Performance royalties

Performance royalties are paid to composers and publishers by Performing Rights Organizations (PROs) when works are played publically (concert halls, bars, churches, etc.) or recordings are broadcast (radio, television, film, etc.). Most classical and jazz composers belong to one of the two largest PROs: The *American Society of Composers, Authors, and Publishers* (www.ascap.com) or *Broadcast Music, Inc.* (www.bmi.com). Though these organizations have slightly different policies and royalty formulas, both are ardent advocates for members.

In order to get paid, each composition must be registered on the composer's PRO website. This is the publisher's responsibility, which means you if self-publishing. To ensure that each performance is noted, send programs or other documentation to your PRO. The amount paid in royalties depends on a number of variables, and is divided equally between publisher and composer. Royalty checks are mailed on a quarterly basis.

PRIVATE TEACHING

Basics

Becoming a music teacher can be exceedingly gratifying. Not only does it provide a regular and sometimes substantial income, but it allows you to impact students positively, translating into immediate personal fulfillment. Self-employed private teachers can set their own hours and rates, handpick students, and be their own boss.

Thorough organized bookkeeping skills are particularly essential for private teachers. Not only will you need to coordinate a potentially complex schedule, but meticulous payment records must be maintained for tax purposes. Even if you typically collect payment each lesson, some clients prefer to pay at the beginning of the month or semester, and others will forget their checkbook from time to time.

Setting Up Shop

The first line of business is identifying an appropriate location for lessons. Find a convenient and safe site that provides a comfortable learning environment. Teaching from home offers several advantages. It avoids commute time, gas expenses, eating out, inconveniences when students cancel at the last minute, and the need to rent a separate space.

If considering this option, be clear about responsibilities that will be placed on members of your household, such as taking good phone messages, keeping things clean, and being quiet during lessons. When working from home, it is best to isolate a room or two solely for teaching purposes, separating personal from work life.

There are many other potential places to offer instruction. Music stores and school lesson programs often designate quarters specifically for teaching. They may even recruit students for you. In some cases, you set the lesson price, but are required to pay a fixed, hourly rental fee. Other times, they handle all money matters and offer you a set rate. There are even public schools that allow music teachers to use facilities free of charge, since it benefits their program without requiring the music director to do additional work.

Rooms can also be rented in office buildings or churches, perhaps just for the hours needed. Another option is travelling to students' homes. While this eliminates certain kinds of overhead, extensive driving can be time-consuming and pricey. Is travelling an hour round-trip for a 30-minute lesson really reasonable? Add a "travel fee" for substantial commutes.

PREPARING YOUR STUDIO

Regardless of where you teach, prepare a nice working environment for students:

- **Cleanliness.** The room should be organized, orderly, and sanitized.
- **Distractions.** Keep interruptions such as pets and ringing phones to a minimum.
- **Equipment/supplies.** Recording equipment, a metronome, music books, manuscript paper, CDs, stickers, and music stands should be easily accessible.
- **Storage.** Designate a convenient place for instrument cases, coats, and shoes.
- **Seating**. At the least, you will need chairs for yourself and the student. It is also nice to have a sofa for parents and other visitors.
- **Decorations**. Create a warm inviting environment that is appropriate and fun. There are a number of music posters available for teachers. Beware: Wall colors affect the mood of students, so opt for something fairly mellow.
- **Waiting area.** It's nice to have a room available to parents, siblings, and students who arrive early. Recordings, music DVDs, magazines, games, snacks, and coffee all contribute to a nice atmosphere.

Recruitment

The process of enlisting students is comparable to the marketing of any product. Strong promotion, people skills, and widespread visibility are all invaluable. The good news is that once committed students have been engaged, they often remain a source of dependable income for years.

As with any product, word-of-mouth is the most effective marketing tool. Parents of students, in particular, can become powerful allies. If they like you, they will not only provide referrals, but also become more involved in their children's education. Ask for leads. Sweeten the deal by offering discounts to families that initiate interviews with prospective students. Some teachers even coordinate "parents-only" events.

Becoming involved with local music programs (youth symphonies, school ensembles, church choirs, summer camps, etc.) is a great way to bolster enrollment. Befriend the directors and ask them to send traffic in your direction. Better yet, get to know participants directly. Volunteer to lead sectionals, offer master classes, or provide other services.

For some instructors, a handful of students is more than enough, while others pack a full-time, seven day per week enterprise. At one point, a good friend of mine taught 80 students weekly! When starting out, you may need to instruct anyone who expresses interest, even if it requires long commutes or tolerating those who are attitudinally challenged (brats). With time and smart planning, however, it is possible to sculpt a workload that fits professional goals.

Earning Students

Guitarist Eric Clemenzi (www.ericclemenzi.com) began teaching privately through a music center. Frustrated with the low wages and environment, he set up a teaching studio at home. Within five years, his student list has grown from a handful to 70+ with a waiting list. The secret?

Eric began a weeklong summer camp for guitarists in a small community center, which generated interest in local newspapers. He began selling retail products in his basement, bringing new faces to the house and offering students a great deal. His acoustic guitar duo performs family oriented shows in places like apple orchards and ice cream shops, allowing him to interact with young, awe-struck admirers. And he initiated a guitar festival which presents concerts, clinics, classes, and equipment to teenagers. Each endeavor brings him students. "I want people to call me before anyone else." They usually do.

More than Just Lessons

Go beyond simply teaching private lessons. There are many ways to create a sense of community among your students. The following techniques not only strengthen their commitment and experience, but also distinguish your studio and help with recruitment.

- **WEBSITE.** In addition to its marketing function, turn your URL into an interactive center where students communicate, work through exercises and games, and learn about studio happenings. *PracticeSpot* (www.practicespot.com) offers a number of beautifully designed site templates for music teachers.

- **NEWSLETTER.** At least once a semester, create a studio bulletin that includes important dates and policies, student achievements, interesting performances, musical puzzles, etc.

- **RECITALS.** Host a student recital at least once a year. If your studio can't accommodate that many people, see if a parent will volunteer their home. Other possible venues include music stores, bookshops, churches, temples, museums, and schools. For a special treat, make sure to feature yourself on at least one short piece.

Jerry's Music Lesson Contract

www.jerrys-music.com

The following represents the lesson policies for **Jerry's Music**. The lessons are booked in 30-minute time intervals, with students attending their lessons once each week. There is a $15 registration fee per student at the time of enrollment. We also require a current Visa or Mastercard number to be kept on file. If you do not have a credit card, we require a one month security deposit.

Tuition – You must pay the **full monthly tuition to receive the monthly rate** and have a permanent spot in the schedule book. Tuition is due before the first of the month. After the 7th of the month there will be a $5.00 late charge and your credit card will be billed for the monthly tuition plus the late fee. If your card is declined, you will be removed from the schedule and billed for the unpaid lessons.

Single Lesson – The single lesson rate is $35 and must be prepaid.

Monthly Lessons – The monthly rate is $120 for 4 lessons or $150 for 5 lessons (based on $30/lesson).

Family / Multiple students – There is a $2.50 monthly discount for each student.

Payment – Payment must be made before the 1st of the month. If you choose autocharge, we will handle the billing. If not, all lessons must be prepaid.

Attendance: Students are expected to attend their lesson(s) each week. **If you cannot attend a lesson, you must notify us before noon the day of the lesson (Monday through Friday) or before 6pm on Friday for Saturday lessons. All scheduling must be handled by the staff at the front counter of the store.** If cancellation is received before the deadline, you will receive a make-up lesson. Cancellations must be rescheduled within 15 days, and are subject to availability. Jerry's Music allows a maximum of 2 cancellations per month. Any additional cancellations will be forfeited. If Jerry's Music cancels a lesson, you will receive a pro-rated credit. The credit can be used toward the next month's tuition. If your teacher cancels, we will supply a substitute. If we are unable to, we will give a credit.

Refunds: Jerry's Music will not refund tuition for lessons cancelled by the student. Make-up lessons due to student cancellation cannot be used in lieu of regular scheduled lessons.

Termination: This contract will automatically renew each month and will remain in effect until written notice is given at least 24 hours in advance of your intent to terminate or in the case of nonpayment.

NAME (please print);____________________STUDENT NAME____________________
ADDRESS: ____
CITY/STATE: ____________________________________ ZIPCODE_______________
PHONE: ______________________EMAIL:___________________________________
VISA/ MC #____ EXP___________

I HAVE READ AND AGREE TO THE TERMS OF THIS CONTRACT.

SIGNATURE & DATE: ____

• **FIELD TRIP.** Arrange for studio outings. Many orchestras present exciting children's concerts, and some chamber groups specialize in educational events.

• **STUDENT AWARDS.** Bestowing the title of "Student-of-the-Week/Month" to outstanding students can be a great motivator. As a prize, perhaps you can loan them a special music DVD or book. Be sure to list the proud winner, along with their "bio" and accomplishment, on the studio website and newsletter.

• **OTHER ACTIVITIES.** Practicing or composition competitions, trivia challenges, and group projects all facilitate a higher level of student commitment.

Expanding the Business

To increase income, consider expanding your teaching enterprise. Group lessons, small ensembles, and classes allow you to earn higher wages while charging reasonable rates. For example, a 60-minute theory class with eight students paying $12 would rake in just under a hundred bucks—not bad for an hour's worth of intervals and scales. By growing your "school" through contracting additional teachers, you can offer additional instruments, styles, and approaches, while earning a commission for work done by others.

Growing a School

After teaching private piano lessons for 5 years, Junko Takahashi decided to expand the business. She created *Musical Expressions* (www.musicalexpressions.com) and obtained a home occupation license. Hiring college classmates and other young professionals, lessons were arranged in client's homes and her own house.

ME has since developed into a sizable enterprise, now employing over 15 teachers in areas such as piano, guitar, strings, woodwinds, and drums. As the business grew, she approached a nearby church about renting classrooms that were vacant during the week.

In addition to teaching, a big part of Junko's job is bookkeeping. Though payment for lessons is due by the end of each month, there are times when no check comes and parents must be tracked down and "reminded." She earns a respectable commission on each lesson taught, but before claiming her cut, that money must pay for an administrative assistant, teaching and recital room rentals, promotional materials, stamps, and other overhead.

Other Freelance Teaching

In addition to private lessons, freelance teaching opportunities include teaching assistants at public and private schools, adjunct professorships at universities and community colleges, master classes, seminars, workshops, and educational residencies. Courses on music appreciation, literature, Kindermusik®, and other subjects can be offered to students or the community.

ADDITIONAL SELF-EMPLOYED OPTIONS

Music Technology

Many freelance options exist for those with music technology expertise, including work as an engineer, mixer, editor, or producer. Owning and operating a recording studio requires an upfront investment, as does any small startup business, but the potential payoff from a well run company is significant. The marketplace is flooded with books, seminars, and music school programs focusing on technology related issues.

From Studio Apartment to Apartment Studio

Guitarist Jay Weaver (www.soundcolorproductions.com) operated a small recording studio out of his apartment and taught 50 private students through a music store when the shop declared bankruptcy. Instead of giving up the students, he moved his teaching practice and recording studio to a rented centrally located building. Five years later, Jay now employs eight private lesson teachers and records everything from bands to commercials and voiceovers. "When I began, almost all of my income came through teaching and gigging. Today, around 55% of my work is engineering, and I hope that number will continue to increase over the coming years."

Many clients from the lesson program have recorded in his studio, and vice versa. In fact, one interesting course places high school students into bands which receive training by the faculty, perform a public concert, and record a studio demo.

Instrument Retail

Some instrument retailers specialize in just one or two instruments, while others carry a wide variety. Small, startup merchants often operate as a home business, relocating to a separate location only if necessary. Dealers commonly offer additional services: repairs, private lessons, recording facilities, the sale of sheet music and merchandise, etc.

Double Reed This Story

For years, oboist Shawna Lake (www.oboechicago.com) helped students and colleagues identify instruments suited to their strengths, just as a favor. So turning this hobby into a business was a natural transition. Shawna now purchases instruments directly from manufacturers of her favorite brands and then retails them for a profit. She also vends used instruments on consignment and does repair work. The business is operated directly out of her home studio. One room is dedicated to teaching, reed making, and business transactions, while the "showroom" is used for testing instruments and performances.

Repair Technician

Skilled technicians are necessary to repair and restore every type of instrument. They are hired by music stores, school districts, and independent customers. The two routes to developing these skills are 1) apprenticing a master technician and 2) attending a trade school. Of course, many people with this interest begin by working their own magic on beat up instruments purchased at pawn shops or stolen from junkyards. For a glimpse into the profession, join an organization focused on your area of interest. These associations offer conferences, educational resources, career advice, and networking opportunities.

SPECIALTY	ORGANIZATION	WEBSITE
Strings	Violin Makers Association of Arizona International	www.vmaai.com
Band Instruments	National Association of Professional Band Instrument Repair Technicians, Inc.	www.napbirt.org

Piano	Piano Technician's Guild	www.ptg.org
Electronic Keyboards	Musical Instrument Technicians Association International	www.mitatechs.org
Pipe Organ	American Institute of Organbuilders	www.pipeorgan.org
Guitar	Guild of American Luthiers	www.luth.org

Music Author

An array of possibilities is available to musicians with writing skills. Journalists and reviewers write for the media; freelancers compose program notes for orchestras; publicists draft news releases for ensembles; grant writers create proposals for arts organizations. For those interested in authoring a text, possibilities include educational materials, how-to manuals, text books, musician biographies, and novels or children's books with musical themes.

Getting Booked

While a musicology student doubling as a babysitter, parents began asking Anna Celenza (www.charlesbridge.com) to introduce their children to music. Obligingly, she chronicled engaging tales about classical masterworks, always concluding by playing the recording. Years later, Anna converted these storytelling abilities into a book based on Haydn's *Farewell Symphony*. She now has a line of illustrated publications, complete with CD, focused around classical compositions. A jazz collection is in the works.

Finding Your Place

The last two chapters explored some of the numerous freelance possibilities available to musicians (for more ideas, see Appendix A). Coupled with traditional jobs, non-music employment, and other financial generators, it becomes clear that a vast array of possibilities is available. The trick is finding your place within this maze of potential, creating a professional life that is financially feasible and personally rewarding.

Chapter Eleven

FUNDING YOUR DREAMS

Chapter 11

FUNDING YOUR DREAMS

For 30 years, the rich and influential Prince Esterházy served as a patron for the great classical composer Joseph Haydn (1732-1809). His generous sponsorship allowed Haydn to pursue numerous musical ventures without worrying about financial implications. Unfortunately, this kind of limitless financial support from a single source is no longer available, excepting perhaps the independently wealthy. Savvy musicians hoping to tackle various projects are typically left to their own devices and entrepreneurial knowhow in order to raise necessary funds.

Most musicians have no problem dreaming up inspired undertakings: buying an instrument, recording a CD, attending a festival, studying abroad, hosting a series, founding a camp, hiring an accompanist, commissioning a composer. Many worthwhile projects, however, are eventually aborted due to a lack of finances.

The good news is that there are many possible sources of capital. Obtaining these resources can require substantial time and energy, but *if the vision and will is strong enough, there is often a way to bring dreams to fruition*. While the first three points below were addressed previously, this chapter focuses on the final three:

- **SAVINGS.** Allocate personal money that was previously saved.
- **INCOME.** Devote a percentage of earnings into a project fund.
- **LOANS.** Borrow from a bank, relative, or acquaintance. Since loans must be repaid with interest, inflating the overall price, exercise caution before traveling this route.
- **GRANTS.** Obtain grants, awards that must not be repaid.
- **DONATIONS.** Acquire financial gifts from family, friends, fans, and other patrons.
- **FUNDRAISING ACTIVITIES.** Host a moneymaking activity earmarked for your cause.

Whichever methods are used, open a bank account solely for the project at hand. This makes it possible to monitor exactly how much money is available at all times, without confusing personal finances.

Dream the Impossible Dream

When cellist Aron Zelkowicz got the improbable idea of founding the *Pittsburgh Jewish Music Festival* (www.pjmf.net), the notion was met with a combination of enthusiasm and skepticism. His proposal to host an orchestral concert plus two chamber recitals, costing nearly $25,000, seemed overly ambitious for a fledgling series. But he was determined to make it happen.

Aron began by visiting the local *Foundation Center* (www.foundationcenter.org), the nation's leading association focusing on philanthropy. Cross listing "Performing Arts" and "Jewish" they came up with several possible funding sources. He wrote to a dozen potential patrons, but even with follow ups, got no response. However, a local arts foundation grant came back positively with an offer of $6000. Aron then shared his vision with a neighbor who was the president of a Jewish federation. This connection, in turn, persuaded several organization members to make significant donations. Local venues gifted the rental fees of their halls, friends helped behind the scenes, and businesses advertised in the program booklet. The rest of the money was raised through ticket sales.

Not only did the Festival break even, but it was a roaring success. The next year, raising money was easier because he now had a successful track record. *Most philanthropists are more willing to invest in projects or artists with a proven history.* Now in its sixth season, the PJMF continues to grow artistically and financially.

STRUCTURE & BUDGET

Nonprofit vs. For-Profit

A music business can be operated as a *charitable nonprofit (*also known as 501(c)(3)) or *for-profit* enterprise. Each structure has unique strengths and weaknesses.

NONPROFIT	FOR-PROFIT
donors can make tax deductable donations	donations are not tax deductable
many grants are open only to nonprofits	not eligible for those grants (may be allowed to partner with a nonprofit)
no income taxes must be paid	income taxes must be paid
though allowed to pay "reasonable" salaries, surplus must be reinvested into the nonprofit	any amount may be earned, and it can be spent as owners/shareholders wish
all activities must help achieve a mission statement, which describes how the nonprofit contributes to the "public good"	can have any mission it wants, including simply earning a high profit margin
excellent records must be kept of all finances and activities	keeping excellent records has many benefits, but legal requirements are not as stringent
must maintain a board of directors	not required to have a board, but can opt to
if going out of business, assets must be donated to another nonprofit	if going out of business, assets may be distributed among owners/shareholders

It typically takes at least six months to be processed and approved as a nonprofit. To apply, you must write a mission statement, establish a board of directors, prepare articles of incorporation, incorporate, draft bylaws describing how the organization will be run, and complete the *Internal Revenue Service's* (www.irs.gov) form 1023. Most organizations hire an attorney to help them navigate this complex and time consuming document. Needless to say, this is not the most efficient way to run a business, in some cases requiring more work and expenses than it is worth. But the advantages of taxation, grant eligibility, and tax deductable donations make this structure worthwhile for some organizations.

Do not fool yourself into believing that nonprofit status will permit you to raise unlimited funds for any pet project you imagine. As with for-profit enterprises, investors—in this case donors and grant-givers—are probably only interested in activities that have an audience. Whichever format you choose, *fulfill a real need and create demand for what you do.*

Doubleheader

A group of performers interested in working together began discussing how to best organize their business. To maximize earning potential, they formed two separate entities:

1) Fifth House Ensemble (www.fifth-house.com), a nonprofit chamber group specializing in concertizing, educational events, and community outreach (unlocking eligibility for donations, grants, and corporate sponsorships); and 2) Amarante Ensembles, LLC (www.amarantechicago.com), a Limited Liability Company that books members to play private parties (including for-profit work falling outside the "public good" requirements).

Though most organizations applying for nonprofit status hire an attorney to complete the requisite paperwork, flutist and executive director Melissa Snoza took this on herself. After reading several books on the topic, she spent three days drudging through the IRS application. In the end, however, Melissa was glad to have gone through the process because it forced her to solidify the organization's mission and taught valuable lessons about tax implications. After 8 months processing time, FHE was granted nonprofit status.

Assembling Your Board

A *board of directors*, compulsory for nonprofits, is helpful with for-profit operations as well. A good board fulfills a range of functions such as fundraising, planning events, strategizing to attract wider audiences, and overseeing a number of operational issues (concert setup, taking tickets, organizing receptions, selling merchandise, etc.). Usually they are not involved with artistic decisions, though some groups have unfortunate tales of overzealous board members who overstep their responsibilities. Some boards meet regularly, while others convene only when there is a particular need or upcoming event.

Though a board can technically consist of just one or two people, 5-15 members are typical. Young organizations often recruit family and friends, but the most effective boards include individuals with a wide variety of interests, backgrounds, and experiences. Members are elected or appointed, and may include ensemble participants, prominent musicians, donors, fans, community leaders, individuals with special skills, and others interested in the group. Involving non-musicians is an excellent way to glean fresh perspectives and reach new constituents. Always be on the lookout for prospective board members.

Advisory boards typically include established experts in the field. Though not required to attend meetings, they make themselves available to contribute advice and brainstorm solutions.

Getting Board

Fifth House Ensemble (www.fifth-house.com) spent a good deal of time recruiting its Board of Directors. Identifying individuals who would be active, understand the group's mission, and offer something of value, members have included:

- Donors who invest in the group and have access to other possible contributors.
- Employees of grant making organizations who can offer proposal advice.
- Lawyers and accountants who contribute their professional services.
- Entrepreneurs who have started their own arts organization.
- Interested individuals who have great ideas and are willing to share the gift of time.
- Musician members, keeping the board and artists in alignment.

FHE also has an active Professional Advisory Board, comprised of individuals who make themselves available to provide professional services and consulting. A number of prominent musicians from around the country serve as "artistic advisers."

Budgeting

Whether planning a single project or business venture, assemble and maintain a comprehensive written budget. This should include both projected and actual figures for income and expenditures. Be as precise as possible, breaking down large categories into specifics so you can accurately assess financial standing.

Unfortunately, things often cost more than anticipated. Labor may take longer than predicted, and other expenses often arise. Aim to raise an extra 10-30% emergency cushion, just in case. It would be a shame to complete the majority of work and then be forced to freeze progress because funding has run dry. Worse yet would be plunging into unforeseen debt. If, on the other hand, there is money to spare, the surplus can be applied towards future ventures.

With a little creativity, there are often ways to curb expenses. The more you do yourself, the less work must be outsourced. Though you won't want to skimp on certain aspects, there are often ways to reduce other costs dramatically. In fact, a smaller budget may force you to make imaginative decisions that ultimately strengthen the outcome. Perhaps friends, fellow musicians, and local students will donate their services. When budgeting, consider which expenses can be shaved and which should not.

Prioritizing

For his self-released debut album *Mirror*, jazz guitarist Miles Okazaki (www.milesokazaki.com) had one overriding goal: deliver a recording of extraordinarily high quality on a relatively low budget. He decided to pay top dollar ($175 per hour) to work in a first-rate studio, guaranteeing an outstanding and efficient recording team. On the flip side, he saved money composing the music, producing the album, and designing the cover himself. Other expenses included paying musicians, duplicating CDs, and hiring a publicist who offered a discounted rate in exchange for a logo Miles designed.

Though he worked hard to be disciplined, unexpected expenses arise with almost every project. In this case, Miles expected mixing to take one day—in reality, it required three. With the budget tapped out, he was forced to borrow from family members, but it was worth it. "After all, you have to live with the product forever."

GRANTS

Not only do grants provide capital that mustn't be repaid, but some sources give repeatedly to appealing projects. Unlike competitions that allow just one winner, grants are typically awarded to multiple recipients, increasing the odds of being chosen. It is no wonder that so many artists and organizations depend heavily on grant dollars. The downsides are that it requires careful, advanced planning to apply—up to a year—and funding is by no means guaranteed.

Grants are not free money! Funders expect a return on their investment. They look to support endeavors that will realistically be completed as described in the proposal and add something of true value to society (as opposed to "vanity projects").

Call & Response

The Cypress String Quartet (www.cypressquartet.com) has been particularly effective at raising capital through grants. "We have received funding for most of our better ideas," explains violinist Tom Stone. He attributes their success to project proposals that are not only meaningful to the group, but also beneficial to the community. One undertaking, now in its tenth season, is entitled *Call and Response*.

Based on the concept of compositional modeling, the CSQ selects two related pieces and then commissions a third that references the others. From that point, they conceive and deliver an educational program to 20-25 schools, many of which are located in underserved communities. All this precedes a concert premiering the new work alongside the other two.

As a result of their workshops, 200 students typically attend (given complimentary tickets funded by donors), substantially affecting the event's dynamic. As the adult classical music buffs look around, they are surprised to see so many young people in attendance, and shocked to observe their knowledge about and engagement with the music.

Types of Available Grants

An array of grants for music related endeavors are awarded by universities, foundations, religious institutions, musical societies, art councils, corporations, private endowments, and government agencies. They range in value from a few hundred dollars to $100,000+. It may be possible to receive multiple awards from a single organization over time, though many require a specific period to pass before reapplication is allowed.

Grant givers engage in this philanthropic tradition in order to fulfill some aspect of their mission, while contributing to the community in positive meaningful ways. Sometimes this goal is as simple as fostering art for art's sake, but there is often a more specific agenda such as developing

Award Winning Projects

- Composer Byron Au Yong (www.hearbyron.com) was awarded a grant from the MAP Fund to produce *Kidnapping Water: Bottled Operas*, a set of 64 musical miniatures performed in waterways throughout the Pacific Northwest.
- Pianist Kathleen Supové (www. supove.com) received a grant from the Mary Flagler Cary Charitable Trust to commission Lukas Ligeti (www.lukasligeti.com) to compose a work for Disklavier and Laptop based on African rhythms.
- Ethnomusicologist Holly Wissler (www.qerosmusic.com) won a Fulbright grant to investigate indigenous, ritualistic music from a remote region of Peru, researching how various aspects of music-making reflect cosmological beliefs.
- The Mallarmé Chamber Players (www.mallarmemusic.org) received a grant from the Aaron Copland Fund to record a CD featuring music by African American composers.
- QuinTango (www.quintango.com) was awarded a Chamber Music America Residency grant that took them to the outer banks of North Carolina for a 5-day program in two rural counties.
- Annually since 1992, Drummer Robert Jospé (www.robertjospe.com) has won grants in consistently increasing amounts from the Virginia Commission for the Arts. Funding, which must be matched by presenters, helps support concerts and educational workshops for his jazz and world music groups.

a type of experience or exploring a social platform. Some sources are open to anyone, while others back only members of a particular region, race, ethnicity, religion, age, profession, etc. Grants are available for the following types of undertakings:

- Career fellowships
- Collaborative projects (often interdisciplinary)
- Commissioning
- Community engagement programs
- Copy work
- Educational programs
- Finishing a project
- Hosting a concert series/festival
- Programs with a social agenda
- Recording
- Researching
- Residencies

- Unique projects
- Studying domestically/abroad
- Touring
- Working with a mentor
- Writing about music

The majority of grants are earmarked for nonprofits. However, even if you are not affiliated with one of these organizations, there may still be a way to qualify. One possibility is joining forces. For example, a composer in search of financial assistance may be able to apply in conjunction with a nonprofit performing ensemble.

Another option is working with a nonprofit umbrella organization that specializes in partnering with for-profit entities, known as a *fiscal agent* or *conduit*. They claim a certain percentage of grant funds acquired, typically 2-7%, in exchange for this relationship. *Fractured Atlas* (www.fracturedatlas.com) is an example of a large conduit that works with artists.

Some grants are available to individuals, though the amounts conferred tend to be lower than those for nonprofits, usually in the $500-10,000 range. Often, these awards are sponsored by nonprofits. Employees or organization members are eligible for *internal grants* (universities, churches, etc.), whereas *external grants* are open only to those who have no prior relationship with the funding institution, preventing bias and ensuring fairness.

There are a number of ways to identify grant sources. Your local library is a good starting point—do not be shy about asking librarians for assistance. Several annual grant directories detail opportunities, requirements, amounts available, deadlines, and contact info. Local, regional, and state arts councils often maintain funding lists, as well as artist organizations in each field such as the *American Composers Forum* (www.composersforum.org) for composers. Universities often house a development office which assists faculty in locating and applying for grant support, and musician bios may provide further clues. Visit *The Savvy Musician* (www.savvymusician.com) for additional resources.

To increase your chances of success, apply for multiple grants when possible. Winning a particular award is far from guaranteed, and most are not designed to single-handedly finance a project. Consider how many ways your proposal can be positioned, targeting even opportunities not specifically designed for musicians. For example, when hoping to tour an educational program of Latin American sacred music, search for grants geared towards music, arts, touring, Latin American culture, education, and religious organizations.

Compiling the Submission

An assortment of materials may be requested when applying for grants: submission form, abstract (short summary), project proposal, resume or CV, work samples, budget, agreement letter from collaborating parties, references, etc. Every aspect of the instructions must be followed meticulously; feel free to ask for clarification if guidelines are ambiguous in any way.

For best results, your proposal should be superior to the competition in *every* aspect. Solve a real problem, present a thorough vision, write with crystal clarity, and make documents beautiful. If you really want the award, blow everyone away. Make the decision easy for jurors.

While all submitted materials are important, none hold as much weight as the project proposal. This document typically describes your interest in the award, the problem at hand, how your project provides a solution, and your qualifications. The best proposals:

1. DON'T GET DISQUALIFIED. Review committees do not begin by looking for winners, but rather for red flags that justify elimination. One misstep can get a file purged.

2. PROVE SUITABILITY. Address *every* point in a grant description, demonstrating that your qualifications and aspirations are in complete alignment with stated preferences. Every sentence should bolster credibility; extraneous elements may turn off reviewers. Read between the lines, assessing exactly which qualities are sought.

3. ARE EXCEPTIONAL. After passing the first two tests, projects with some outstanding distinguishing feature fare best. Why should jurors choose your work over other qualified submissions?

In the project proposal, don't worry about repeating information that appears in supporting materials. In fact, this document should stand on its own—make sure every point you want to emphasize is included here. Place the most important information towards the beginning, so the committee does not stop reading before discovering these assets. Focus on the project's value, not just the ways in which you will be benefited. Support all arguments with specifics.

Grant committees often include members who are not specialists in your field. In fact, many have just one music representative, or zero. Assume nothing. Avoid technical terms, and explain the significance of claims. Your winning the planet's most prestigious viola award may be mind-blowing to those in the know, but simply saying the name will have little impact on an architect or lawyer.

A HIDDEN BENEFIT

Composing a grant proposal can be valuable even if no funds are awarded. The writing process forces you to flesh out details of your vision, focusing on what is truly important.

Sometimes, it is advantageous to alter the design of a project slightly in order to align it with a particular set of requirements. However, never make a "false sale" by fudging the facts. Not only will this dishonesty burn bridges with the granting institution, but word has a way of travelling; it can slam shut additional doors in the future.

Before mailing an application, take great care to proofread and run your proposal by trusted colleagues or past award winners. There may be someone from within the organization willing to provide feedback. If suggestions are offered, follow them!

Though even top-notch proposals are not guaranteed success, a large number of denials often indicate a fundamental problem with submissions. Either the project is a weak fit for available funding or documents are poorly framed. Many grants are NOT offered to the most qualified applicants. Instead, those with clear and well-crafted materials are favored.

The Selection Process

Judges who award grants are most often good people who truly want to make a positive difference. Though there may not be enough money to aid every worthwhile project, most jury members are not corrupt insiders, simply there to reward friends. Adjudicating panels, made up of past award winners, experts in the field, and employees of the grant giving institution, really want to identify excellent projects and provide assistance to deserving artists.

The first step for judges is to eliminate weak applications. Below are the most common reasons proposals are rejected:

- **INCOMPLETE.** Incomplete applications are disqualified.
- **LATE.** Late applications are not considered either.
- **EXTENSION REQUESTED.** Judges do not look favorably at those who ask for more time.
- **NOT ELIGIBLE.** Perhaps the applicant is from the wrong region or age group.
- **WRONG FORMATTING.** The length, format, and number of copies should be as specified.
- **NOT A GOOD FIT.** If your project doesn't align with the mission of the program, there is little reason to apply.
- **POORLY WRITTEN.** Judges won't have the patience or energy to plow through weak writing.
- **SLOPPY PRESENTATION.** Jurors assume that messy documents equal poor workmanship.

• **LACK OF GRACIOUSNESS.** Always treat employees of the organization with the utmost respect, even if an error is made. If not, your negativity may come back to haunt you.

After the disqualification round, jurors rank the remaining files in order of merit. Some aspects considered are:

1. **NECESSITY.** Does the project tackle a real or manufactured need?
2. **EFFECTIVENESS.** Will the need be successfully and creatively addressed?
3. **IMPACT.** How will it affect involved artists and the community?
4. **QUALITY.** Will the value be high?
5. **LIKELINESS.** Is it probable that the project will be completed as described?
6. **HISTORY.** Does the applicant have a proven record of success?
7. **SUSTAINABILITY.** Is there potential for long-term growth? Will this project lead to others?

Grant Advice from a Veteran

Composer Mary Ellen Childs (www.maryellenchilds.com), best known for her "visual percussion" creations, has learned a great deal about grant writing over the past 25 years. In addition to applying for over 100 awards, she has frequently served as a panelist.

"Grants are not a crap shoot, though it can feel like that at times because many deserving people apply for most opportunities." In order to advance, it is imperative to spell out your message and assume nothing. Jurors do not have time to read between the lines or dig through mountains of prose. Mistakes as basic as failing to state your area of expertise early on (i.e. *Mary Ellen Childs, composer*), or listing the dates of activities when a proven history of success is required, are enough to get an application passed over.

People often ask "what do panels look for?" but perhaps this is the wrong question. Instead, figure out what you truly want to do. Early in her career, Mary Ellen applied for a grant with a proposal that fit the guidelines perfectly. But her heart wasn't into the project. After receiving the award, she was stuck working on it. Now, she only pitches projects that truly excite her.

If you receive a grant, follow through with all requirements. Many awards necessitate a report once the project has been completed. Make sure your account is high quality and completed in a timely fashion. If not, the organization will black list you from future awards, and may also circulate your lack of compliance.

DONORS

We have all made requests for "contributions" before, whether hitting up our parents or pleading with a scholarship office. Most musicians are comfortable selling tickets for an upcoming event and will happily push CDs or candy bars for an ensemble fundraiser. Yet somehow, directly requesting financial support for a personal aspiration can feel selfish, intimidating, or even terrifying. With all of your talent and training, must you really resort to "begging?"

The short answer is yes. The amount of government funding for the arts has dropped dramatically, and not all proposals can be supported through grants. Pursuing a musical life is expensive, and there are simply not enough funds available to artists through traditional sources to facilitate all worthwhile projects.

There is absolutely no reason to feel guilty for soliciting financial support for meaningful projects. The worst potential outcome is a denial, and as long as you are gracious, no one will hold the inquiry against you. In fact, creating a community of donors does a lot more than raise capital. It causes supporters to take ownership in your success, becoming active advocates.

In some cases, effective fundraising requires adjusting your vision to create a product with wider appeal. But if this ultimately makes your pursuits more relevant and wide reaching, it becomes an incredibly positive process. Fan-based funding will become increasingly important over the coming decades, presenting savvy musicians with a challenge and an opportunity to expand their impact while realizing their dreams.

"Go to China!"

Harpist Lana Greenawald was ecstatic when she won a spot in the local youth symphony. The problem was the requisite $4000 in membership and travel fees for the year, covering a tour to Asia. Determined to raise this money, she recorded 30 minutes of Christmas music in a home studio. Then, after explaining her situation to friends, neighbors, and members of the Harp Society, she raised $2000 fairly effortlessly by selling 200 units at $10 apiece.

One neighbor, impressed with Lana's determination, decided to help even more. Unprompted, she mailed a check for $2000 with the memo line: "Go to China!"

Understanding Potential Donors

You may be shrugging, despairing that there are simply no rich people in your life, and certainly not anyone who wants to finance your project. The known, wealthy, music patrons are already inundated with major requests for support: build a concert hall, begin a scholarship fund, underwrite a music school, back a symphony. Is there any realistic chance these patrons will support the work of a little known, emerging artist?

This is the wrong way to approach a fundraising campaign. Instead, consider people you already know, the members of your network. Most individuals have a certain amount of discretionary income, and those who already like you and your music are more likely to help than complete strangers. In fact, you may be surprised how much family, friends, and fans are willing to give to an appealing cause.

However, consider the psychology behind philanthropy. People do not donate simply because they urgently need to unload cash from a bulging bank account. In a sense, the motivation behind giving is a bit like any other non-essential "purchase"—the donor feels their life will somehow be enhanced. This statement is certainly not discounting the value of altruism. Most people truly feel good about themselves when helping others and that is the payoff. However, there is no shortage of meaningful charities vying for hard earned cash in exchange for a spoonful of "personal fulfillment." Donors typically give for some of the following reasons:

1) To help someone they care about.
2) To support a project or cause in which they believe.
3) To feel important.
4) To be part of a movement.
5) To live vicariously (for closet musicians).
6) To wield influence.
7) To obtain an incentive.
8) For tax breaks. *Remember that only donations to nonprofits are tax deductible.*

By this point, you probably have a clear idea about what you hope to accomplish, how much needs to be raised, and why this project is important to you. But consider what is in it for "investors." Of all the laudable causes in the world, why does yours merit attention?

Socially meaningful (i.e. presenting to children or the underserved) or tangible projects (recordings, commissions, etc.) generate more interest than appeals for logistical support (food, lodging, transportation). Beyond that, a theme that resonates with donors is more likely to win their backing. Make sure your proposition is a compelling one.

Smart Stewardship

Michael Stephenson of the New Century Saxophone Quartet (www.newcenturysax.com) describes donor fundraising as a two-step, cyclical process. The first stage is *cultivating relationships*. "We meet most of our major donors at concerts or through colleagues, and get to know them over time. We enjoy their friendship, as we hope they enjoy ours." They invite these individuals to concerts or dinner, and mail them new CDs gratis, with no agenda other than staying connected.

The next phase is *soliciting funding*. Requests for major donations are typically made during face-to-face meetings. Because of the camaraderie that has been built between musicians and donors over time, this process never feels awkward or uncomfortable. In fact, patrons are often anxious to help. Of course, the NCSQ is careful not to abuse these relationships, pitching only projects that will likely be of interest to each donor.

Afterwards, the cycle of friendship and support continues. One thing they never do is disappear until the next fundraiser!

Preparing to Fundraise

Before commencing a fundraising campaign, create an attractively designed, single sheet *case statement*. Longer is possible, but keep it from becoming overwhelming. Without this, it is difficult to make a convincing argument for your cause—plans somehow don't seem as serious or real until they are concretely set in writing. Succinctly noting the essence of your plight also provides an outline for donor presentations.

In many ways, a case statement is similar to a business plan (see Chapter 2), but geared specifically to the donor. Make this document easy to read at a glance, perhaps using outline form. Describe your background, the nature of the project, and the desired outcomes and benefits. Include the overall amount that needs to be raised and progress thus far, including support from grants, other patrons, or even your own piggy bank. *Donors are much more likely to consider projects that already have financial momentum.*

When approaching donors, one essential consideration is how much to request. If that figure is unrealistically high, you may immediately shut down any possible donation. On the other hand, a number that is too low might result in a smaller pledge than the donor would be willing to give otherwise. Often, the best solution is to suggest a range. Consider the project needs, donor's financial resources, and depth of your relationship. Someone you just met is unlikely to pour thousands of dollars into your dream even if they have the means. It takes time to cultivate relationships that result in major gifts.

People may want assurance that their donation will be put to good use and that your fundraising target is attainable. One helpful strategy is breaking down larger goals. In fact, some contributors like the option of determining where their money will be directed (i.e. travel, reception food, recording one piece, etc.), rather than simply adding to a generic pot. By doing this, they can be thanked not only for their gift, but also for making one specific aspect possible.

Labor of Love

Nokuthula Ngwenyama (www.ngwenyama.com) was asked to oversee all aspects of the 2008 *Primrose International Viola Competition*, a contest she had won at the age of 16. Giving 500 hours of her time preparing for this ambitious weeklong event, Nokuthula ultimately raised $85,000 with the help of a committee and advisory board. "It was definitely a labor of love," and her enthusiasm resulted in a supportive and motivated donor base. Funds were raised through the following activities:

- **In-kind contributions.** A significant part of the budget was covered by in-kind donations: the use of facilities (practice rooms, concert halls), piano tuning, catering, live audio streaming, and even a $20,000 viola that was awarded to the winner.
- **Secured donors.** Donations from individuals, many of whom Nokuthula solicited in person, contributed a total of $4100.
- **Phone-a-thon.** American Viola Society members donated $1500 collectively after being phoned.
- **Benefit concerts.** Two benefit concerts in different states raised a total of $4000.
- **Sponsors.** A violin shop and one foundation donated $5000 each. Another foundation contributed $10,000.
- **Registration.** The registration fee of $180 by 78 participants brought in over $14,000.
- **Advertising.** Ads in their programs raised $1200.
- **Miscellaneous.** Ticket sales, t-shirt sales, parking, etc. raised a small amount.

Soliciting Funding

If you have never asked for a donation before, the prospect can be nerve racking. Before making an actual pitch, you may want to practice with friends or mentors to organize your thoughts and get comfortable. For the first actual request, start with someone you trust and know well. This way, even if you have the heebie-jeebies, she will certainly understand. After a few attempts, fundraising may not feel as daunting a task as it once seemed. In fact, you may find it enjoyable to share your story with others.

The most effective way to ask for a donation is in person. People are exponentially more apt to give when there is personal human interaction, and such encounters allow you to have the patron's undivided attention. Face-to-face meetings are especially critical when asking for larger gifts or beginning a new campaign. Depending on the nature of your relationship, it may be appropriate to meet over coffee or a meal.

Begin with a warm welcome and perhaps some small talk to break the ice, but quickly move on. You certainly don't want to waste the donor's time. Continue with a project overview, using the case statement as a guide. Allow the other person to ask questions and share feedback. Always maintain a comfortable atmosphere, and observe signals projected by the patron. Though you certainly don't want to come off as greedy, convey enthusiasm about your plans and proudly ask for the donation.

Sometimes an initial meeting is just used to plant an idea. No contribution request is made until a subsequent appointment. Another technique is foregoing the donation inquiry altogether. Instead, simply ask your confidant for advice on reaching financial goals, allowing them to 1) make a donation; 2) volunteer to host a fundraiser; 3) offer to solicit others on your behalf; 4) help you design a plan to raise the money. Most close members of your network will try to help in some way when asked.

Politely accept contributions of any amount—never haggle—and expect to receive rejections. These are simply a part of fundraising. Always give people who are unwilling or unable to donate an out, without resorting to high pressure tactics. When turned down, don't take it personally, and express appreciation for the time spent. You never know who will have a change of heart or donate to the next project.

There are other methods for soliciting potential donors. Telemarketing (telephoning) still has the advantage of human contact. This is a good way to engage old friends and those who are geographically distant. If no previous relationship exists, however, many people become annoyed by unsolicited contacts.

Direct mail is another possibility. For best results, each note should be personalized, since most people instantly discard anything that resembles "junk mail." A handwritten message on an otherwise typed letter is always a nice touch.

Though highly personalized e-mail requests may yield results occasionally, don't expect a high response rate. Most people ignore and delete this kind of informal request for money, and if it comes off looking "spam-y," you may wind up burning bridges at the same time you are not raising money. However, if a fundraising campaign is detailed on your website, feel free to direct fans there through e-mail or newsletters.

Donor Love Letters

The Ōn Ensemble (www.OnEnsemble.org), a Japanese taiko drumming quartet, hosts a fundraising drive each year. Beautifully formatted, 3-page, double-sided letters, complete with color photos, are sent to prospective donors. In 2008, it began:

Dear Friend of Ōn Ensemble,

*Ōn Ensemble is gearing up for our annual home-concert, and this year's show is set to be our biggest and best self-produced endeavor yet! We've arranged our best songs, hired our favorite lighting and sound engineers, and reserved the Japan America Theater in Little Tokyo, with over 800 seats! The event is intimidating and exciting...**and I need your help!***

I'm writing today to ask you to make a donation toward Ōn '08: Yubu. By making a donation of any amount, you become a member of the Foundation Team, Ōn Ensemble's core group of supporters. In the next few moments, I think I can prove three things:

- *You can make a major impact on Ōn Ensemble.*
- *Arts funding needs your support more than ever.*
- *Donating is the best deal in town!*

It sounds like a stretch, but let me explain...

The following pages described the group's mission, history, and future; their need for donor support; a statement that any amount, even $3, is helpful; a description of thank you gifts (for $300, their top level, supporters receive quarterly "love letters" from members "complete with a bag of spices and seasonal recipe"). Progress is updated regularly on their website.

Incentives

Many people happily donate to good causes on their own merits, but the deal can be sweetened when privileges or goods are acquired in exchange for contributions. The types of incentives possible are limited only by your creativity: pre-release CDs, autographed paraphernalia, VIP season tickets, private house concerts, an iPod filled with your favorite music, a piece dedicated to the donor, etc. Of course, always consider the amount a gift (and shipping) will cost you.

Unsung Tales & Motivated Fans

Jazz vocalist Allan Harris (www.allanharris.com) funded a set of albums called *Cross That River* through incentive-based programs. Donations unlocked various perks including access to web materials (interviews, rehearsal videos, blogging), special release CDs, signed sheet music, backstage passes, dinner with the artist, public acknowledgement, and permission to attend events (rehearsals, recording sessions, radio interviews). For each album, he received around 100 donations ranging from $25-$15,000; the most common levels were $500-1000.

Allan organized these efforts through *ArtistShare* (www.artistshare.com). "Working with this company loaned an air of legitimacy to my fundraising efforts." However, simply signing on with them hardly guaranteed that money would flow freely. Allan and his wife/manager Pat worked pro-actively to interest friends and admirers in the project. He travelled across the country to perform private house concerts. Additionally, the unique theme of the recordings—unsung tales of black cowboys in the American West—spawned enthusiasm.

In-Kind Contributions

In addition to capital, it can be extremely beneficial to receive *in-kind contributions* (non-cash gifts): the use of a rehearsal space, free housing, transportation, frequent flier miles, reception catering, an instrument loan, free services, etc. Graciously accept these gifts, since they alleviate expenses and reduce the total amount that must be raised.

Corporate Sponsorship

While few corporations are willing to donate significantly to individual musicians or chamber groups, many will consider offering in-kind contributions. The Rose Ensemble (www.roseensemble.org), a vocal group focusing on ancient music, has forged relationships with several companies. A local magazine offers $15,000 of free advertising yearly; a wine vendor provides complementary alcohol for receptions; a photographer documents events gratis. In exchange, TRE graciously acknowledges these businesses in print materials. Without exception, such affiliations have grown out of personal relationships rather than cold calls and unsolicited requests.

FUNDRAISING ACTIVITIES

There are literally thousands of fundraising activities, ranging from bake sales to car washes. A simple web search unveils myriads of companies eager to meet with you about moneymaking solutions. Though capital from any source is helpful, a few music-related suggestions follow. Many variations can be spun from each theme, and all are adaptable to individuals, ensembles, and larger organizations. Be creative.

Concerts

What better way to raise money for a musical project than giving a benefit concert? Though the event is "free," audience members are encouraged to leave contributions in tip jars, donation boxes, or church style pass-the-plate collections. People are often willing to give far more under these circumstances than the typical ticket price.

> **An Amazing Benefit**
>
> José Gomez was devastated when his two clarinets were stolen. To raise money for new ones, he organized a benefit concert in a local church. José opened the event by explaining his situation and asking for donations. A flyer describing the instruments he hoped to purchase was distributed, and performances by several prominent local musicians followed. The event raised just shy of $3000.

Services

Why not hire yourself out to deliver singing telegrams or make surprise appearances as a strolling performer? In fact, if you have much success with these novelty services, consider morphing them into a regular business.

Pre-Sales

For recordings, *pre-sales* (selling the product before it is available) are a great way to raise money. Obviously, established fans and members of your network are most likely to take a chance on a recording that hasn't yet been completed. One possible twist permits "pre-orderers" to download tracks as they become available, in advance of the physical copy.

Buying Ahead

A year before Boston Secession (www.bostonsecession.org) recorded *Surprised by Beauty: Minimalism in Choral Music*, they began fundraising. In addition to seeking large contributions, they pre-sold the album at concerts, on their website, and through direct mail. An autographed disk could even be pre-purchased for a few dollars more than the sticker price. Fans also had the option of being listed as "Executive Producer" in exchange for a substantial donation.

Games

If raising money for a private lesson studio, try holding a *Practice-A-Thon*. Students get sponsors to pledge a certain amount for each hour they practice over a certain period. The biggest earner wins a prize. Not only is money raised, but students practice more!

Similarly, a band could schedule a *Play-A-Thon*. Attempting to stage a 24-hour show, pledges donate a fixed fee for every hour the group is able to perform without collapsing.

A *Battle-of-the-Bands* competition raises funds for multiple groups. Each ensemble plays short sets, and guests place money in a can for their favorite act. Cash is counted at the end of the evening, and the group with the most is declared royalty. How's that for beefing up your resume: "Winner of the Walnut County Battle of the Bands!

Auctions

Auctions have been successfully employed by numerous musical organizations. In the *live auction* format, people openly bid against one another and items go to the highest bidder. A common variant is the *silent auction*, where visitors stroll around displayed items and mark offers on paper. For *raffles*, participants purchase tickets and winners are drawn at random. In all cases, begin by obtaining items gifted by individuals and businesses. Musical products can include autographed CDs, concert tickets, private lessons, piano tunings, music books, posters of musicians, and cell phone ring tones.

A Night to Remember

Each year, the trio Chatham Baroque (www.chathambaroque.org) hosts a major fundraising event entitled *Twelfth Night Gala*. The occasion includes a silent auction with 100 donated items (smaller gifts are bundled into packages); a live auction of 8-10 unique or costly items (house concert, limo ride and a performance, etc.); a short CB performance of around 25 minutes; gourmet catered food; and a wonderful opportunity to mingle. Its unusual and festive nature attracts media attention and a fresh assortment of guests.

Logistically, Twelfth Night is organized largely by board members and volunteers, with the assistance of staff members and musicians. Funds are earned through 1) *underwriting* (patrons donating $500+ to help facilitate the event in exchange for complimentary event tickets, advertising in program books, and more), 2) *ticket sales* (priced at $100 apiece), 3) *auction items*, and 4) *additional donations*. The committee works diligently to increase the net profit each year, focusing special attention on securing new underwriters for the event.

Ads

Businesses may be interested in purchasing ad space in your brochure, newsletter, program booklet, or website. Ads can also be projected onto a screen before performances begin, as is common in movie theaters. Obviously, you will have more luck convincing business owners to advertise if your clients consist of likely consumers for their product. Consider approaching nearby restaurants, music stores, concert venues, and arts organizations.

Joint Ventures

If financing a project is simply out of reach on your own, why not pool resources with other organizations, sharing expenses, responsibilities, and glory? With more people involved, it may also be easier to create a buzz and attract an audience.

Strength in Numbers

The Junior Symphony of Vancouver (www.oregonchamberplayers.org) was founded in order to fill a cultural void in a small Northwestern town without a single concert venue. Their events often combine forces with other local organizations. "As a community, we are stronger when working together," claims co-founder and oboist Victoria Racz.

One fundraising alliance involved the library, which made fliers, arranged for a performance site, and oversaw catering. JSV wrote news releases and prepared a concert during which student participants spoke about their favorite books. Patrons of both organizations attended, and proceeds were split down the middle. This event was so successful that it has become an annual event.

Raising Money in Difficult Times

No matter how savvy you are, raising money is rarely easy. This challenge becomes more acute during difficult financial times. As I write this, the world economy is in recession, with less money available for just about every sector of society. That includes musicians, and as families and businesses tighten spending, artists will have a tougher time.

Yet even under such conditions, raising capital is possible. However, it is more essential than ever that your product solves a real need and your case is absolutely compelling. In fact, an economic downturn provides a unique prospect for musicians. As society re-examines its priorities, music has the potential to provide a sense of hope, community, and joy in ways that material items can hardly compete.

Chapter Twelve

OUTSTANDING PERFORMANCE PLUS...

Chapter 12

OUTSTANDING PERFORMANCE PLUS...

Music has played a vital role in every culture since the inception of humanity. For most of that time, there were just two ways to engage in this mystical phenomenon: witness a live performance or create the sounds yourself. In stark contrast, the ways music is experienced today has exploded. It bombards us from all directions: radio, television, film, CDs, iPods, websites, shopping malls, cell phones. The extraordinary prominence of music is exciting, but what does that mean for the state of performances?

For the tried and true, there is no substitute for a live presentation. The world's best recording somehow doesn't compare with the vitality of an ensemble working together in real time. This demographic, however, is relatively small. More often, people view concerts as one of many options competing for their attention. To take time out of their busy schedule, drive downtown, and pay for tickets and parking, the experience better be—well—extraordinary. To even warrant consideration, it should provide *something* significantly different than that which could be created in the comforts of their family room:

1. **ENTERTAINMENT.** A fun, engaging, and interactive event.

2. **NEW OR EXCEPTIONAL EXPERIENCE.** Some element, musical (i.e. a new composition not yet recorded) or extra-musical (i.e. interdisciplinary or multi-media), that cannot be reproduced at home.

3. **SIGNIFICANT HAPPENING.** A "must see" show that everyone is talking about, perhaps featuring a hip aspect or someone famous.

4. **SOCIAL FUNCTION.** A participant is a friend, acquaintance, or family member, or the event fulfills some kind of social function (entertaining guests, a singles mixer, etc.).

5. **PERSONAL CONNECTION.** The concert's theme connects with a personal interest.

6. **EXCITEMENT OF LIVE PERFORMANCE.** For some people, live music is a compelling enough rationale on its own merits.

If your concerts consistently draw packed houses, be proud of this accomplishment. Obviously, something is going right. But if not, there is a problem with: 1) the perceived relevance of your event; 2) your marketing campaign; 3) a combination of the two. In any case, perhaps it's time to reevaluate what motivates people to witness live music.

Most musicians prioritize outstanding playing, and you should strive for nothing less. But *great execution alone rarely brings people to the concert hall.* Musical performances are not gymnastics competitions! If excellence is the only thing of interest to be offered, why not just check out the recording? After all, there is little chance a live presentation can compete with the perfection of a digitally edited, flawlessly mixed sound file.

This chapter focuses on the rest of the package. Of course, not every event must evolve into a circus to prove relevant, and interdisciplinary experiences do not inherently improve the marketability of a presentation. In some cases, such choices actually diminish its power. But savvy musicians consider the full gamut of possibilities. They look for ways to breathe new life, credibility, and relevance into live performance. Once the floodgates of creative potential have been opened, a new kind of artist is born.

MUSICAL CONSIDERATIONS

Form, Cohesion, & Progression

How many times have you attended a concert featuring wonderful individual selections that somehow didn't make sense together? This kind of mish-mash is equivalent to a fascinating museum salon with random unrelated displays. The experience can be confusing.

Consider the overall form, flow, and logic of your program. Is there enough variety? Continuity? Will the opener engage the audience, with the closer bringing them to their feet? Does each piece lead logically to the next? What kind of logistical concerns does the program create?

Programmers often begin by choosing random musical selections they enjoy. This strategy may produce outstanding results, but there is also the danger that works will not satisfactorily combine into a unified whole.

Instead, think of each concert as a single entity made up of several episodes (compositions). Evaluate the role of each, deliberating the kinds of threads, narratives, and recurrent motives that hold together the show. Consider how energy flows from one work to the next. Beginning with a title or theme can be helpful. This doesn't have to place you in handcuffs. In fact, it may even serve as a creative muse.

Edible Music

American Modern Ensemble (www.americanmodernensemble.org) director Robert Paterson built a program around one of his favorite themes: cuisine. "Food and Music," which included Marc Mellits's *Fruity Pebbles*, William Bolcom's *Lime Jell-O Marshmallow Cottage Cheese Surprise*, and Aaron Kernis's *The Four Seasons of Futurist Cuisine*, was followed by a festive reception featuring drinks and edibles referenced in the show.

Duration

Nothing kills an otherwise outstanding concert more than having it last too long. This is equivalent to hosting a wonderful houseguest who, unfortunately, outstays their welcome. Only under extreme circumstance should a performance extend beyond the two-hour mark (i.e. operas, all-night fundraisers, installations where the audience is free to enter and exit).

Sometimes musicians are shocked when a performance lasts longer than intended. This demonstrates poor planning. It is better to leave an audience wanting more than to have them fidgeting in their seats, grudgingly wishing they'd left twenty minutes earlier!

Carefully time all pieces, and overestimate to be safe. When moving to a more reverberant hall, tempos tend to slow slightly, adjusting for the acoustics. In your calculations, don't forget to include time for applause, talking, beginning late, set changes, and intermission.

Also consider the duration of individual works. A standard "song" on the radio is three-minutes, so the general population is not accustomed to concentrating on music for extended periods. This certainly doesn't mean that only miniatures should be considered. Under the right circumstances, extended works are quite effective. But consider short pieces as a contrast to long ones. A 45 second interlude can be refreshing, especially in the midst of half hour masterworks.

On a related note, it is *not* a criminal act to program individual movements in isolation, or to space them throughout the event. Within the right configuration, this can facilitate a fascinating approach to programming. Similarly, for jazz performances, not everyone must solo on every tune.

Short and Sweet, in 3/4 Time

Pianist Stephen Hough (www.stephenhough.com) compiled a program of short, 19th Century waltzes. "It's a great mistake for people to assume that something has to be long to be a masterpiece. To be able to say a lot in a few words is one of the hallmarks of an artistic genius—whether poet or musician."

Memorization

Classical music is one of the few artistic fields in which players commonly use "notes" during performance. Actors reading lines or dancers referencing sketches would be totally unacceptable. Though memorizing music may be unreasonable for large ensembles, this goal is often feasible for soloists and chamber groups. Though the process requires more preparation time, it offers many benefits: facilitating a deeper understanding of works performed, permitting more interpretive and physical freedom, and breaking down barriers with the audience.

A Piece to Remember

Alarm Will Sound (www.alarmwillsound.com), a 20-member band specializing in contemporary music, takes issue with the traditional prestige surrounding premier performances. "So many groups commission a new piece, play it once, and then throw it in the trash. This is not the best way to build a performance tradition," states cellist and composer Stephen Freund.

When AWS champions a new work, they commit to programming it multiple times, providing members an opportunity to internalize and develop true fluency with the music. Members memorize and stage pieces, creating a greater level of audience engagement. In addition, fans associate particular compositions with the group, a model employed by virtually all pop bands.

ENGAGING THE AUDIENCE

Let's face it—most performers want their offerings to be wildly received. Numerous benefits could arise as a result: personal validation, monetary payoff, raving reviews, future opportunities, the satisfaction of moving others. Oddly, many musicians spend little energy considering the experience of their audience when planning a performance.

Your audience's perspective is of paramount importance, maybe even more than your own. Without a doubt, taking these critical supporters for granted can lead to dissatisfaction. One goal of performers should be to move viewers so they will be eager to attend other events. Delivering a meaningful experience not only builds your fan base, but also benefits others by bolstering the image and relevance of musical experiences.

To create a healthy bond with an audience, you must first gain their trust. A crowd that likes and connects with you will be more eager to engage in the music. They may even follow you with an open mind when presented with challenging artistic journeys. If performing repeatedly for the same people, trust (or distrust) may be carried over from previous encounters. With new viewers, it is essential to gain a faithful commitment early on.

Love Thine Audience

It seems that Boston Brass (www.bostonbrass.com) is able to captivate any audience. During concerts, each player chats with the crowd, sometimes even joking about the overly serious nature of typical "chamber music concerts." They have been known to perform *a capella* vocal numbers, and the trombonist accompanies himself on guitar while singing comedic originals. Funnier moments are followed with serious masterworks. Players roam the lobby during every intermission to meet and mingle with fans. With so much audience interaction, it is no wonder that BB has experienced widespread success.

The Music

Winning over an audience can occur by simply performing well received music. Such enthusiasm may be generated from familiar or accessible tunes, breathtaking virtuosity, or high-level performance. However, it often requires more.

Stage Presence

The ways in which artists present themselves, from the opening entrance to the closing bow, significantly shape the overall experience for spectators. Players who smile and physically interact with the music are more likely to engage than those who stiffly and unemotionally hide behind music stands. Though each instrument has its own physical limitations, any performer can communicate passion for their art.

What messages do you convey as a performer? To find out, study a mock performance video, perhaps with the volume down. Do bows communicate warmth and sincerity or sterility and detachment? Do physical gestures radiate joy or awkward nervousness? Do you broadcast mistakes by making faces? During multi-measure rests, is your attention focused on the source of the music, or are you lost in an alternate reality? Audiences immediately pick up on these signs. Whether you look disconnected or joyously involved, viewers will likely follow your lead.

Seeing Music

New Triad for Collaborative Arts (www.newtriad.org) is an organization with a mission of developing a "new kind of performer" that creates classical music experiences accessible and moving to a wide variety of audiences. Through seminars and consultations, they encourage musicians to think beyond the notes played, incorporating drama and psychology. One area of emphasis focuses on connecting visual aspects of performance– movement, facial expressions, and the ways in which an instrument is held–with the artist's vision of the character, meaning and, subtext of each piece.

Public Speaking

Audiences appreciate getting to know performers as human beings. Spoken words break down barriers as almost nothing else, whether introducing the group, describing musical content, or sharing a peculiar story. When addressing the crowd, consider their background and experience. Avoid technical jargon unless performing for experts.

Rather than regurgitating historical facts from program notes, find ways to hook the listeners. One effective technique is demonstrating short musical excerpts in combination with verbal explanations. When the full version follows, listeners recognize those moments and experience a deeper connection, feeling they "got it." Another possibility is sharing a personal anecdote. Why did you choose this work? What crazy thing happened during rehearsal?

Curated Concerts

Insistent that audience members play an active role in shaping recitals, pianist Adam Marks (www.adammarks.com) developed a format he calls "curated concerts." Before shows, he prepares by learning as much as possible about programmed works: historical context, composer information, extra-musical relationships, intriguing stories, etc. During performances, he not only talks to the audience, but allows them to direct interactive discourse. Multiple presentations result in unique discussions depending on the interests, backgrounds, and input of each crowd. "Great concert musicians must possess extraordinary listening abilities," says Adam. "My approach is just a logical extension of that process."

PUBLIC SPEAKING TIPS

Good stage presence combined with a likeable demeanor can help win over even the toughest of crowds. Remember, the purpose of talking is much more than conveying information. It is a tactic for building positive rapport.

- **Think things through.** Before the engagement, consider what to say. Determine a strong opening, and keep the rest interesting and focused.
- **Attitude**. Treat listeners with respect. Just as a thoughtful talk can place them in the palm of your hand, a rude or condescending remark can turn them against you.
- **Humor**. Laughter seems to be a taboo action in many classical music settings. There is only one explanation for such condescension: the Snob Factor. Humor is every bit as valid an emotion as any other, and a fantastic way to engage audiences. *We can all use more laughter in our lives!*
- **Do not read.** Some players memorize their music, but read speeches verbatim! The lack of spontaneity conveyed by reading comes across as stilted, robotic, and disingenuous. If you aren't an expert public speaker, practice until it feels comfortable and natural.
- **Body language**. Wear an appropriate facial expression and make direct eye contact with audience members. Do not play with your hair, fidget with hands, pace aimlessly, or succumb to other nervous habits.
- **Conviction.** Speak loudly and clearly with energy and enthusiasm. Be careful not drop the ends of sentences.
- **Pause.** Consider the pacing, and frame sentences and important concepts with pauses. Give listeners a moment to absorb what has been said.
- **Do not ramble.** Keep talks concise. Too much verbosity is just as irritating to audience members as being ignored. Two minutes is often enough.

Toastmasters International (www.toastmasters.org) is a wonderful organization that helps individuals develop their public speaking abilities.

Audience Participation

Most audience members enjoy participating, making them feel like cherished contributors rather than dispensable onlookers. A lucky thirteen ways to accomplish this are: 1) making them laugh; 2) asking questions requiring a response; 3) having them clap or conduct; 4) hosting a sing along; 5) call-and-response singing; 6) whistling a familiar tune; 7) requesting a volunteer; 8) inviting individuals on stage; 9) playing from the audience, intersecting their space with the performers; 10) encouraging people to roam, experiencing music from different locations; 11) constructing improvisations based on themes suggested by the audience; 12) creating opportunities for spectators to dance; 13) allowing the audience to choose program order.

The Audience Votes!

The Chamber Orchestra Kremlin (www.chamberorchestrakremlin.ru) presented a concert entitled *The Audience VOTES!* Season ticket holders received a CD with 21 compositions, from Mozart to Schnittke, and a booklet containing program notes. They were allowed to cast votes for their favorites, and the top choices were performed.

Pre- & Post-Concert Activities

A crescendo of pre-concert happenings can generate excitement. Recordings and live opening acts create a musical atmosphere before the featured ensemble sets foot on stage. Performers, ushers, or other "characters" can roam the hall and engage with the audience. Here's another approach: have a comedian warm-up the crowd. This technique is common in Hollywood before live show tapings, so why not music concerts?

A Musical Feast

The Garth Newel Music Center (www.garthnewel.org) has architected an event model that places musicians and spectators side by side. Evening shows begin with a cocktail hour, during which guests mingle with one another. At a certain point, performers from the resident piano quartet enter to lead a pre-concert talk combining musical information, engaging tales, and banter with the regulars. After the musical performance, the night caps off with a 4-course gourmet meal for all. In fact, performers have even doubled as servers. By closing time, musicians and visitors have become great friends.

Pre-concert talks allow interested audience members to invest in the show's energy before it begins. Informational lectures and interactive discussions may be led by group members or external guests such as local educators, scholars, or artists. This is an ideal time to introduce a soloist or play and explain excerpts. Also possible is addressing broader philosophical issues such as how to approach listening to unfamiliar music.

A post-concert wrap-up, or "Meet the Musicians and Their Instruments," allows audience members to ask questions and offer feedback. On-line blogs take the pre- or post-concert ideas further, allowing participants to ask questions and express beliefs well before or after the show.

INTRODUCING...THE CROWD!

During intermission and after the event are wonderful times to interact directly with audience members. Make a commitment to greet your fans. Fight the temptation to hide out. Their appreciation will grow if they learn you're a great performer onstage AND a real likeable person. A nice reception allows artists and audience to mingle, and everyone is happy when eating! Please be gracious if someone asks for an autograph. This is a form of flattery—some people religiously collect signatures of people they admire.

Applause Etiquette

Classical concerts have strictly regulated policies about when clapping is appropriate and when it is not. Maintaining this order is so critical that audience members often police those around them, ensuring that no such indiscretion is made. The rationale is that an ill-timed show of appreciation is distracting, disrupting the music's flow and continuity.

The danger is that this practice often leads to disengagement and passive listening, opposite its original intent. Enthusiasm during performances is accepted and encouraged in most other performing art environments: opera, figure skating, drama, the circus, and concerts of other genres. If an "uneducated" audience claps at the "wrong" time, please be gracious in accepting their zeal. It simply means they are enjoying themselves.

Surprises

An unexpected treat can keep people talking for months. Possibilities include:

- Instrumentalists performing a vocal number
- Vocalists performing an instrumental number
- Cameo appearances by a local celebrity

- Costumed characters
- Bringing an animal or child onto the stage
- Introducing a musical genre that is out of character with the rest of production

EXTRA-MUSICAL ELEMENTS

Music is theatre. Concerts are visual. Strong extra-musical elements can transform an event. Musicians should evaluate every aspect of their presentations, from the moment people enter the venue to the time they leave. Everything matters, from bows and smiles to lighting and staging, since all contribute to the overall experience of viewers.

In the early twenty-first century, human beings are arguably more visually sophisticated than any other time period. Thanks in part to television, film, and the Internet, people are accustomed to complex quickly changing imagery in ways never before imaginable.

Many extra-musical options are described here. Obviously, not all elements are appropriate for every occasion. Some require impractical financial expenditures and/or time commitments. While a savvy use of these ingredients can be transformative, nothing should be inserted gratuitously. A belly dancer, snake charmer, or fire breather will do little to help your cause if utilized in an insincere, contrived context!

It seems that most performers either consider many of these elements or none of them; few incorporate only a couple. However, the inclusion of a single visual aspect may be enough to transform a performance, like a stroke of red paint against a black and white canvas.

Venue

Performances can be held virtually anywhere, and an event's location significantly impacts the experience. Each venue has its own unique acoustical properties, stage size, general décor, and potential. Find ways to take full advantage of the space, exploiting its shape and idiosyncrasies. In addition, the character and ambiance of a site can be integrally linked to the overall concept of an event. For example, a modern art museum would be ideal for a performance from graphic notation, perhaps projected. A park concert could be planned around nature themes.

If you have the option of choosing a venue, several factors in addition to price should be considered. What is the audience capacity? (Nothing is more discouraging than performing to an empty house. The energy of 200 people packed into a room that has only 180 seats is completely different than 200 spread throughout a 1500 seat stadium.) Are their lighting capabilities? What are the stage dimensions? Do they have a decent piano? Before settling on a location, think through all issues that will affect your event.

Music Everywhere

- The Olympic Music Festival (www.olympicmusicfestival.org) offers chamber music concerts in a barn, complete with wandering donkeys. Partly as a result of their unusual setting, they typically attract more than 12,000 visitors each summer season.
- The Canadian composer's collective Redshift Music Society (www.redshiftmusic.org) created *Vertical Orchestra*. Concerts are housed in unlikely venues such as the Vancouver Public Library's beautiful, open atrium. Performers placed throughout the building's seven floors coordinate by following synchronized stopwatches.
- Musicians from the Royal Philharmonic Orchestra (www.rpo.co.uk) performed the music of Elgar in a London rubbish dump on instruments made from found materials.

Setup

Traditionally, performances are centered on stage. If more than one ensemble plays, the area is reset so the next group will also be centered. Alternative formations offer several potential advantages: eliminating downtime, fresh relationships between audience and sound sources, the element of surprise. When evaluating a hall's potential, consider using different parts of the stage, pit, balcony, aisles, backstage, or even audience area.

PRISM CONCERTS

"Prism Concerts" (aka "Collage Concerts") offer an exciting way for audiences to experience music in live surround sound. The idea behind the event: uninterrupted music featuring a variety of ensembles and artists. Such continuity is possible because each subsequent group is placed in a different location. Some events have a unifying theme, while others attempt to be as diverse as possible. This model can extend beyond music to include dance, acting, or film.

Set Design

A set defines the physical environment where a performance is held. Contributing to this milieu is everything from instruments and chairs to elaborate sets and props. An intriguing design can capture an audience's attention before the show begins, and needn't be expensive. In fact, because classical and jazz concerts typically offer little creativity in terms of set design, a small effort goes a long way.

Unusual music stands and chairs add pizzazz. Backdrops can be created by dispersing instruments across the stage (be careful where you step!) or creating asymmetrical structures incorporating platforms of various heights. Borrowed lamps, tables, sofas, or other props from your living room make the audience feel right at home.

Setting the Stage

Composer Paul Dresher's (www.dresherensemble.org) involvement with new opera and music theater taught him that visual aspects are just as important as sonic ones, affecting focus, counterpoint, and atmosphere. Taking pains to keep the stage area from looking cluttered, he carefully considers the placement of musicians (often incorporating risers of various heights) and lighting/color scheme, sculpting a unique look for each work.

Props and more elaborate sets often play a central role within his productions. For example, *Sound Stage* is framed around a 17½ foot tall set built entirely of invented instruments. It is played by performers moving around the base, elevated in the air, and maneuvering the insides of this massive structure.

Staging

It often feels odd, uncomfortable, and unimaginative when musicians remain frozen stiff. Natural, spontaneous movement connects body with sound, and can influence interpretation.

More deliberate choreography is also possible. Something as simple as standing while playing makes a difference. Another possibility is having performers change locations periodically. For example, why not reposition members of a quintet for each movement? In addition to the visual impact, new musical relationships will be highlighted. Extensive staging for performers of portable instruments can be particularly effective, as show choirs and marching bands regularly demonstrate.

He was Staged!

Swedish clarinetist Martin Fröst (www.martinfrost.se) is more than your average virtuoso. Whether performing new works or the classics, he finds ways to make them his own through miming, choreography, costuming, and lighting. He even performs on roller skates.

Interdisciplinary Options

In addition to fresh and powerful results, a well done collaborative venture can draw diverse crowds. Interdisciplinary options include partnerships with dancers (ballet, jazz, tap, modern, ethnic), poets, actors, visual artists, cinematographers, aerialists, circus performers, pantomimes, magicians, balloon artists, hand/shadow puppeteers, comedians, and chefs (why not?).

Total Art

Interdisciplinary collaboration is at the heart of VisionIntoArt (www.visionintoart.com), a collective co-founded by composer Paola Prestini in 1999. Comprised of eight musicians (three of whom are composers), a poet, an actor, a filmmaker, and a visual artist, all performing members sing, improvise, and move. They begin conceptualizing each production by workshopping newly composed music for two weeks, 4-5 hours per day. During this time, the non-musicians observe, offer feedback, and begin crafting their role. Though composers generally direct their own work, everyone in the ensemble is free to add creative input.

In addition to full productions, VIA also performs what they call "Traveling Songs," or sets of variable pieces offered in club settings. These songs represent the international nature of the collective, extending across culture, discipline, and training.

Technology

Technology allows for an infinite variety of possibilities. Beware of technical glitches and bugs that add stress and complications.

TECHNOLOGY	NOTES
Sound Reinforcement	Music and speech amplified to affect loudness or balance.
Surround Sound	Sounds recreated by speakers placed in different parts of the hall.
Sound Modifiers	Effects that modify reverb, echo, distortion, and addition parameters.
Instruments	Electric guitars, electric violins, synthesizers, samplers, etc.
Recordings	Recorded material, including music and sound effects, may be played alone or accompany acoustic performance.
Sequencers	Computer programs that replay pre-programmed sequences.
Interactive Programs	Some computer software, such as MAX, allows for acoustic instruments to interact with electronic sources, creating unusual algorhythms and sound potential in real time.

Lighting	Effective lighting can transform a performance, affecting the mood, focusing attention, and contributing to the set's appearance. *Please note: poorly integrated attempts can be worse than not using lighting at all, so proceed with caution.*
Super Titles	Projected translations or texts above the stage or onto a screen.
Slide Shows/Videos	Projected onto a screen or various parts of the venue.
Video Feed/ Live Projections	Projected live images of players or the audience. Can be focused on the fingers of a pianist, bodies of musicians, or the entire stadium. Some groups incorporate complex rigs with multiple cameras.

Electric Performances

The mission of early music ensemble Hesperus (www.hesperus.org) is to "bring the past into the present." One way they do this is by accompanying silent films, marrying technology with tradition. For example, *Robin Hood* is supported with English Renaissance tunes representative of the period when the story takes place. Audience members shift attention between the screen and musicians, who rotate through an impressive array of period instruments.

Squonk Opera (www.squonkopera.org) is an interdisciplinary multimedia ensemble. Their show *<Put Your Hometown's Name Here>: The Opera* is custom tailored to each location. Weeks before a given town's show they film local sites, interviews with residents, "imagination maps" drawn by children, and other items of regional interest. During performances, this video is projected onto a large screen. To create a more unique visual experience, props such as umbrellas and "projection puppets" (small, round "lollipop" screens on black poles) capture parts of the image during various scenes, highlighting close-ups of eyeballs, mouths, etc. The mobile musicians, who combine acoustic and electric instruments, move artfully to weave in and out of the foreground.

Attire

Attire frames the tone of an event and image of performers. Traditional dress may look nice but will soon fade into the background, while challenging the norm immediately makes an impression (for better or worse). Before selecting the default choice, consider the impact of other options.

Would you like to establish a formal or casual tone? Does a color represent the group? Period outfits, ethnic clothing, full-blown costumes, or accessories such as shoes, hats, jewelry, and scarves add a distinctive touch. Also consider whether ensemble members should dress similarly or in contrast, and if performers should undergo a metamorphosis during intermission.

Dressing the Part

The Mozart Festival Orchestra performed a program called *The Four Seasons by Candlelight* in full 18th century period costume, transporting the audience back in time.

Downtime

Downtime during concerts is a peculiar classical music tradition. It interrupts the continuity of an event and often looks unprofessional. No respectable rock group would permit such a blatant waste of time. Even operas requiring significant set changes find ways to maintain momentum.

Perhaps the logistical dilemma of an event with multiple ensembles can be a creative point of departure. For example, utilizing various parts of the hall eliminates the need for downtime while creating a unique experience. Set changes are ideal for addressing the audience, showing a short film, reciting poetry, or offering incidental music. It is even possible to choreograph these interludes. At the least, minimize downtime through careful planning.

Wall to Wall Concert

The show *REWIND*, produced and executed by the concert production company Sympho (www.symphoconcerts.org), features 90 minutes of continuous playing. In fact, electronic music begins before the audience enters and continues after they leave. Eleven previously existing compositions programmed in reverse chronological order, from Schnittke to Purcell, are adjoined with newly commissioned connectors. As one piece concludes, the next begins, overlapping like music played by a disk jockey. Events also incorporate visual art, lighting, and musicians placed unconventionally throughout the hall.

Intermission

Many concerts planners automatically incorporate intermission. However, there is no cardinal law requiring a break in the middle of musical events. While this practice allows people to mingle, claims that intermissions are necessary for spectators to use the restroom are clearly bogus. Movies often extend 2-3 hours and viewers seem to survive. A break also provides the opportunity for people to sneak away. And because they are standard fare, omitting intermission can distinguish your show.

In some cases, intermission is necessary and desirable. Some performers, particularly singers and wind players, have endurance issues that require downtime to rest their "chops." It may be preferable to let the audience wander rather than forcing them to wait through major costume or set changes. Intermissions can be used to sell food, drinks, recordings, t-shirts, raffle tickets, and other merchandise. A number of additional activities are possible, such as performer interactions with guests, instrument demonstrations, and gathering written feedback. A fun idea for family programs is to set up activities for kids such a face painting or game playing.

A DIFFERENCE OF OPINION

When brainstorming with a friend about ways to add zing to an upcoming concert, he showed me the program: Beethoven, Copland, Ravel, Intermission, Bach, Ligeti. I started talking about the six pieces listed, but he corrected me, insisting there were only five. This highlighted a significant philosophical difference. I view intermission as an integral part of the experience, and one to be considered as much as any other. In this case, it would last longer than two of the pieces! If you program an intermission, be sure to ponder its impact on the concert's form.

Is All This Really Appropriate?

As argued in the next chapter, much of society views classical music as a thing of the past, an historical relic. But here's the kicker—many classical musicians agree! They fight passionately to preserve the authenticity and integrity of The Great Tradition, playing standard lit, wearing standard attire, following standard concert etiquette. In their minds, any twist to this model is a gimmicky cheap trick that detracts from the performance. With the power of history on their side, they stay true to authentic practices, longing nostalgically for an earlier period when audiences were more sophisticated and great music alone reigned supreme.

In response...First, time does not stand still. Traditions that cease to evolve render themselves irrelevant or obsolete. And what's the problem with inventing new performance practices? Are customs being slandered? Do successful alternatives diminish the value of traditional ones? *The argument that musicians must embrace conventional rituals is just as perilous as unilaterally rejecting them.*

Second, the basic premise is flawed. In Kenneth Hamilton's book "After the Golden Age," he describes various recitals from the 19th Century which, astonishingly, have little to do with the way we "remember" them. Isolated movements were oft performed, applause during flashy numbers was desirable, and many presentations favored the variety show, anything goes model. Concerts were entertaining and interactive—even rowdy. And it was Wagner who coined the term *gesamtkunstwerk*, or total artwork, which combined music with theater and visual arts. Paradoxically, it seems that many of our practices today are based on faulty revisionist history.

As a savvy musician, you are in the driver's seat. No fines will be imposed on those who break from The Great Tradition. The way things are typically done does not have to be the way you do it. Just remember that challenging status quo *will* yield results, positive or negative, so make decisions carefully.

Our job as musicians is not to keep Bach, Beethoven, or Bird from rolling over in their grave. It is to contribute something personal and meaningful. If your performance does that, there is no reason to apologize, whether it challenges every convention in the book or religiously adheres to them. Isn't the most important tradition the one of preserving vibrant live performances for generations to come?

Chapter Thirteen

ARTISTRY & RELEVANCE

Chapter 13

ARTISTRY & RELEVANCE

To succeed as a professional musician, you must consider two critical overriding elements: 1) business concerns that allow you to develop a prosperous career, and 2) artistic issues that enable you to offer something meaningful (both to yourself and others). Balancing these considerations is sometimes challenging, but they need not be mutually exclusive.

To the first point...Success in any business requires a clear understanding about what society values and why. *No matter how much talent, dedication, and creativity you have, only products with an audience can sell.* Even brilliant marketers would fail miserably if peddling telegrams, for example, or the horse and buggy. There is simply no demand (perceived relevance) for these items. True, clever vendors could probably grow a small niche market, but large-scale sales are unlikely. Savvy musicians must understand current trends and create products with the potential to thrive within that framework.

To the second point...*There is more to life than money.* Artistry, at its best, allows us to share things that no amount of currency can replicate. If your quality music does not currently attract the amount of attention desired, there is often an alternative to throwing in the towel and selling out your convictions. Reframing, repackaging, and remarketing are all ways to breathe new life into your musical product.

It is often possible to capture both artistry and relevance. True, this combination may require creative strategizing and atypical approaches. But in the end, musicians who produce meaningful art that is also commercially viable will harvest substantial successes on a number of levels. On the other hand, one without the other is likely to lead to frustration or even resentment. A musician who makes great music but lives in near poverty, or one who gets rich pursuing avenues she deplores, will not be a happy one. To ensure a rewarding musical life, discover that magical equilibrium.

This chapter is not an ironclad treatise on the state of music in the early twenty-first century. Nor does it offer aesthetic judgments towards or against any style of music or type of experience. Instead, it is offered as a catalyst for discussion and action. Only by realistically comprehending challenges can we create solutions that keep our musical offerings vibrant for years to come.

Though this chapter addresses "classical" and "popular" styles of music making—challenges they face and possible solutions—connecting claims with jazz and other genres doesn't require much of a stretch.

Please note: There are many musicians, including quite a few featured in this book, working actively to solve the following challenges. Additionally, there are welcome exceptions to the troubling assertions outlined on the next several pages. Broad generalizations are included only to make a point and foster discourse.

CHALLENGES

Conventions

CLASSICAL	POPULAR
The event, called "Chamber Music Recital," featured a regionally known, variable instrumentation ensemble performing works written 100 to 250 years ago. Prior to the concert, audience members entered the brightly lit hall and took their seats. Music stands and folding chairs were placed in a neat semi-circle on the stage. *The lights dimmed and a quartet wearing tuxedos entered and bowed. The audience politely clapped as players assumed their positions without offering a word. Silence engulfed the hall, and audience members sat quietly and attentively. Each musician was a virtuoso, and the ensemble was tightly rehearsed.* *The first movement ended 12 minutes later, received by silence. (Actually, a few people clapped, but others responded with looks of disgust so they aborted further expressions of enthusiasm.) The lyrical middle movement lasted 7 minutes, followed by a rousing 9-minute finale. The audience applauded this astounding performance as players bowed and exited. A crew then took 5 minutes to reset the stage. This routine duplicated itself for the other high quality works on the show.* *After the closer, musicians walked to center stage for a closing bow as the audience rewarded them with applause and a few hoots. When exiting the hall, someone said, "What extraordinary performances! But did you notice that not one player smiled?" Someone else declared, "I concentrated so hard, I'm exhausted!"*	*The event, titled provocatively, featured a regionally known rock group performing original music. Prior to the concert, audience members entered the dimly lit hall and took their seats. Instruments were displayed onstage along with an elaborate set. Smoke rose from the floor and recorded music pumped through speakers.* *The band entered, dressed in wild costumes. They moved theatrically and energetically through various parts of the venue, accompanied by a light show. The audience went wild, jumping enthusiastically out of their seats and screaming at the top of their lungs. Each musician was a showman, and the choreography was tightly rehearsed.* *As the music began loudly, spectators danced along while singing (shouting) at full blast. The first song ended 3 minutes later and the crowd went wild. The lead singer then welcomed the audience with questions requiring a group response. The next song began. Such a routine duplicated itself throughout the event. Players constantly moved about the stage area while playing, and even charged through the audience at one point.* *After the closer, musicians ran to center stage for a closing bow as the audience rewarded them with applause, whistles, and screams. When exiting the hall, someone said, "What a crazy performance! Did you notice how much fun the players were having?" Someone else declared, "I danced so much, I'm exhausted!"*

No value judgment is expressed for or against either archetype. There is certainly a place for both formats, but these descriptions highlight fundamental differences of approach. To those familiar with classical models, the rock concert may appear offensive and superficial, with theatrical elements and ear piercing amplification distracting from core musical content.

Similarly, this comparison partially explains the perspective of the public majority, more familiar with pop music antics. In their experience, highly interactive productions engulf the senses, combining visual and aural stimulation. Under this light, average classical recitals fall short, illustrating a core challenge facing the relevancy of this music.

"Classical" Has an Image Problem

Unfortunately, this assertion is not difficult to prove. When asked to describe fun, exciting, engaging music, most people don't even consider classical genres. Try taking your own survey at the local grocery, aquarium, or school gymnasium. You will likely hear that classical music is:

- Boring
- Overly formal & stuffy
- Elitist, high-brow, & snobbish
- Old-fashioned
- For old people
- Relaxing
- Irrelevant

For much of the public, "classical music" conjures images of geeks wearing tuxedoes listening to "pretty-pretty music" written centuries ago. Often the butt of jokes in sitcoms and locker rooms, its creators and devotees are stereotyped as "unhip" and out of touch with pop culture. By any measure, the support base of classical music pales in comparison to popular styles.

Being presented with such sentiments makes me squirm, as you may be doing right now. I'd like to believe that classical music is passionate, revolutionary, breathtaking, subtle, and so many other wonderful things. But those are not the perceptions of the vast majority. Unflattering connotations may arise from ignorance, a single negative experience, damaging media portrayals, or a lack of linguistic comprehension. But for whatever reason, these opinions exist widely.

Why is there such a disconnect between the product offered by most classical musicians and the general public? Though stereotypes can be deeply troubling, they are often based in half-truths and partial realities, not total mythology. By comparing classical performances with their pop world counterparts, perhaps these perceptions become a bit more comprehensible.

- **BORING.** As described previously, classical and popular concert conventions are polar opposites. Popular shows tend to create visually spectacular environments, while classical performances play down these elements in favor of focused auditory emphasis. For audiences accustomed to "watching concerts," the lack of visual stimulus may seem humdrum and uninspired.
- **OVERLY FORMAL AND STUFFY.** For many classical events, performers wear tuxedos and visitors are required to dress up. Humor and audience interaction are oddly missing; at times, whole concerts elapse without a spoken word. Movement and the outward show of emotion by audience members are often frowned upon.
- **ELITIST, HIGH-BROW, & SNOBBISH.** Many classical musicians scoff at presentations that incorporate non-classical genres, unorthodox interpretations, or extra-musical elements, discounting them as mere gimmicks. And do not even think about clapping between movements—you will surely get the evil eye from everyone in the know.
- **OLD FASHIONED.** Non-connoisseurs often believe that "classical music" implies tunes written by dead white guys from a long time ago, performed within a concert model that hasn't changed much since the 19th Century. Not so ironically, many classical performers play only music by dead white guys from a long time ago, clinging to concert models that haven't changed much since the 19th Century.

• **FOR OLD PEOPLE.** Younger generations often associate classical genres with their grandparents and others enjoying their golden years. This perception is often mirrored by reality: 95% of audience members for many classical events fall into this demographic.

• **RELAXING.** Perhaps classical marketers themselves have reinforced this notion. Classical radio stations often favor literature that is inoffensive and can function as background music at the dentist office. There is a series of recordings called "The Most Relaxing Classical Music in the Universe." Where can we purchase "The Most Vibrant (Controversial, Violent, etc.) Classical Music" albums?

• **IRRELEVANT.** Considering the explanations above, it is no wonder that many view this experience as foreign, disconnected, and largely irrelevant.

Having an image problem is bad news. It means fewer people purchase the product, which in turn diminishes impact and opportunities available. With such public perceptions, it is no wonder that classical audiences have dropped significantly since their heyday. The perception of this music is tarnished, desperately in need of reparation and reinvention.

Compare, for example, our situation with that of the Kodak Corporation. Kodak was so central to the world of photography that the two terms were almost synonymous (i.e. "A Kodak moment"). They produced the highest quality product in the business, but were slow to adapt as the digital photography revolution approached. As a result, their operation was severely crippled. Kodak is but a footnote in terms of market share today. Evolution cannot be stopped!

There are, of course, devoted classical music lovers. Worrisome, however, is that this small fan base seems to be limited to two demographics in many communities: other schooled musicians and an increasingly aging audience that is not replenishing itself. No guardian angel is protecting this music. Savvy musicians must take steps that stimulate interest in their art.

"Popular" Has A Musical Problem

When it comes to relevance, the popular music world has done a lot right. Pop styles reach almost everyone in some capacity on a daily basis. They dominate radio airwaves and are increasingly the soundtrack for film and television. Trendy primetime TV shows such as *American Idol* glamorize popular styles of music making. Many bands create spectacular presentations that attract huge audiences, even when charging significant admission fees. Promoters know how to market not just the music, but also the image of artists.

Pop stars have, for better or worse, become icons of our society. We scrutinize and obsess over intimate details of superstars' lives that we have been fed by tabloid paparazzi and, increasingly, the mainstream media. Popular music has infiltrated its way into the core fabric of our society. The perceived value of its products and performers is extremely high.

While it's exciting to see music playing such a significant role in so many lives, the tactics of the pop music industry come with unfortunate downsides. While many of these issues are social in nature, the argument here focuses on a specific shortcoming: popular styles have a musical problem. This is not an overriding aesthetic criticism. It is by no means an indictment of certain grooves, offensive lyric content, wailing electric guitars, or repetitive electronica.

However, in the pop world, the desire to ensure maximum profitability often comes at the detriment of the product's artistic integrity. Many record labels and managers seek formulaic easy graspable tunes with the hopes of spurring the hit flavor of the week, dismissing creative alternative voices that push the envelope in any direction. By design, musical output is often dumbed down to the lowest denominator, marginalized so that it may be fully absorbed in a single hearing by the most unsophisticated of listeners.

This troubling aspect helps explain why so many people have a difficult time comprehending more intricate expressions. In fact, the musical critiques commonly waged against classical music actually illustrate some of the ways in which this kind of pandering has dwarfed the general public's overall musical literacy.

1. "TOO COMPLEX." Many pop tunes are boiled down to one or two ideas, with limited variety and excessive repetition. As a result, many pop listeners relegate music to a background role, instead of devoting the linear concentration necessary for, say, reading a book. Lay listeners are not used to following counterpoint, transforming melodies, harmonic and rhythmic sophistication, involved formal structures, etc.

2. "TOO LONG." To receive radio play in the pop world, songs are normally limited to three minutes. Classical pieces are often much longer—consider a Mahler symphony!—and require intense concentration. In today's society, plagued by Attention Deficit Hyperactivity Disorder (ADHD), many people are not used to listening actively for extended periods.

3. "NO WORDS; NOT GOOD FOR DANCING." Popular tunes often fulfill a specific function other than pure music: a vehicle for presenting lyrics, dancing, etc. For someone with those expectations, processing sound on its own merits as is required in many classical presentations may feel unfulfilling and daunting.

Complexity, development over time, pure music—such classical elements may actually be strengths. But the average pop listener raised without these priorities may struggle to get past such differences, discounting experiences that do not fit into their comfort zone.

A DYSFUNCTIONAL RELATIONSHIP?

The relationship between musical choice and audience is analogous to marriage partners. Constant in-fighting is not healthy and often leads to divorce, but placating one another by trying to never offend is equally dysfunctional. Yes, being asked to grow in new directions can be difficult. But without this, evolution becomes impossible. *Challenging listeners, at times, to think and listen in new ways is an important responsibility bestowed upon artists.*

Much of our population has had few opportunities to experience the fruits of classical music, or at least not in a positive inviting manner. As a result, some people project unflattering impressions on these experiences they don't fully comprehend. The consequences of commercialization and artistic dumbing at the expense of all else has been detrimental not only to musicians with profound and unique artistic visions, but also to the public.

By failing to challenge the intellect, stimulate the imagination, or engage observers in creative thought, a listener's musical comprehension is significantly diminished. Imagine what would occur if the average English speaker's vocabulary were drastically reduced. Communication would still be possible, but the range of nuance, sophistication, and expressive potential would be greatly restricted. In a sense, it would negate centuries of linguistic and sociological evolution. Such is the case when it comes to music and our public majority.

Who's to Blame?

Who is to blame for challenges facing the classical music community? Some accuse the media. Others complain about the lack of government funding and a failed education system. Fault can be placed on capitalism, the nature of consumer-driven societies, corrupt managers, or musicians who "just don't get it." In fact, there are many places to point the finger, and most of these arguments make legitimate claims.

But playing the blame game does little to help. The world simply changes, and we have no choice but to adapt or go the way of the dinosaurs. Why waste energy on negativity when you can focus on discovering exciting new solutions? Look at it as an opportunity. There is a lot we can do, as individuals and a community, to turn things around.

UNDERSTANDING OUR ROLE

Are We Merely Entertainers?

Some artists claim it doesn't matter how successful music is with audiences as long as the product itself is of high quality. There are certainly many wonderful reasons for playing other than connecting with listeners: personal, inner fulfillment; improving technique; developing music literacy; learning performance practice.

However, artists who do not value their listeners often wind up turning them off. This, in turn, creates obstacles for those who want this music to enjoy an active and healthy life. Dedicated music connoisseurs may be willing to weather a handful of performances they don't love, but a newcomer testing the waters is less likely to return to similar events if an enthusiastic reaction isn't elicited the first time.

EAR CANDY

A colleague of mine suggested that musicians are simply entertainers. He referred to our services as the "cotton candy of society." At first, I was taken aback, interpreting the declaration derogatorily. Is there not more to what we do? Is our sole function to provide "ear candy?" Clarifying his statement, he explained that musicians do not supply any basic necessities of survival—food, clothing, or shelter—and a life devoid of classical music (in this case) is possible. Our job is to add "the good stuff, the sweetness of existence."

Musicians are encouraged to assign their audience a central role. It is recommended that every project actively address several of the following goals, listed in no particular hierarchy:

1) Inspire *the audience*
2) Amuse *the audience*
3) Educate *the audience*
4) Heal *the audience*
5) Communicate something to *the audience*
6) Create community with and among *the audience*
7) Stretch and challenge *the audience*

Perhaps the word "entertain" subsumes all of these possibilities, perhaps not. The definition is inconsequential. More important is that when audience members are involved, their role is not taken for granted.

Please note that "appeasing the audience" is not listed. Dumbing down your product as a means to attract bigger crowds is not a practice endorsed here. Interestingly enough, "impressing the audience" doesn't appear either. While spectators may be astonished by your high level musicianship, hopefully the performance offers something deeper than showing off how great you are. This is one area where pop artists have it right. *In order for fans to take ownership, something has to be in it for them.*

Embracing a Middle Ground

It seems that many musicians are squarely positioned on one side or the other when it comes to music and audience. Are there just two extreme, polar-opposite options: interactive user-friendly formats with shallow expressions, or intimidating academic presentations with depth? Whether musicians offer profound statements but fail to connect with their audience, or dumb down their product in order to attract one, they are making sophisticated music less relevant.

Musical integrity is often compromised by presenters who believe the public only gravitates towards uncomplicated products. Yet much of the populace craves the new, the exciting, the unfamiliar. Audiences frequently want to stretch and grow. They do it all the time, eagerly flocking to the latest gadget, film, or Internet trend. *Many people love the roller coaster ride, as long as they know they'll be safe at the other end.*

When entering a foreign environment, it is normal to feel lost and helpless. Such is the case when many people observe classical concerts, overwhelmed and detached from this exotic and alien atmosphere. If on the other hand open-minded observers find some way to connect, the music's mysterious power and multiple levels of depth often captivates and mesmerizes them. But an "in" is required. If the tunes are unfamiliar, the presentation seems sterile, and there are no other clues, how can we realistically expect to connect with new listeners?

A third archetype exists—one that seeks a happy medium between accessibility and integrity. The more foreign, complicated, or out of the comfort zone an experience is for observers, the more essential audience-engaging tactics become. On the other hand, when extra-musical elements and accessible formats are embraced, programmers should not cower at the incorporation of profound adventurous musical offerings. Perhaps this hybrid can engage proponents of both sides, submitting a middle ground that can be embraced by both the musical bourgeoisie and the masses.

In today's fast food society, many people feel unfulfilled by the superficiality and lack of depth that is too often prevalent. True, there are plenty of individuals who have no interest in being challenged, enlightened, or pulled in new directions—they watch only feel-good films and read cheesy romantic novels—but a sizeable chunk of society seeks meaningful stimulating encounters. Classical music has the potential of adding significant value to their lives. Savvy musicians can become part of that community's solution, just as they can be a part of ours.

Can Classical Be Popular?

Can classical music be popular in the current era?

RESPONSE #1: Absolutely, but the packaging is crucial. Many American families religiously attend Tchaikovsky's *Nutcracker Ballet* year after year, and celebrate every 4th of July by attending outdoor orchestral concerts. The movie *Shine* transformed many viewers into avid Rachmaninoff lovers. Other musician-based films such as *Amadeus* and *Immortal Beloved* have similarly inspired, as have soundtracks like Tan Dun's Grammy winning score for *Crouching Tiger, Hidden Dragon.*

Following the tragic events of September 11, 2001, endless citizens attended classical memorial concerts to find solace. The Three Tenors, Josh Groban, Bobby McFerrin, Yo-Yo Ma, Joshua Bell, the Canadian Brass, Wynton Marsalis, and André Previn have all inspired vast audiences beyond the usual suspects. Rock singer Sting's 2006 release *Songs from the Labyrinth* brought the name John Dowland, a relatively unknown English Renaissance composer, to the attention of millions. These success stories, along with countless smaller-scale examples, suggest that classical music can indeed be popular when marketed and framed effectively.

RESPONSE #2: Maybe this is the wrong question. *Perhaps priorities should be broadened, instead asking if output from classically trained* *musicians can be popular.* Approaching from this angle changes everything. It expands the potential of what we have to offer beyond a single "style," unlocking possibilities of additional genres, secondary talents/skills, new concert formats/venues, and daring initiatives. It emboldens the savvy performer, composer, teacher, or administrator, allowing them to embrace past models when desirable, but without enslavement.

Third Viennese School

The Austrian group Mnozil Brass (www.mnozilbrass.at) considers the full potential of its participants. Throughout their virtuosic memorized spectacles, members play multiple instruments (including recorders, sometimes through their nose), sing, act, and execute choreographies. Individually, they take on character roles based on unique talents and personality traits. Arrangements highlight player's individual strengths; for example, the lead trumpet player has strong jazz chops. One of their shows, *The Trojan Boat,* is essentially an opera. The seven contributors are featured as vocal soloists, the chorus, and the orchestra.

REBRANDING CLASSICAL MUSIC

To ensure the longevity of classical music, artists must build new audiences while presenting their product in ways that resonate with current lifestyles. Musicians who realistically accept and respond to challenges presented by a quickly changing world will not only reap the benefits personally, but advance the cause of the music community at large.

Bring Music to the Audience

Music can, and should, be performed just about anywhere. Location directly affects audience. Some people love fancy, downtown, sprawling music centers. Others refuse to deal with the traffic and paying for parking, but eagerly anticipate events in their own community. Find ways to bring your art directly to new audiences.

Chamber Music in Any Chamber

The Chiara Quartet (www.chiaraquartet.net) began their professional existence with a two year rural residency grant that placed them in Grand Fork, ND. During this period, they played at nursing homes, psychiatric wards, town squares, and every public school in town, often multiple times. They scheduled interviews with local radio stations, including those that had not previously featured musicians, and presented concerts. In a small town with little existing musical activity, enthusiasm about their work grew steadily. "The smaller the place you are, the more readily and quickly you can make an impact," claims violist Jonah Sirota.

This experience heavily influenced the group's philosophy. Disenfranchised with the idea that simply going into schools will fuel a return of audiences to the concert hall, they became insistent that "outreach" and "performance" should not be separate entities. The CQ began an initiative called *Chamber Music in Any Chamber*. Scheduling concerts in unexpected places—clubs, galleries, bars—these events are intimate, personal, and accessible.

Filling the Void

There is a treasure trove of opportunity for savvy musicians, not only professionally, but also to increase impact. To discover them, simply brainstorm places where music is *not* happening: corporate offices, universities (outside the music school), underserved communities, government centers, hospitals, community clubs, etc.

Concert of Ideas

Creative Leaps International (www.creativeleaps.org), founded by operatic baritone John Cimino, has delivered keynote presentations to Fortune 500 companies, leadership institutes, universities, business schools, and even top White House government agencies. The team of six musicians draws together multiple disciplines—music, the arts, sciences, humanities—in imaginative collisions and juxtapositions.

Programming typically begins with a custom designed *Concert of Ideas,* fluidly fusing musical and theatrical works with themes such as leadership, diversity, creativity, and innovation. This interactive and playful performance is followed by debriefing discussions, facilitated by CL members, to bring out participants' individual insights and reflections. The effect is energizing, uplifting, and thought provoking, opening participants to candid heartfelt conversation with one another.

For multiple day presentations, CL offers a range of workshops, often ensemble-based. They culminate with a *Harvest of Learnings*, performed in partnership with attendees and based on insights generated and synthesized by the participants themselves.

In many ways, these environments can benefit the most from musical contributions, especially if programs interface directly with their needs and concerns. In fact, individuals who do not typically attend concerts may appreciate your efforts more than seasoned aficionados.

Thematic Connections

Musical or programmatic themes that connect with the general public increase perceived relevance while providing a point of entry for new listeners. Possible links include current events, community causes, charity benefits, politics, religion, holidays, sports, and pastimes.

Making Connections

Themes that resonate with the general public often result in heightened enthusiasm and the ability to engage new audiences.

- The text from Joseph Schwantner's (www.schwantner.net) composition *New Morning for the World* is based on speeches by Martin Luther King, Jr. The premier performance featured Willie Stargell, former Pittsburgh Pirate all-star, as the narrator.
- Jazz composer Fred Sturm (www.fredsturm.com) constructed an entire program of orchestral music entitled *The Baseball Music Project* (www.baseballmusicproject.com). In addition to arrangements of baseball related tunes, the centerpiece is his extended composition *Forever Spring.*
- JacobTV (www.jacobtv.net), aka Jacob Ter Veldhuis, has a series of works for boom box and instrumentalist(s) based on speech melody. His piece *Heartbreakers* is for jazz combo and a soundtrack + video of dysfunctional clips extracted from American talk shows from the 1990s such as Jerry Springer.

Multi-Genre Concerts

The "iPod generation" consists of countless open-minded music fans who eagerly embrace the widest possible variety of musical experiences. In some cases, the less commercially viable something is the better. For this breed of open-minded listener, multiple-genre concerts offer the quintessential post-modern experience. Whether alternating between groups performing vastly different genres or featuring a single versatile ensemble performing wildly diverse literature, classical music can play a prominent role.

A Study in Post-Modernism

- The 2007 Bang on a Can Marathon (www.bangonacan.org) featured over 27 hours of non-stop music, including an ensemble of 9 bagpipes, 2 rock bands, a hip hop group, a youth choir, and many ensembles performing works by contemporary concert music composers.
- Jerseyband (www.jerseyband.com) created its own style of music called *Lungcore*, a horn-driven concoction which fuses heavy metal with jazz and classical influences.
- During a Mozart violin concerto, Gilles Apap (www.gillesapap.com) created a cadenza that referenced bluegrass, Irish fiddling, Eastern European dance, blues, Indian ragas, and Prokofiev. He also whistles, sings, and gets percussive effects from his instrument.

Contemporary Music

In the popular world, "new" has enormous appeal. Pop fans consistently seek the hippest, freshest hits. Similar arguments could be made about classical taste, at least in the past. People lined up in droves for the premier of a Rossini opera or new piano work by Liszt. But many classical audiences today reject the very notion of contemporary music, sometimes harshly, demanding "war horses" of the past instead. As a result, recent works are often presented almost as an apology, sandwiched between standard lit. Other times, they are omitted completely.

Programming with this bias, however, fails to recognize another truth. *Novice or non-classical audiences, particularly younger ones, often react more favorably to contemporary works than older relics.* The power, expanded sonic palate, and aesthetics of these compositions are actually closer to their experience than, say, Mozart or Bach. In fact, some contemporary ensembles are leaders in the quest to cultivate fresh fans for classical music.

Of course, there are also outstanding new music groups whose events are barely populated. So what's the problem? In many cases, these performances are sold like any other classical event, marketed only to a subset of existing classical fans. The music may be innovative or even accessible, but promotion and presentation vehicles are not. To generate ecstatic buzz, find ways to brand modern creations as the hippest thing in town. New venue, new presentation, new marketing, new audience, new education: New Music.

Contemporary Music for Contemporary People

Performances by Present Music (www.presentmusic.org), a contemporary ensemble based in the "conservative" city of Milwaukee, typically attract audiences of 750+. Their relatively young crowds consist largely of doctors, lawyers, teachers, and other non-musician adventure-seekers. "Most people love new things. They flock to buy the latest novel, see a recent film, or witness cutting edge visual art," claims artistic director Kevin Stalheim. "New music can be received the same way, if you just get people in the door. Our audiences are known for how carefully they listen, and their response is incredibly positive and enthusiastic."

One appealing feature of contemporary music is the enormous aesthetic variety available. "As with a meal, you don't want to eat just potatoes!" Programs usually feature around ten contrasting shorter works linked by a common theme. Kevin also notes that many composers are influenced by popular and world music, both which resonate with the public.

Events—and they truly are events—have taken place in venues like museums, cathedrals, zoos, science centers, and swimming areas, often integrating features of the locale. Collaborative efforts have incorporated other music ensembles (one show included a 50-person flute choir), dancers, gymnasts, film, visual art, and even animals. Without pandering, experiences are framed in relevant ways that create a true sense of community.

An Argument for "Bands"

One of the challenges in the classical music world is the lack of "bands." Instead, many promoters market music in isolation, a difficult proposition. True, audiences will ultimately be moved by works performed, but it is tricky to build a following for a composition alone. The concept of "generic performer playing great music" is a tough sell on a large-scale. The problem is that you can't gossip about a rhythmic motive. It is essentially impossible to get an autograph from a harmonic progression or interview a *cantus firmus* (pre-existing melody to which contrapuntal voices are added).

People become devoted to bands and artists, just as they follow teams and players in the sports world. They like to know about the personalities, quirks, and accomplishments of participants. Music may make the world go 'round, but in today's tabloid society, it is the personalities behind the art that have the best chances of developing a devoted following.

From a commercial standpoint, many of the most successful classical projects center on artists, not music. Devoted followers attend their concerts and purchase recordings regardless of material programmed. Yes, promulgating great literature should be a central premise, but a band with a brand may be able to pack the house on that aspect alone.

A Classic Band

The Kronos Quartet (www.kronosquartet.org) is one of the highest profile classically trained chamber ensembles in existence. They have released 40+ recordings, commissioned 600 pieces, and average more than 100 concerts per year. This group has defied conventional wisdom in just about every aspect of classical music performance. They play works almost entirely by living composers, ranging from the avant-garde to world music. Members frequently double on percussion and other instruments, and some pieces are staged.

Precisely because of this quirky, alternative approach, fans have come to expect thrilling, out of the ordinary presentations. No matter what or where they play, audiences appear en masse. The "band," their concept and history, is what draws the crowd.

Pop Culture Connections

Elevating classical music within the context of pop culture can earn bundles of new patrons. Though some of the following suggestions are too grandiose for individual artists to accomplish, they demonstrate the kind of progressive thinking that can advance classical music.

- **AWARDS SHOW.** A major televised classical music awards show, demonstrating the breadth and vibrancy of activities being pursued.
- **INTERNET INGENUITY.** Trendy interactive websites, podcasts, webcasts, and other uses of the Internet designed to attract new audiences.
- **MULTI-EXPERIENCE TICKET PACKAGES.** Season tickets that combine classical concerts with theater, dance, and other cultural events.

• **MULTI-GENRE TICKET PACKAGES.** Season tickets that combine classical events with music of other styles.

• **MUSIC FILMS.** Films about music and musicians generate publicity and excitement.

• **REALITY TV.** Since writing this, the BBC announced *Maestro*, a reality show where eight celebrities compete to become top conductor (www.bbc.co.uk/musictv/maestro).

• **SIMULCASTING.** The Metropolitan Opera (www.metoperafamily.org) has achieved success simulcasting productions in high definition to movie theaters around the country. Preceding viewings with a local live music act makes this idea even more stimulating.

Concerto for DJ and Orchestra

Composer Anthony De Ritis (www.deritis.com) asked himself "what could make a symphony orchestra more relevant today?" The result was *Devolution*, a concerto for DJ and orchestra originally performed by Paul D. Miller aka "DJ Spooky, That Subliminal Kid." It features spun beats over orchestral interludes, three drummers fading in and out of textures, and even a DJ cadenza. Extensive news coverage surrounding the premier resulted in a packed hall, bringing many enthusiastic audience members previously unfamiliar with orchestral music.

Education

While not every musician teaches formally, all should contemplate their educational mission. Whether offering private lessons, side-by-side concerts, open rehearsals, pre-concert talks, music blogging, or educational workshops, carefully consider which lessons are offered. Education, combined with unbridled enthusiasm, is the most powerful tool proponents have to rebrand classical music and keep it relevant for decades to come.

Audience of the Future

The Pittsburgh Symphony Orchestra (www.pittsburghsymphony.org) hosts a program called the *Audience of the Future Project*. Over the course of a year, students from several local high schools are invited to visit the concert hall on six different occasions. After watching the orchestra rehearse, participants break into teams that oversee various aspects of an upcoming concert. They select the repertoire, write program notes, promote the concert, produce the event, provide verbal introductions, and film a behind-the-scenes video.

Not only is this eye-opening activity valuable for students, but it provides the orchestra's management a rare candid glimpse inside the minds of young people. This kind of experiment can be adapted to chamber ensembles and other arts organizations.

Full Speed Ahead!

The issues addressed in this chapter are important on both micro- and macro-cosmic levels. It is certainly not your responsibility to single-handedly save classical music! But it is essential to have an accurate assessment of the scene in order to create products that can prosper. And when creative artists band together to address current dilemmas, they become an important lobby.

Savvy musicians can do a lot to make classical music "hip" again. Our biggest asset is our artistry; the main liability has been our inability to adapt. As savvy musicians, let us work towards solutions that maintain integrity *and* relevance at the heart of our activities.

Chapter Fourteen

LEAVING A LEGACY

Chapter 14

LEAVING A LEGACY

As we have seen, many kinds of issues are crucial to the success of a savvy musician. But in conclusion, here is a one of paramount significance: What kind of legacy will you leave? How will you affect the lives of those around you? When your name arises in conversations down the road, how will you be remembered?

As a musician, it's easy to become overwhelmed by the requirements of just "getting by." Determining a larger-scale purpose may seem like icing on the cake, an extra that is worthy of consideration, but one that must be placed on the backburner until a series of more pressing items fall into place. Of course, that list grows exponentially as we age and are faced with an ever-increasing body of responsibilities: marriage, kids, mortgage, making a living. Sure, we want to leave a special mark, but that will just have to wait or happen by accident.

Consider for a moment that legacy *is* the cake, while everything else qualifies largely as icing. Discovering the impact we hope to make—in essence our life's meaning—influences everything: the way we spend our time, the work we pursue, and the relationships we build. *A sense of higher purpose focuses priorities and gives us strength during the most difficult of times.*

Legacy through Outreach

Rob Levit (www.roblevit.com) is a jazz guitarist with more than 15 recordings to his name and a busy performing schedule. But his desire to affect change and impact the lives of others has led him to initiate some unusual projects.

Rob founded a summer program for underserved children called *The Arts Mentorship Academy*. Each morning, students convene for an interactive talk on creativity. Days are filled with multi-disciplinary experimentation: photography, African drumming, jazz dance, and mural design. The week concludes with "Community Sharing," a public forum for displaying their creations. The experience has proven deeply moving and life altering for this community of young people.

Rationales

Philanthropy and having children are two wonderful acts that many people choose to define their legacy. For the moment, however, let's reflect on some of the many ways in which addressing this issue can influence our musical life.

1. FOCUS. Defining a legacy dream leads you to favor certain activities over others.

2. OPPORTUNITY. This calling may actually unlock professional opportunities as you establish yourself as an expert or advocate in that area. It also distinguishes your work.

3. FULFILLMENT. A sense of purpose keeps you happy, motivated, and energized.

4. VALUE. A meaningful mission allows you to touch the lives of others.

5. COMMUNITY. Communities benefit and evolve when members bequeath meaningful contributions.

Few people have the luxury of directing 100% of their efforts towards their life's primary motivation. We all have to pay our dues and our bills, and sometimes that means tackling work or projects that are not in perfect alignment with overriding goals. However, with a bit of ingenuity, there may be ways to transform even these tasks from grunt labor into something that helps achieve a higher purpose. This approach also makes your activities more enjoyable. But if work consistently leaves you feeling empty, perhaps it's time to reevaluate what you do.

Legacy through Benefit Concerts

After the 2004 tsunami devastated Southeast Asia, jazz saxophonist Shirantha Beddage (www.shiranthabeddage.com) felt a deepened connection with his Sri Lankan heritage. The horrific stories that emerged motivated him to organize a benefit concert. Working with his father, who served as the Lion's Club president in his hometown, they organized and promoted an event that took place in a high school auditorium. In addition to the admission fee, guests were encouraged to make contributions. In total, the effort raised over $20,000—enough to construct three homes.

One teacher who attended was so moved he began his own Sri Lankan fundraiser, which ultimately collected enough money to build one house and a Children's and Maternity Day Clinic. Legacies are often contagious.

Defining Your Legacy

Legacies come in all shapes and sizes. Some emerge as the result of a simple interaction, while others require a lifetime of work and dedication. The primary legacy we hope to leave often evolves over time, or is different for each community and cause that touches our life. Though this calling may be discovered by accident, sharing our passion usually results from deliberate action. So take a moment to consider what kind of impact you hope to make.

Legacy is not simply what you do. It doesn't necessarily result by completing the requirements of a job, even if those tasks are done extremely well. Some people work compulsively, yet fail to leave much of an impression whatsoever. Therefore, with each undertaking, consider which priorities are stressed. *What you do with your time on Earth is significant; equally essential is how you do it.*

Take, for example, teaching. Many educators effectively impart information, but only some will be remembered forever. And the primary lessons that live on do not always equate to core class content. Even if you are the best music theory professor in the world, some alumni may recall little about proper voice leading years later—they might not even care (sorry). Instead, your name may trigger memories about your quirky sense of humor, sincere interest in their success, or the way you pushed them to take chances. These admirable qualities may even seep into their own interactions. *That* is the legacy.

Legacy through Teaching

The teaching of violinist Mimi Zweig (www.stringpedagogy.com) has impacted the lives of countless individuals, directly or indirectly. Not only has she developed music programs throughout the U.S. (from string academies to teacher training), but the priorities stressed in her approach make a lasting impact: 1) fostering a love for music; 2) creating a non-judgmental learning environment; 3) helping students reach their potential for excellence; and 4) the insistence that anyone can become a successfully music maker. Her high school ensemble, *The Indiana University Violin Virtuosi*, has toured the globe.

Mimi's impact becomes apparent through the actions of disciples like Sherry Sinift (www.sawyoming.org) and Hong Shapiro (www.violonissimo.ch), who have begun their own string academies based on her approach, and William Harvey (www.culturesinharmony.org), founder of an organization that forges musical connections across cultural and national barriers. But even former students who no longer play exhibit her influence by attending concerts, becoming patrons of the arts, and seeking music lessons for their own children.

Let's play a game of Mad Libs. How would people who know you, or have seen you in action, complete the following?

"_____ (Your name) is the most _____ (characteristic) person I've ever known!"

"More than anything else, _____ (your product) makes me _____ (action)!"

"_____ (Your name) revolutionized the way I think about _____ (subject)!"

"My life changed after _____ (event you initiated)!"

"_____ (Your name) is responsible for _____ (meaningful accomplishment)!"

What would they say? What would you like the response to be? Consider some of the various "legacy categories:"

- **INSPIRATION.** Touching people's lives in a special way through music or actions.
- **MISSION.** Advocating and fighting for a cause in which you believe.
- **NICHE.** Addressing an area where there is a shortage of resources.
- **UNIQUENESS.** Expressing art in an unusual distinctive manner.
- **PROJECT.** Organizing an exceptional project that makes a lasting impression.
- **ONGOING PROJECT.** Initiating a project that continues after you leave.
- **EDUCATION.** Teaching a particularly meaningful (life) lesson.
- **PERSONALITY.** Being the nicest, sweetest, funniest, quirkiest, etc. person around.
- **PASSION.** Exuding a contagious kind of love for what you do.
- **COMPASSION.** Playing a supportive role for a person or community during a time of need.
- **TEAM BUILDING.** Creating or strengthening a sense of community.
- **SERVICE.** Donating time, talent, or money to a worthy cause.
- **EXCELLENCE.** Being the top in your field. However, few of us can be the greatest in the world at what we do. And even if you are the preeminent trombonist to surface from your rural Southern Mississippi village, aiming to leave only this legacy is kind of a selfish one. Being a strong player is wonderful, but what you do with your talent and how it affects the lives of others is more important than the aptitude itself.

Legacy through Commissioning

For years, the Imani Winds (www.imaniwinds.com) have been setting precedents and challenging conventions about what it means to be a chamber musician. This African-American woodwind quintet frequently features improvisation, collaborations with other artists, and a fusion of musical styles within a traditionally classical context.

For their 10th Anniversary, the group initiated a *Legacy Commissioning Project*, working with ten composers of color. "When compared with string quartets, the literature available to our ensemble is quite limited," claims flutist Valerie Coleman. This project is just one way they are working to expand and reshape that tradition.

It's never too early to begin thinking about legacy, nor is it too late. If you're in school, consider ways to evolve and elevate your institution. Start a club. Begin an outreach tradition. Mentor younger students. Similar thinking can be applied to musicians in any area. What overriding feature will be your stamp? How do you define your mission? What actions are you taking to get that across?

The impact of a powerful legacy is felt long after the initiator's name has been forgotten. If you found an organization that changes lives 15 years after your retirement, the gift continues to give even if your name is omitted from the brochure. Similarly, if you positively touch someone's life and they spread that sentiment in turn, your influence is felt. Legacy is not just self-preservation and glorification—it is about making a true difference.

Legacy through Cultural Diplomacy

In February 2008, the world took notice when the New York Philharmonic (www.nyphil.org) became the first orchestra ever to perform in the communist republic of North Korea. With a single presentation, they broke down barriers that no political or military unit had been able to crack in decades. Though a colossal budget was required to facilitate this high profile event, cultural diplomacy is possible on a smaller scale.

American Voices (www.americanvoices.org), a nonprofit founded by pianist John Ferguson, has shared American music with over 200,000 people in 95 countries on five continents. Their efforts focus on offering concerts, workshops, and master classes in nations emerging from isolation and conflict.

Their 2008 *Unity Youth Performing Arts Academy* in Iraq placed 750 young performing artists side by side with ten American teachers specializing in classical and jazz music, theater, film, and dance styles ranging from ballet to hip hop. Participants from violence-prone cities like Mosul, Kirkuk, and Basra put their safety at risk to engage in contact with the outside world for the first time in their lives. Performances open to the public and broadcast extensively showcased citizens of these two nations producing something beautiful and powerful. Artists, at their best, can truly change the world.

Coda

On the surface, it may seem that the choice to become a musician is a selfish one. Though certainly not an easy career path, the option allows participants to pursue an arena that they truly enjoy. But music, and the actions of its creators, has the power to heal, inspire, amuse, challenge, communicate, entertain, educate, fulfill, and create community. Whether engaging an extensive audience or individual soul, savvy musicians with a mission can influence the world in powerful ways, big and small. We can leave meaningful legacies that truly make a difference.

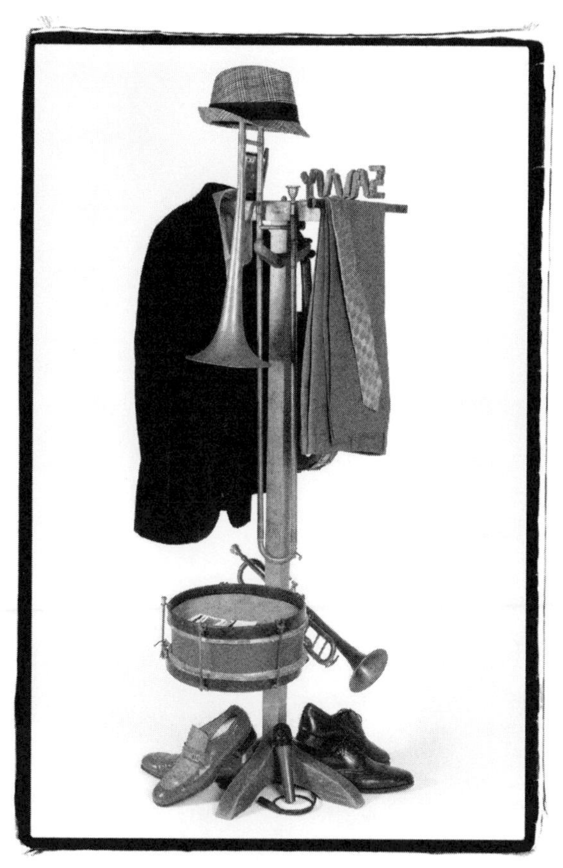

Appendices

Appendix A

OPPORTUNITY BRAINSTORM

The following brainstorm not only demonstrates the vast amount of music opportunities available, but can also serve as a launching pad for exploration. If an opportunity catches your imagination, use the Internet, your network of contacts, and other available resources to investigate further.

Ensembles

- Ballet orchestras
- Barbershop quartets
- Big bands
- Brass bands
- Broadway touring companies
- Classical chamber ensembles
- Chamber choirs
- Circus bands
- Concert choirs
- Church choirs
- Church bands
- Church orchestras
- Community theater groups
- Contemporary music ensembles
- Cruise ship bands
- Dance bands
- Early music ensembles
- Educational groups
- Festival orchestras
- Festival choirs
- Folk groups
- Gospel choirs
- Jazz combos
- Jazz choirs
- Light opera companies
- Light opera orchestras
- Marching bands
- Military bands
- Military choirs
- Military jazz groups
- Military orchestras
- Musical theater companies
- Musical theater pit orchestras
- Opera companies
- Opera orchestras
- Performance art ensembles
- Pop groups
- Religious bands
- Symphony orchestras
- Touring ensembles
- Wedding bands
- Wind ensembles
- World music ensembles

Freelance Performance

- Alumni associations
- Anniversary parties
- Art councils
- Association meetings
- Audition accompanist (pianists)
- Awards banquets
- Baby showers
- Bar/bat mitzvahs
- Bars
- Bachelor(ette) parties
- Background music
- Banquets
- Baptisms
- Barbeques
- Benefits
- Birthdays
- Block parties
- Bookstores
- Business luncheon
- Busking (street musician)
- Cabarets
- Ceremonies
- Church gigs
- Circuses
- Chamber music societies
- Christmas parties
- Club dates
- Clubs (Rotary, Elks, etc.)
- College events
- Comedy shows
- Community events
- Company picnics
- Concert series
- Concerto soloist
- Conferences
- Corporate engagements
- Country clubs
- Cruise ship work
- Dance class accompanist
- Demonstrations
- Dorm events
- Educational concerts
- Educational residencies
- Embassies
- Ensemble member
- Ensemble sub
- Expositions
- Fairs
- Fashion shows
- Festivals
- Fraternities & sororities
- Fundraisers
- Funerals
- Grand openings
- Guest artist
- Graduation ceremonies
- Graduation parties
- Historical associations
- Hobby related events
- Holiday parties
- Hospital events
- House concerts
- Hotels
- Instrumental accompanist
- Jam sessions
- Memorial services
- Military events
- Museum events
- Music conferences
- Music festivals
- New Year's Eve parties
- Office parties
- Opening acts
- Pageants
- Parades
- Parties
- Performing on TV/film project
- Picnics
- Political conventions
- Radio concerts
- Rallies
- Rehearsal pianist
- Rehearsal dinners
- Religious ceremonies
- Resorts
- Restaurants
- Retreats
- Reunions
- Revivals

- Ringer
- Romantic dinners
- School events
- Silent film accompanist
- Sing-alongs
- Singing telegrams
- Singles events
- Social dances
- Strolling violins
- Summer camps
- Surprise parties
- Studio work—jingles
- Studio work—movies
- Studio work—radio
- Studio work—television
- Studio work—record dates
- Temple gigs
- Theatrical incidental music
- Touring shows
- Trade shows
- University events
- Variety shows
- Vocal accompanist (pianists)
- Yacht clubs
- Wedding ceremonies
- Wedding receptions
- Wedding showers

Performance Venues

- Amusement parks
- Antique galleries
- Aquariums
- Art galleries
- Atriums
- Auditoriums
- Bars
- Backyards
- Barns
- Beach
- Bed & breakfasts
- Botanical gardens
- Bookstores
- Cafés
- Cafeterias
- Carnivals
- Casinos
- Churches
- Colleges/community colleges
- Comedy clubs
- Concert halls
- Convention centers
- Country clubs
- Cruise ships
- Clubs
- Department stores
- Discotheques
- Embassies
- Exhibits
- Factories
- Fairs
- Farmer's markets
- Firehouses
- Fitness centers
- Food courts
- Golf courses
- Grocery stores
- Historical properties
- Homes
- Hospitals
- Hotels/motels
- Libraries
- Malls
- Military bases
- Music stores
- Museums
- National parks
- Nightclubs
- Nursing homes
- Open air theaters
- Opera houses

- Orphanages
- Outdoor bandstands
- Parks
- Prisons
- Private schools
- Public schools
- Radio stations
- Resorts
- Restaurants
- Retirement communities
- Rooftops
- Schools
- Sports stadiums
- Stadiums
- Staircases
- Subway stations
- Supermarkets
- Synagogues
- Temples
- Tents
- Theaters
- Town squares
- Universities
- Warehouses
- Wineries
- Yacht clubs
- Zoos

Composing Opportunities

- Arrangements
- Ballets
- "Books on tape"
- Children's books with CDs
- Ceremonial music
- Commercials
- Commissions as gifts
- Commissions by artists in other disciplines
- Commissions by individual musicians
- Commissions by musical ensembles
- Community ensembles
- Competitions
- Concert music
- Copy work
- Cruise ship shows
- Dance
- Day time television
- Documentary scores
- Educational ensembles
- Film scores
- Incidental music
- Industrial videos
- Internet greeting cards
- Jingles
- Method books
- Music for beginners
- Musicals
- On-line greeting cards
- Operas
- Operettas
- Professional ensembles
- Radio themes
- Recordings
- Regional ensembles
- Re-orchestrations
- Ring tones
- Sacred music
- Songs
- Television scores
- Theme songs
- Theater music
- Toys playing music
- Transcriptions
- Video game music
- Website music
- Wedding music

Teaching Subjects

- Accompanying
- Arranging
- Choral
- Composition
- Conducting
- Ear training
- Ensembles
- Eurhythmics
- General music
- Guitar class
- Improvisation
- Instrumental lessons
- Keyboard class
- Kodaly
- Music appreciation
- Music business
- Music education/ pedagogy
- Music entrepreneurship
- Music history
- Music literature
- Music technology
- Music theory
- Music therapy
- Notation
- Orchestration
- Orff
- Percussion
- Score reading
- Sequencing
- Strings/orchestra
- Suzuki
- Winds/band
- Vocal lessons

Teaching Opportunities

- Adult/continuing education
- Adjunct college teaching
- After school programs
- Band/orchestra/choir assistant
- College/university professor
- Community college teaching
- Community groups
- Day care music instructor
- Drum corps assistant
- Education department of orchestra (or other group)
- Educational residencies/ workshops
- Festival adjudicator
- Instructional videos
- Kindermusik
- Music teaching assistant
- Public school—elementary to high school
- Pre-school/kindergarten
- Private lessons—community program
- Private lessons—music store
- Private lessons—school music program
- Private school (K-12)
- Private studio
- Settings for social change
- Special needs kids
- Substitute music teaching
- Summer camps
- Summer festivals
- Teaching artist
- Tutoring
- Vocal coach
- Workshops

Writing Opportunities

- Blogging
- CD liner notes
- Children's books (music themes)
- Educational books
- How-to books
- Instructional books
- Journal articles
- Magazine music journalist
- Museum notes on music exhibits
- Musician biographies
- News releases/publicity
- Newsletters for musicians
- Newspaper music journalist
- Novels about music/ musicians
- Online articles
- Program notes
- Reviews of performances
- Reviews of recordings
- Scholarly text
- Text books

Music Related Jobs

- A & R administrator
- A & R scout
- Accompanist
- Accountant for musicians
- Arranger
- Artist manager
- Audio technician
- Booking agent
- Cantor
- Competition judge
- Concert producer
- Concert promoter
- Conductor
- Contractor
- Copyist
- Disk jockey/announcer
- Director of publicity
- Entertainment attorney
- Grant writer
- Instrument builder
- Instrument restorer
- Instrument technician
- Instrumental performer
- Lyricist
- Mastering engineer
- Minister of music
- Music author
- Music critic
- Music documentary maker
- Music editor
- Music journalist
- Music librarian
- Music program director
- Music publisher
- Music retail sales manager
- Music school dean/ administrator
- Music software designer
- Music software consultant
- Music store employee
- Music store owner/ manager
- Music therapist
- Music video producer
- Orchestra librarian
- Piano tuner/technician
- Pipe organ tuner/ technician
- Photographer of musicians/events
- Private music teacher
- Publicist
- Radio announcer
- Radio programmer

- Recording studio owner
- Record producer
- Recording engineer
- Recording mixer/editor
- Retail sales management
- Road manager
- Salesperson
- Singer
- Songwriter
- Sound designer
- Sound engineer/mixer
- Stagehand
- Stage manager
- Talent agent
- Teacher/professor
- Transcriber
- Tour coordinator
- Videographer of musical events
- Web designer
- Web master

Marketing Tactics

- Advertisements
- Alliances
- Audio postcards
- Auditions
- Articles
- Autographing
- Banners
- Billboards
- Bios
- Blogs
- Bookmarks
- Books
- Booths
- Brand identity
- Brochures
- Bulletin boards
- Bumper stickers
- Business cards
- Bus bench ads
- Buzz
- Calendar listings
- Canvassing (door to door)
- Cards
- Catalogues
- CD-Roms
- Chalking
- Chat rooms
- Classified ads
- Client referrals
- Cold calling
- Concerts
- Concert program ads
- Conventions
- Co-sponsoring
- Coupons
- Customer service
- Curriculum vitae
- Direct mail
- Direct marketing
- Directories
- Demo recordings
- E-mail
- E-mail signature
- Exhibits
- E-Zines
- Feature articles
- Finder's fees
- Flyers
- Free consultations
- Free demonstrations
- Free seminars
- Free services
- Fundraisers
- Gifts
- Gig marketing
- Giveaways
- Internet
- Internet bulletin boards
- Internet radio
- Internet registries
- Interviews
- Invitations
- Lawn signs
- Letters
- Letterhead
- Links

- List-serves
- Logos
- Magazines
- Magazine ads
- Marketing "parties"
- Marketing teams
- Mementos
- Movie ads
- Multiple streams (aim for 7+)
- Name
- Name recognition
- Networking
- News releases
- News stories
- Newsletters
- Newspapers
- Niche marketing
- Organization websites
- Outstanding/unusual offerings
- Packaging
- Pins
- Permission marketing
- Photos
- Podcasts
- Pre-concert concerts
- Press kits
- Professional referrals
- Program ads
- Postcard drops
- Postcards
- Posters
- Print Ad
- Public service announcements (PSA)
- Public relations (media)
- Public speaking
- Quick follow-through
- Reputation
- Radio
- Resumes
- Reviews
- Satisfied customers
- Seminars
- Showing up
- Signs
- Slogans
- Social networking websites
- Special events
- Stationary
- Staying current
- Store windows
- Strategic alliances
- Street marketing
- Telemarketing
- Television
- Thank you notes
- Three dimensional items
- T-shirts
- Trade publications
- Trade shows
- Video postcards
- Video-sharing websites
- Vlogs
- Web calendars
- Web-based media
- Web presence
- Webvertising
- White pages
- Writing ability
- Word of mouth
- Yellow pages
- Your website
- Your passion

Target Audiences

- Alumni
- Amateur musicians
- Associations/guilds
- Business communities
- Children
- Colleagues
- College students
- Communities
- Clubs
- Donors
- Ethnic groups
- Families
- Fans of other music genres
- Film enthusiasts
- Fraternities/sororities
- Gays/lesbians
- Grandparents
- Groups for which you fulfill a need
- Hobby participants
- Immigrant communities
- Internet "friends"
- Like minded individuals
- Literary buffs
- Locals
- Men
- Music buffs
- Music majors
- Organization members
- Parents
- Past clients
- People connected to a theme
- Performing arts fans
- Political groups
- Professional musicians
- Religious groups
- Restaurant patrons
- Retirees
- Rural communities
- School-aged musicians
- Seniors
- Singles
- Social organizations
- Special needs individuals
- Spiritual groups
- Sports fans
- Students
- Teachers
- Teenagers
- Travelers/vacationers
- Underserved communities
- Visual art fans
- Volunteers
- Wealthy individuals
- Whites
- Women
- Young Adults

Networking Opportunities

- Activities with your kids
- Acquaintances
- Advisors
- Airplanes
- Alumni events
- Artist colonies
- Arts events
- Arts administrators
- Arts organizations
- Board of directors meeting
- Businesses
- Cafés
- Career fairs
- Chambers of Commerce
- Charities
- Civic organizations
- Classes
- Clients

- Collaborators
- Colleagues
- Community college courses
- Competitions
- Concerts
- Conductors
- Conferences
- Continuing education
- Cultural events
- Donors
- Everyday life
- Family
- Fans
- Festivals
- Former acquaintances
- Fraternities/sororities
- Friends
- Friends of family
- Friends of friends
- Gigs
- Guest artists
- Guilds
- Gyms
- Health clubs
- Happy hour
- Hobbies
- Homeowner's associations
- Industry employees
- Industry events
- Internet
- Karaoke
- Leisure activities
- Like-minded people
- Lessons with "celebrities"
- Luncheons
- "Meal networking"
- Media personalities
- Meetings
- Mixers
- Music enthusiasts
- Music festivals
- Music schools
- Nature settings
- Neighbors
- Networking clubs
- Networking meetings
- Parents of your children's friends
- Parties
- Poker night
- Political organizations
- Post concert "hangs"
- Private clubs
- Professional organizations
- Receptions
- Restaurants
- Schools
- Seminars
- Showing up
- Social events
- Social networking websites
- Sporting events
- Students
- Summer festivals
- Teaching
- Travelling
- Rehearsals
- Relatives
- Religious organizations
- Retreats
- Reunions
- Teachers
- Universities
- University events
- Vacationing
- Volunteering
- Work colleagues
- Yoga classes

Appendix B

ASSEMBLING THE TEAM

Being a savvy musician does *not* mean you have to do everything yourself! On the contrary, work hard to build a team of outstanding individuals who understand your vision and help bring it to fruition. Employing specialists in various areas allows you to benefit from their strengths, expertise, and network of contacts, while saving a great deal of your own time. Of course, each employee costs money, either in the form of an upfront fee, commission, or both. Carefully consider which work to contract out and which to self-produce.

In some cases, it is possible to have close friends or family members help, but proceed with caution. If something goes wrong, it can be taxing or even detrimental to the relationship. Another possibility is seeking assistance from college students or young professionals who are willing to assist at reduced rates (or even gratis) in exchange for the experience. Some groups even organize internships for that purpose. A final option is inviting skilled individuals to serve on your board, which may result in donated services.

In addition to artistic collaborators, key individuals in the life of a musician often include:

- **ACCOUNTANT.** Prepares tax returns; assists with tracking income and expenses.
- **ADMINISTRATIVE ASSISTANT.** Aids with paper work, phone calls, setting appointments, organizational issues, and additional errands.

- **ARTIST MANAGER.** Books local, national, or international concerts; negotiates salaries; supervises promotional materials; advises the group. Concerned with long-term career development of artists they represent.
- **ATTORNEY.** Should be consulted before entering into any major or complicated legal contract. Failing to understand the ramifications of major deals can have damaging consequences.
- **BOOKING AGENT.** Secures gigs; drafts contracts; serves as a liaison between clients and musicians. Typically focuses on local, as opposed to national or international, markets.
- **CONCERT PRODUCER.** Handles logistical aspects of a performance: finding the venue, setting up rehearsals, overseeing sound check, communicating with lighting and sound engineers, making sure people are where they're supposed to be.
- **CONTRACTOR.** Hires musicians to fill out ensembles; communicates details of services; disburses payment.
- **COPYWRITER.** Writes content for print ads, radio ads, brochures, and other promotional tools.
- **FINANCIAL MANAGER.** Oversees investment portfolio; makes suggestions about general financial issues.
- **GRANT WRITER.** Composes grant proposals.
- **GRAPHIC DESIGNER.** Designs logos, business cards, programs, brochures, newsletters, CD booklets, and other promotional materials.
- **PHOTOGRAPHER.** Photographs musicians.
- **PUBLICIST.** Writes and mails news releases to newspapers, magazines, newsletters, radio, and television, capitalizing on angles that make your story newsworthy. Can be hired on a per project basis or for long-term employment. It is not the job of a publicist to sell your product, although that is often the result of their efforts.
- **PUBLISHER.** Packages and duplicates compositions, collects payment, oversees copyright, licenses music.

- **RECORD LABEL.** Duplicates, designs, and distributes recordings. Some labels also cover or contribute to recording expenses.
- **RECORD PRODUCER.** Responsible for realizing the vision of a recording project. Involved with all phases of process: liaison between musicians and engineer; checks that all passage are adequately recorded; provides suggestions; keeps session focused; makes edit choices. Part music director, part psychologist, part cheerleader.
- **RECORDING ENGINEER.** Records, edits, mixes, and masters recordings.
- **TRAVEL AGENT.** Books air, land, or sea travel reservations; arranges hotels and car rentals; helps with other travel issues (tour guides, advice on vaccinations, etc.).
- **WEB DESIGNER.** Designs and maintains website.

Appendix C

THE ENTREPRENEUR'S BOOM CHUCK

Words & music by David Cutler

In my experience, if there are three things that savvy musicians love, it's entrepreneurship, comedy, and song. The following tune combines all three. Check out the recording at www.savvymusician.com.

10
B
mp
trade it for some cash.
eight for the price of three!
Please let me tell you
When there are roadblocks,
ff
mp
13
What I can sell you, 'cause I can mar-ket e - ven a tar-pit.
I see ri - sing stocks. I find po - ten - tial in things tan-gen-tial.
16
ff
I found a tou-pee, sold it on e - Bay. It made a real big
Here's an i - de - a: des-sert tor - ti - lla that's served with squid and
ff
19
f
C
splash! I am proud to be an en - tre-pre-neur. I can find
tea! I am proud to be an en - tre-pre-neur. The o - ther
f

22
p
op - por - tu - ni - ty e - ven when life hands me ma - nure. I own a
day to make a buck I gave a cow a pe - di - cure. I'm an in-
p
25
cen - ter with a ren - ter and a phone line that's se - cure. And I
ven - tor and a men - tor and a bus - 'ness con - noi - sseur. Would you
27
f
run a cor - por - ra - tion...
like your pack - age gift wrapped?
1.
mf
Would you
f
ff
8vb
30
like our new bro - chure?
mf

BE SAVVY,
but
HAVE FUN!

Appendix D

RESOURCES FOR SAVVY MUSICIANS

SavvyMusician.com

Rather than printing an incomplete list of resources here, and one that will soon be outdated as new organizations arise and old ones move or disappear, please visit The Savvy Musician (www.savvymusician.com) online. This indispensible website includes:

• **FEATURED ARTISTS.** Updated links to artists featured in *The Savvy Musician.*

• **RESOURCE CENTER.** An extensive catalogue of over 1000 resources beneficial to musicians: magazines, blogs, organizations, funding sources, artist colonies, social networking sites, free business tools, and more.

• **BOOKSTORE.** *The Savvy Musician Bookstore*, operated through Amazon, specializes in books that help musicians become more successful. In fact, many titles have reviews describing specifically how the text benefits musicians. For each purchase, a small percentage is earned by www.savvymusician.com. All proceeds are invested directly into making this website one of the most valuable resources on the Internet for musical artists and organizations.

• **NEWSLETTER.** Join a community of thousands to receive the free *Savvy Musician Newsletter.* Featuring artist profiles and articles by leaders in the field, you can even submit your questions or stories (from unprecedented successes to disastrous nightmares) to be considered for inclusion. This is the rare breed of newsletter, designed with *your* interests in mind, that you will eagerly anticipate each time!

- **ARTICLES/VIDEOS.** Focusing on a variety of issues relevant to aspiring and established musicians.

- **SERVICES.** Information on mentoring, consulting, and presentations.

- **PRODUCTS.** Purchase this book and other products for savvy musicians.

Books

Below are recommended books that expand upon themes from each chapter. For reviews of these (and more!) titles, specifically addressing how and why they are beneficial to savvy musicians, visit The Savvy Musician Bookstore (www.savvymusician.com).

CHAPTER 1-THE ENTREPRENEURIAL MINDSET

- *The Art of Possibility: Transforming Professional and Personal Life*, by Rosamund Stone Zander & Benjamin Zander. ISBN: 978-0142001103.

- *Awakening the Entrepreneur Within: How Ordinary People Can Create Extraordinary Companies*, by Michael E. Gerber. ISBN: 978-0061568145.

- *Make the Impossible Possible: One Man's Crusade to Inspire Others to Dream Bigger and Achieve the Extraordinary*, by Bill Strickland. ISBN: 978-0385520546.

- *Mindset: The New Psychology of Success*, by Carol Dweck. ISBN: 978-0345472328.

- *The Rise of the Creative Class: And How it's Transforming Work, Leisure, Community, and Everyday Life*, by Richard Florida. ISBN: 978-0465024766.

• *So You Want to Be an Entrepreneur: How to Decide if Starting a Business is Really for You*, by Jon Gillespie-Brown. ISBN: 978-1841128030.

• *Tribes: We Need You to Lead Us*, by Seth Godin. ISBN: 978-1591842330.

CHAPTER 2-MINDING YOUR BUSINESS

• *The Brand Called You: Make Your Business Stand Out in a Crowded Marketplace*, by Peter Montoya. ISBN: 978-0071597500.

• *Branding for Nonprofits*, by DK Holland. ISBN: 978-1581154344.

• *How to Form a Nonprofit Corporation*, by Anthony Mancuso. ISBN: 978-1413306477.

• *The One Page Business Plan for Nonprofit Organizations*, by James T. Horan Jr.. ISBN: 978-1891315022.

• *Purple Cow: Transform Your Business by Being Remarkable*, by Seth Godin. ISBN: 978-1591840213.

• *The Successful Business Plan: Secrets and Strategies*, by Rhonda Abrams. ISBN: 978-0966963526.

• *You, Inc: The Art of Selling Yourself*, by Harry Beckwith & Christine Clifford Beckwith. ISBN: 978-0446578219.

CHAPTER 3-MARKETING IS EVERYTHING

• *101 Ways to Promote Yourself: Tricks of the Trade for Taking Charge of Your Own Success*, by Raleigh Pinskey. ISBN: 978-0380810543.

• *Arts Marketing Insights: The Dynamics of Building and Retaining Performing Arts Audiences*, by Joanne Scheff Bernstein. ISBN: 978-0787978440.

• *Getting Noticed: A Musician's Guide to Publicity & Self-Promotion*, by James Gibson. ISBN: 978-0898792850.

• *Guerrilla Marketing, 4th edition: Easy and Inexpensive Strategies for Making Big Profits from your Small Business*, by Jay Conrad Levinson. ISBN: 978-0618785919.

• *Guerrilla Music Marketing Handbook: 201 Self-Promoting Ideas for Songwriters, Musicians, and Bands on a Budget*, by Bob Baker. ISBN: 978-0971483804.

• *Lexicon of Musical Invective: Critical Assaults on Composers since Beethoven's Time*, by Nicolas Slonimsky. ISBN: 978-0393320091.

• *Marketing for Cultural Organisations: New Strategies for Attracting Audiences to Classical Music, Dance, Museums, Theatre, and Opera*, by Bonita M. Kolb. ISBN: 978-1844802135.

• *Permission Marketing: Turning Strangers into Friends and Friends into Customers*, by Seth Godin. ISBN: 978-0684856360.

CHAPTER 4-PRINT MATERIALS THAT SCREAM SUCCESS

• *Keys to Great Writing*, by Stephen Wilbers. ISBN: 978-1582974927.

• *Made to Stick: Why Some Ideas Survive and Others Die*, by Chip Heath & Dan Heath. ISBN: 978-1400064281.

• *The Non-Designer's Design Book, 3rd Edition*, by Robin Williams. ISBN: 978-0321534040

• *Resume Magic: Trade Secrets of a Professional Resume Writer*, by Susan Britton Whitcomb. ISBN: 978-1593573119.

• *Words that Sell*, by Richard Bayan. ISBN: 978-0071467858.

CHAPTER 5-POUNDING THE VIRTUAL PAVEMENT

• *Best Websites: Simple Steps to Successful Websites*, by Nelson Bates. ISBN: 978-1419690006.

• *The Big Red Fez: How to Make Any Web Site Better*, by Seth Godin. ISBN: 978-0743227902.

• *How to Promote Your Music Successfully on the Internet: 2007 Edition*, by David Nevue. ISBN: 978-1439208649.

• *The Musician's Internet: Online Strategies for Success in the Music Industry*, by Peter Spellman. ISBN: 978-0634035869.

• *MySpace Music Marketing: How to Promote & Sell Your Music on the World's Biggest Networking Website*, by Bob Baker. ISBN: 978-0971483842.

• *The New Rules of Marketing and PR: How to Use News Releases, Blogs, Podcasting, Viral Marketing, and Online Media to Reach Buyers Directly*, by David Meerman Scott. ISBN: 978-0470113455.

CHAPTER 6-THE NEW RECORDING PARADIGM

• *All You Need to Know about the Music Business, 6th Ed*, by Donald Passman. ISBN: 978-0743293181.

• *The Future of Music: Manifesto for the Digital Music Revolution*, by David Kusek & Gerd Leonhard. ISBN: 978-0876390597.

• *Record Label Marketing*, by Tom Hutchison, Amy Macy, and Paul Allen. ISBN: 978-0240807874.

• *Start and Run Your Own Record Label*, by Daylle Deanna Schwartz. ISBN: 978-0823084333.

CHAPTER 7-EXTRAORDINARY PEOPLE SKILLS

• *The Art of Mingling: Easy, Fun, and Proven Techniques for Mastering Any Room*, by Jeanne Martinet. ISBN: 978-0312083168.

• *Cold Calling for Cowards: How to Turn the Fear of Rejection into Opportunities, Sales, and Money*, by Jerry Hocutt. ISBN: 978-0615138756.

• *How to Win Friends & Influence People*, by Dale Carnegie. ISBN: 978-0671027032.

• *Make Your Contacts Count: Networking Knowhow for Business and Career Success*, by Anne Baber & Lynne Waymon. ISBN: 978-0814474020.

• *Never Eat Alone: And Other Secrets to Success, One Relationship at a Time*, by Keith Ferrazzi. ISBN: 978-0385512053.

CHAPTER 8-PERSONAL FINANCE FOR MUSICIANS

• *The Automatic Millionaire: A Powerful One-Step Plan to Live and Finish Rich*, by David Bach. ISBN: 978-0767923828.

• *Investing from Scratch: A Handbook for the Young Investor*, by James Lowell. ISBN: 978-0143036845.

• *The Millionaire Next Door*, by Thomas J. Stanley and William D. Danko. ISBN: 978-0671015206.

• *The Money Book for the Young, Fabulous, & Broke*, by Suze Orman. ISBN: 978-1594489136.

• *Your Money or Your Life: Transforming Your Relationship with Money and Achieving Financial Independence*, by Joe Dominguez & Vicki Robin. ISBN: 978-0140286786.

CHAPTER 9 & 10-NICE WORK IF YOU CAN GET IT

• *Beyond Talent: Creating a Successful Career in Music*, by Angela Myles Beeching. ISBN: 978-0195169133.

• *Career Opportunities in the Music Industry*, by Shelley Field. ISBN: 978-0816059966.

• *Getting Gigs! The Musician's and Singer's Survival Guide to Booking Better Paying Jobs With or Without an Agent*, by Mark W. Curran. ISBN: 978-0970677310.

• *How to be Your Own Booking Agent: The Musician's & Performing Artist's Guide to Successful Touring*, by Jeri Goldstein. ISBN: 978-0960683055.

• *Make Money Performing in Schools: Definitive Guide to Developing, Marketing, & Presenting School Assembly Programs*, by David Heflick. ISBN: 978-0963870582.

• *The Music Teaching Artist's Bible: Becoming a Virtuoso Educator*, by Eric Booth. ISBN: 978-0195368390.

• *Making Money Teaching Music*, by David & Barbara Newsam. ISBN: 978-1582971568.

• *Making Music in Looking Glass Land: A Guide to Survival and Business Skills for the Classical Performer*, by Ellen Highstein. ISBN: 978-1892862051.

• *The Plain & Simple Guide to Music Publishing*, by Randal Wixen. ISBN: 978-0634090547.

• *Promoting Your Teaching Studio: How to Make Your Phone Ring, Fill Your Schedule, and Build a Waiting List You Can't Jump Over*, by Philip Johnston. ISBN: 978-0958190510.

• *Reaching Out: A Musician's Guide to Interactive Performance*, by David Wallace. ISBN: 978-0073401386.

• *Your Own Way in Music: A Career and Resource Guide*, by Nancy Usher. ISBN: 978-0312083427.

CHAPTER 11-FUNDING YOUR DREAMS

• *The Ask: How to Ask Anyone for Any Amount for Any Purpose*, by Laura Fredricks. ISBN: 978-0787978563.

• *Breakthrough Fundraising Letters*, by Alan Sharpe. ISBN: 978-0978405106.

• *Guide to Getting Arts Grants*, by Ellen Liberatori. ISBN: 978-1581154566.

• *Yours for the Asking: An Indispensable Guide to Fundraising and Management*, by Reynold Levy. ISBN: 978-0470243428.

• *The Zen of Fundraising: 89 Timeless Ideas to Strengthen and Develop Your Donor Relationships*, by Ken Burnett. ISBN: 978-0787983147.

CHAPTER 12-OUTSTANDING PERFORMANCE PLUS...

• *After the Golden Age: Romantic Pianism and Modern Performance*, by Kenneth Hamilton. ISBN: 978-0195178265.

• *Romancing the Room: How to Engage Your Audience, Court Your Crowd, and Speak Successfully in Public*, by James M. Wagstaffe and Bruce Bean. ISBN: 978-0609805978.

CHAPTER 13-ARTISTRY & RELEVANCE

• *The Art of the Turnaround: Creating & Maintaining Healthy Arts Organizations*, by Michael Kaiser. ISBN: 978-1584657354.

• *Musicians with a Mission: Keeping the Classical Tradition Alive*, by Andrew L. Pincus. ISBN: 978-1555535162.

• *No Vivaldi in the Garage: A Requiem for Classical Music in North America*, by Sheldon Morgenstern. ISBN: 978-1555536411.

• *The Tipping Point: How Little Things Can Make a Big Difference*, by Malcolm Gladwell. ISBN: 978-0349114460.

• *Who Needs Classical Music?* by Julian Johnson. ISBN: 978-0195146813.

• *Why Classical Music Still Matters*, by Lawrence Kramer. ISBN: 978-0520258037.

CHAPTER 14-LEAVING A LEGACY

• *Change the World: How Ordinary People Can Achieve Extraordinary Results*, by Robert E. Quinn. ISBN: 978-0787951931.

• *Life Entrepreneurs: Ordinary People Creating Extraordinary Lives*, by Christopher Gergen & Gregg Vanourek. ISBN: 978-0787988623.

• *The Purpose of Your Life: Finding Your Place in the World Using Synchronicity, Intuition, And Uncommon Sense*, by Carol Adrienne and James Redfield. ISBN: 978-0688166250.

Featured Artist Index

Index

L

M

N

O

P

Y